Brothers,
Sisters,
Strangers

ALSO BY FERN SCHUMER CHAPMAN

Motherland

Brothers, Sisters, Strangers

Sibling Estrangement and the
Road to Reconciliation

FERN SCHUMER CHAPMAN

VIKING

VIKING

An imprint of Penguin Random House LLC
penguinrandomhouse.com

LIBRARY OF CONGRESS CATALOGING-IN-PUBLICATION DATA
Names: Chapman, Fern Schumer, author.
Title: Brothers, sisters, strangers: sibling estrangement and the road to
reconciliation / Fern Schumer Chapman.
Description: New York: Viking, 2021.
Identifiers: LCCN 2020026928 (print) | LCCN 2020026929 (ebook) |
ISBN 9780525561699 (hardcover) | ISBN 9780525561705 (ebook)
Subjects: LCSH: Brothers and sisters. | Brothers and sisters—Family
relationships. | Interpersonal relations. | Alienation (Social psychology) |
Chapman, Fern Schumer.
Classification: LCC HQ759.96 .C43 2021 (print) | LCC HQ759.96 (ebook) |
DDC 306.875/3—dc23
LC record available at https://lccn.loc.gov/2020026928
LC ebook record available at https://lccn.loc.gov/2020026929

Printed in Canada
1   3   5   7   9   10   8   6   4   2

Set in Adobe Caslon Pro
Designed by Cassandra Garruzzo

For my brother

Give me your hand, my brother, search my face;
Look in these eyes lest I should think of shame;
For we have made an end of all things base.
We are returning by the road we came.

SIEGFRIED SASSOON, "TO MY BROTHER"

Contents

Introduction

S ibling estrangement carries profound hurt and a deep stigma. Few can bear to admit to the suffering and shame when the unique bond with a brother or sister breaks. It's even more daunting to expose this emotional abyss in public, opening it up to the larger world.

For the better part of forty years, my only sibling—a brother—and I had almost no relationship. I can't recall a specific fight or incident that led to our estrangement. We simply didn't have much to say to each other, and, in time, we said nothing at all. In the early years of our cutoff, I tried. I reached out many times, but he was unresponsive, so eventually I quit trying. I couldn't force him to have a relationship with me. Eventually I hardly knew who my brother was anymore.

I simply couldn't understand the estrangement. I ruminated endlessly on this incomprehensible situation: an utter contradiction of the very nature of family, an aggressive rejection of the fundamental way most living creatures organize themselves.

Questions nagged at me: *Am I alone in my suffering? Do others live in a constant state of mourning the living? And what did this failure say about me? How should I explain to my children that they'd never know their cousins on my side of the family? Could I prevent other family members from being caught up in the split? How should I portray this cutoff to friends and family when I didn't understand it myself? If I couldn't trust my only sibling to want a relationship with me, whom could I trust? Given my loss, would I ever be able to find a sense of balance and well-being?*

Support groups exist for the estranged, but many who endure this trauma are reluctant to join or to even reveal their heartbreaking stories to others. I realized early on the disturbing nature of how others perceive a sibling rupture. If, for example, I tell someone I'm divorced, that person probably won't flinch. If I say, "I don't get along with my mother," there's a good chance they'll roll their eyes empathetically. But if I say, "I have no relationship with my brother," they might arch their eyebrows, wondering if I'm trustworthy. Questions arise, silent but inevitable: What's wrong with her? Is this a good candidate for friendship? If she can't maintain a relationship with her own brother, is she capable of sustaining *any* relationship?

No one wants to admit to this level of family dysfunction, to face these elemental doubts about oneself. Most of us suffer in silence, isolated twice: not only from our sibling but also from social support against the loss.

Few friends or family members unacquainted with the experience truly understand the depth of this hurt, and even fewer want to talk about it. Some have their own anxieties, fearing that merely engaging with the topic might usher in an estrangement in their own lives. They seem to feel that the condition might be contagious, and they, too, might one day be left lost and alone. At the same time, whenever I tell people that I am working on a book about sibling estrangement, they sit up a little straighter and lean in, as if I've tapped into a dark secret. Those who haven't experienced this loss likely know someone who has, and they welcome insights to understand it.

Even when estrangement is a clearheaded choice—a survival mechanism to move forward from abuse or unbearable discord—the cutoff leaves disconnected siblings in a world of secrecy and shame. The cutoff from a sister or brother becomes a fault line, dividing the family and a life into "before" and "after." The loss can be so deep that it alters who we are and what we become. For a sibling who's been cut off without any choice in the matter, estrangement feels like a chronic rejection and betrayal. This was my experience. Over time, I no longer held the identifying, defining role of sister, sister-in-law, or aunt. My children had no cousins on my side of the family. I dreaded birthdays, holidays, weddings, funerals, family get-togethers—any and every possible encounter with my brother or, perhaps worse, with his glaring absence. Having no explanation of why he wanted nothing to do with me, I was stuck on a Möbius strip of rumination, caught in a constant state of bereavement.

Five years ago, however, my situation changed. A possibility of reconciliation with my brother surfaced. Naturally, I was mistrustful and skeptical; this wasn't the first time I had gotten my hopes up. Rather than jump in and risk further devastation, I sent myself on a quest.

Almost nothing has been written about the challenges of rebuilding a sibling relationship when conflict or abandonment has left little but distrust. As I considered reestablishing contact with my brother, the topic itself seemed grossly unacknowledged and underinvestigated. Yet, to be sure, wherever relationships exist, so, too, do conflicts both major and minor that lead to estrangements.

I decided to take on these topics myself, accumulating information, processing it into knowledge, and applying logic. Above all, I was determined to do everything possible to reestablish a connection with my brother—and never let it go.

I've always been fascinated with the dynamics of family relations. In several books for adults and children, I explored my mother's hidden early life in Nazi Germany. I examined the psychological legacy of children who are separated from parents at a young age and the effect of those early-life traumas on subsequent relationships. Through research and memoir writing, I addressed this central question: How does a woman who feels betrayed by her parents and experiences the trauma of the loss of her family, homeland, and identity in childhood eventually mother her own children?

For this book—also blending research and memoir—I wanted to learn how sibling estrangement affects an individual's relationships with other family members and friends, as well as self-esteem and sense of identity. For my investigation, I relied on recognized experts who are well established in the broad discipline of family studies. I looked for behavioral scientists and authors who had conducted their own comprehensive research on the subject.

I also did fieldwork by creating a survey for siblings suffering estrangement. The shame and humiliation that often accompanies this experience made it challenging to find estranged siblings who were willing to complete my survey or discuss the topic. Estrangement violates society's norms and ideals about family unity, explains Australian social worker and scholar Dr. Kylie Agllias, one of the foremost experts on the subject, who wrote the internationally acclaimed, groundbreaking book *Family Estrangement: A Matter of Perspective*.

Siblings are the building blocks of the family, and those relationships are considered enduring and unbreakable. "In its most fundamental form," Agllias writes, "estrangement might also be viewed as a threat to the human socialization and survival process. It is a breakdown of the attachment bond protecting children in early life, older people in later life, and the weak and ill throughout their lives."[1]

Never intended to be strictly scientific, my survey sought stories and insights from those struggling with estrangement. I also gained knowledge from online chat rooms where brothers and sisters willingly discussed their fractured sibling relationships in an ad hoc, nonjudgmental support group. In the cyberpresence of those with similar experiences, the estranged have conversations about their raw pain, the shock, torment, and heartbreak of their losses, and the many ways the devastating experiences have defined their lives.

In my first foray into these online discussions, I asked the administrator of a British Facebook chat room to allow me to join the group. She greeted me with the following poignant words:

"Welcome to our group. It's not a club most of us wanted to join. You may be estranged, but, here, you are not alone. Our names are different, but our pain and our stories are the same."

I wasn't surprised to hear similar stories and to see patterns in my survey responses of the estranged as well. The information I garnered from my survey and from chat rooms comes not from a laboratory but from the hearts of participants.

Each chapter of this book consists of two parts. The first is a memoir capturing my brother's and my efforts to rebuild our relationship. In the second, I highlight a salient issue of estrangement that occurred in my brother's and my story, explore research on the topic, and feature other people's stories.

My primary aims are to offer comfort, to help mitigate the stigma of estrangement, and to tear down the walls of isolation. I hope that whatever your reasons for picking up this book, you find in its contents something that inspires and guides you and sheds light on how severed relationships might be repaired in your own life or in the lives of others you know. At the very least, you will learn more about who is at risk for sibling estrangement, why these relationships break down, and how cutoffs can define an individual.

The process of writing this book has been its own form of narrative therapy for my brother and me. In many ways, this project has revealed my brother's true self to me, to him, and to our family. His courage in allowing me to tell our story gave both of us the opportunity to bridge our divide and walk together down the road to reconciliation.

PART I

Estrangement

Chapter 1

The Challenges of Sibling Relationships

⊤

I just talked to Scott. He's unbelievably upset. I don't know. I don't know what to do . . ."

The trembling, panicky message on my voice mail is from my eighty-nine-year-old mother. She's talking about my elder brother, who is sixty-one.

"He's just a wreck, and so am I. He sounds awful. . . ."

"I don't know what to do," she continues, with the same high-pitched terror. "I don't know what to tell him. Uhhh, I don't know what to tell you. Please call me back so . . . so we can do something."

We! So *we* can do something?

"I hope."

With those two choked-out words, she is covertly acknowledging that my brother and I have been estranged for decades.

Then she signs off with the same words she has trained herself to use. Through most of my life, my mother has struggled to express her feelings for her children. She's not sure how to give my brother and me the very thing she lost as a twelve-year-old child, when her parents sent her, all alone, from Nazi Germany to America: a mother's love. About ten years ago, though, she began to change. At that time, she seemed to make a promise to herself: Never hang up the phone on one of your children without saying, "Love you. Bye."

After clicking off the frantic voice mail, I say the words out loud, reintroducing myself to the concept. "My brother."

He has been excised from my life for so long that I don't even remember the origins of the rift. Was it a fight or some crisis that set us on our separate paths? Did I mistreat him or his family in some way? Whatever I did, his punishment seems profoundly disproportionate to whatever crime I might have committed.

Yet I doubt it was a single, calamitous incident. Instead, our break was a process of accretion, hurt piled on hurt, slowly building a hard shell of separation.

Indisputably, we were never close as children, and I always yearned for a deeper relationship with my brother. I suppose I was missing what I never had. In fact, we were always near-opposite personalities. I was introspective, self-reliant, invested in a few intense friendships. He was an adventurous risk-taker who couldn't wait to break from the family and live his own life. While Scott sought affirmation outside the family as the leader of a large circle of friends, I stuck close to home, trying desperately to repair my mother's damaged self and my parents' failing marriage. I was hoping that eventually I would be rewarded for my efforts with the family I needed.

Instead, all these years, I've lived in a cycle of injury, anger, and pain—a chronic state of powerlessness and grief. The ache hovers at the edge of consciousness: sometimes the barest wisp of longing, sometimes an ominous pileup of thunderheads rumbling through my mind. I've pushed the pain away, but every now and then, when I notice someone on the street who looks like him, I lose myself, staring at a stranger, not wanting to let the image go.

Some nights I dream about him. In the morning I lie in bed, sifting through memories, replaying moments from our shared past, wondering what I did to drive him away.

How, I've often wondered, can a person erase blood? How can I deny the existence of the only other person walking the earth who knows where I came from? Who can cross-reference my memories? Who shares my story? And most important of all: How can *he* deny *me* and *my* family?

The breach began when Scott and I were in our twenties. He was a newlywed and I was busy making my career as a reporter at a newspaper. I would call him occasionally, but often he wouldn't call me back; I assumed he was busy with his new life. At that time, I didn't give our limited contact too much thought. But when we would see each other, I was struck by the fact that we were traveling in two distinct orbits, and increasingly we were becoming remote to each other. Our conversations relied on superficial topics: "You get a new car?" "You doing golf lessons this year?" "I ran into Mark Leavitts at the mall yesterday. Wasn't he in your class?" More awkward than connected, we couldn't find anything to say to each other.

Maybe when he's older, I'd tell myself. *Or when he has children . . . or when he feels successful . . . or when Dad is gone . . ."* He was also estranged from our father. Neither Dad nor I lived comfortably with the absence of a relationship with Scott, and I held tightly to the tantalizing possibility that maybe, one day . . .

As we both welcomed children into our families, our scanty, sporadic conversations dwindled even more. I invited his family to birthday parties

when my children were young, but they rarely attended. When he recip-
rocated, we went a few times, but the cousins didn't really know one another because they never spent enough time together to build a relationship
and, consequently, none of us felt comfortable at the event. Eventually, we
quit going too. At weddings or funerals, the distance and divide deep-
ened. I would gaze at my brother across the room, looking at the stranger
who once lived with me during my most formative years.

Months, years, and decades piled up. The shell grew into a wall of silence, impenetrable and insurmountable. I began to give up on my fantasies, trying instead to extinguish my feelings, and then to convince myself
I didn't have a brother. It was just easier if he didn't exist; I was sure he
would never be a part of my life again.

Now, after all these years, I try to reintroduce myself to the idea of
him. I hear myself say again, "My brother." The words sound so foreign in
my voice.

Who is he? All I know is the framework of our lives. He was the only
other child in our deeply dysfunctional childhood home, a place steeped
in our mother's Holocaust past—about which she never spoke. Neither
did anyone else. Yet her loss and despair hung everywhere, as obvious as
the stench seeping from the kitchen garbage can.

I suspected our estrangement was tangled up in that history. The bitter
irony was that the Holocaust had robbed my mother's generation of their
families; yet my brother and I, who *could* be in each other's lives, had
somehow re-created the same loss. I wanted a relationship with my big
brother in part to help me sort out our difficult parents: an unknowable
mother, a tyrannical father. But, driven to bury our painful past, both of
us escaped to college and never looked back—certainly not at each other.
Instead, we lived in a legacy of familylessness.

Few pictures or mementos exist to document our shared childhood.
Oblivious to building a family, our parents rarely took pictures of the four

of us together or even of my brother and me as we passed through child-hood. They rarely organized holiday gatherings, birthday parties, or vaca-tions. They never encouraged us to watch out for each other in life.

And we haven't. But even though he has drifted far away from me, I'm constantly reminded of him. Almost every day, someone casually men-tions "my brother" or "my sister"—ordinary words that prick me like a tiny electrical shock. I never say anything; I wouldn't want anyone to feel self-conscious about the expected, natural order of family. Still, when I hear innocuous comments—"We're going to my sister's for Thanksgiving" or "My brother's coming over to fix my bike"—my teeth clench and my fin-gernails dig half-moons into my palms.

Envy courses through me when I see brothers and sisters watching their children's baseball games together. Or having a meal at a restaurant. Or even texting each other. I feel as if I've been expelled from siblingdom. For me, there are few family celebrations; Thanksgiving is a stress-filled scramble to fill the chairs at my table.

I am *not* an only child, but I suffer the isolation of one.

I seem to carry this embarrassing loss alone. When I run into people who knew Scott and me as kids, they naturally assume that we've re-mained connected. "How's your brother?" they'll ask, unwittingly sinking a dagger into me. My features twist as I dodge them with a casual: "Fine. Fine." Then I quickly, skillfully redirect the conversation, asking about their family, avoiding the natural follow-up question: "What's he doing now?" Because I really don't know.

Of course, I'm aware of his outlines: a long marriage; two successful adult sons, both living near their parents—and near me. And every so often—even though I've asked my mother not to discuss him and his fam-ily with me—she can't help but share big news about his family. A few years ago, she told me that one of my nephews was planning to marry. Knowing it would be a large affair, I felt a stirring of hope: Maybe *this* would be my "one day." Maybe my family would be included. Soon I was checking the mail every day for an invitation that never arrived. On the wedding day, I mourned my losses even more intensely, learning again that when estrangement endures, the injuries multiply with every birthday, holiday, family occasion—and every new generation.

To manage my grief, I have strategically avoided certain places in my daily life. I always detoured, often inconveniently, from the street where he lives; I didn't want to see his sons shooting hoops in his driveway. I rarely shopped near his home because I didn't want to run into him or his friends. When my children were teenagers, I dreaded attending their sports events at his sons' nearby high school. Over time, my off-limits zone has expanded farther and farther out, and the "avoid" list has grown longer and longer. It's a relief and a respite that he doesn't have a Facebook page.

My fears were not unfounded. Two decades ago, the high school my brother's boys attended organized a large arts festival that introduced students to various career paths. I was asked to share my experiences as a writer. After my presentation, I was told to pick up my stipend check at a table near the school's entrance.

When I approached the table, staffed by several members of the school's PTO, I scanned the adults and stopped, stunned, at a pair of familiar dark eyes. I needed a moment to place the face: my own brother!

"Hello," I mumbled awkwardly.

"Hi!" he said cheerfully. At first, I couldn't tell if he even recognized me, or if he was just acting as if we didn't know each other. But he didn't ask my name; he handed me an envelope, saying briskly, "I'm PTO treasurer. Thanks for coming today." Then he turned to the next person in line, again introducing himself as treasurer. As he rifled through his pile of envelopes, he asked the presenter, "What's your name?"

That was the last time I saw my brother.

And now—after all this elaborate work of forgetting and avoiding and trying not to care—now what?

Turning back to the phone to return my mother's call, I tap on her name to call the number I know better than my own: ten digits we were assigned fifty years ago, when area codes were introduced, when we moved into the house where Mom still lives. That phone number is a tether to my childhood memories.

At the moment, though, I'm feeling anything but nostalgic.

"Well?" I ask my mother, barely concealing my anger as she answers the phone. "What do you want *me* to do?"

I've always felt she gave in too easily to Scott's cutting me off. I resented her for accommodating him, letting him off the hook, attending family events when she knew I was excluded. If I were in her place and one of my children shunned a family member, I would simply refuse to attend. My philosophy is that my children are free to be as distant or close to one another as they choose, but I expect every family member to be invited to all family events.

But my mother had her own rationalization, an explanation that never varied: She didn't mean to hurt *me*, but she felt her relationship with my brother was tenuous. "If I don't go to his house for Passover or the boys' birthday parties," she would tell me, "I'll never see that part of the family." Afraid of losing her son and grandchildren, she was willing to risk her safe, reliable relationship with me for the crumbs she might collect at my brother's table.

And now—now that he's drowning in troubles—*I'm* supposed to help *her* by rescuing *him*.

My brother was barely a teenager when he fled the family. He organized so many outings to parties, sports events, movies, and other activities that he seemed to come home only to sleep. I suppose he was escaping a place where he felt small and unacknowledged. He lived in the shadow of our highly accomplished, thoroughly self-absorbed father. Dead fourteen years now, Dad had dreamed his only son would follow in his giant footsteps by becoming a doctor. But Scott didn't share that dream; he dropped out of the University of Illinois during his junior year, abandoning premed for a career as a commodities broker.

During his decades of trading, he rode wild swings from stupendous financial success to bankruptcy. Not long ago, my mother confided that he was struggling with grave money problems. The ever-increasing risks of high-stakes trading had engulfed him in a tsunami of financial and personal ruin, resulting in his current severe depression.

"You have to do *something*," my mother sobs into the phone.

"I can't, Mom," I choke, swallowing my own tears. "I just can't."

"But you have to!" she wails. Her sadness and desperation stun me. Like most children whose parents lost everything in the Holocaust, I have tried to shield her from more pain: I can't stand to hear her suffer.

"But Mom! You *know* I've barely talked to him for forty years. And whenever I've tried, he always bails on me."

"I . . . I just don't know what to do," she says through unrelenting tears.

Listening to her sobs, I wobble. I want to ease her pain, yet if I reach out to him, I'm afraid I'll pay a terrible price myself.

But the following thought always haunts me, driving me to do what she asks: *her life has been so much worse than mine.* I hate to be the source of her grief. I worry about the cumulative effect of all she has endured. Will this rob her of years? Deprive her of any joy—even the smallest bit—that she might find in her remaining days?

The scales begin to tilt in her favor.

"You want me to call—"

"Yes!" she says, jumping in before I finish my sentence.

Then I flash on one of the times I gave him another chance, probably fifteen years ago. We had a brief, civilized conversation at a family event and, as we said good-bye, he extended an olive branch: "Maybe we can get lunch," he said.

Stunned, I didn't know how to respond. Did he mean it? Or did it just slip out of his mouth, without real consideration?

Then, in an even more surprising move, he called a week later to ask if we could celebrate my birthday. And so, one November day, we met at a local restaurant.

The minute we pulled our chairs to the table and picked up the menus, I sensed a shift in him, the return of our old breach. He was withdrawn; eyes darting around the restaurant, he barely looked at me. I searched for some way to engage him.

"How are your kids?"

"Fine."

"How's work going?"

"Fine."

"Going anywhere this winter vacation?"

"Nope."

I was trying to dance with an unwilling partner.

Desperately, I tried to catch the eye of the waitress, who lingered at another table, chatting with her customers. I hoped she would rescue me from the existential burden of coming up with something to say to my brother.

Eventually, she approached our table and chirpily asked, "What would you like?"

"A brother!" I wanted to answer.

Instead, I ordered a Cobb salad. He asked for a hamburger, extra well done. I had forgotten that he always ate his meat charred. He conversed more with the waitress than with me, actually looking her in the eye with a hint of a smile.

That distracted us for a few minutes, but ultimately the waitress left. She couldn't save me.

I checked my watch; only ten minutes had passed since we sat down. I considered asking him, "What the hell? Why ask me to go to lunch and then ignore me?" But like my mother, I didn't want to risk the little he was willing to give.

So as we awkwardly waited for our food, I sifted through every topic I could think of that might give our conversation traction, even pitching subjects that bored me to tears.

"Your boys still doing baseball?"

"Nope."

"How's your fantasy football going?"

"Fine."

Finally, to my great relief, lunch arrived, and we directed our attention toward our plates. He barely looked up, taking large bites of his hamburger. Spearing a cherry tomato, I wished he hadn't raised my hopes, hadn't drawn me out of my safe den, where I had achieved a fragile equilibrium.

Shoveling down our food, we finished lunch in a record-breaking thirty-five minutes. We parted in front of the restaurant with a perfunctory, indifferent good-bye, more like business acquaintances than siblings. As he turned away, I blinked back tears and swallowed the familiar lump in my throat. I knew he was done with me . . . again.

"No, Mom," I say firmly into the phone. "I'm not calling him."

My words hang between us; her weeping speaks of decades of pain and family loss.

But I'm not caving this time.

"I'm sorry, Mom."

"Think about it," she sobs.

"Sorry." I dig in. "I just can't."

Scott and I are very different people, and it makes sense that we have carved out distinctly different personalities and characteristics. Brothers and sisters who share parents, home, values, and beliefs often reduce competition by cultivating unique traits and differentiating themselves from one another. But Scott and I seemed to have differentiated ourselves right out of a relationship. "The gene pool is vast," I would tell my two sons and my daughter offhandedly, trying to justify the emotional distance to minimize the pain. Through the decades, they came to understand that I had a brother and that he and I no longer had any relationship.

The Unique Challenges of Sibling Relationships

From birth, siblings are fellow survivors of childhood, witnesses to that elemental world. That front row seat to our formative years is the basis of a crucial, unique, enduring relationship. In fact, as the renowned Yale University professor of psychiatry Theodore Lidz, author of the classic, widely used textbook *The Person* explains, "A person's relatedness to a brother or sister is often closer and more meaningful than the relationship to parents."[1]

In childhood, brothers and sisters instill in one another necessary social qualities—tolerance, generosity, loyalty—that eventually affect relationships with friends, colleagues, and lovers. After all, siblings typically spend more time together than with anyone else; for the fortunate, those relationships may continue for fifty to eighty years, outlasting most friendships, marriages, and even relationships with parents, which generally span thirty to fifty years.

Over the course of a lifetime, sibling relationships are not stagnant but dynamic and sometimes volatile, with peaks and valleys; they wax and wane, grow and change over time. Chronically wrestling with competition, cooperation, and comparison, siblings may have almost nothing to do with each other for years; at other times, they may be in constant contact.

Two opposite, powerful pulls exert pressure on sisters and brothers. First, siblings are hardwired to differentiate themselves so that they can receive the limited, crucial resource for survival—parental care. Second, siblings feel compelled to deeply invest in relationships with relatives to ensure that the family gene pool continues. One evolutionary theory, kin selection, suggests that the more closely individuals are related, the more likely they are to help one another. (Interestingly, siblings are genetically more alike than they are like either parent or anyone else in the world—sharing about 50 percent of genetic material.)

Complicating the sibling relationship is the fact that each child is born into a different family. A first child might enter a family with a mother and father, while a second child born to the same family is likely met by a mother, a father, and an older sibling, thus receiving less parental attention than the older brother or sister did. In addition, mothers and fathers often parent children differently. Each child may be destined to have divergent experiences, as well as his or her own family narrative: I was the outsider; he was the favorite; she was the beauty. These identifications deeply influence how siblings relate to and define one another. This fundamental understanding of the bonds of family make estrangements within it feel so unnatural, and it helps explain why family, friends, and even acquaintances are shaken to the core when sibling relationships shatter.

The more I read and learn, the more I see how our culture has avoided and neglected the sensitive subject of sibling estrangement, which can start with a brief silence and turn into years and decades of cutoff. Eighty percent of American children grow up with at least one brother or sister. Yet, for more than a century psychological research has largely ignored the importance of sibling relationships. Even Sigmund Freud, the founder of psychoanalysis, refers to the sibling relationship only five times in his two dozen volumes of work. Only during the past two decades have researchers conducted meaningful studies on how siblings shape one another's lives.

Those of us who know the pain of living without our siblings don't need studies to tell us the importance of these relationships. But the estranged are a large, undisclosed group—one that's not easily measured. Specific numbers are nearly nonexistent, in part because people are often reluctant to admit they are estranged from a brother or sister. Despite the lack of hard data, some researchers believe that sibling estrangement is grossly underreported, and the phenomenon is epidemic.

Contributing to the epidemic is the fact that the family in the Western world during the twenty-first century is undergoing a profound metamorphosis. Its role as an institutional social anchor is diminishing. *New York Times* columnist David Brooks describes the drastic shift in a March 2020 article in *The Atlantic*, "The Nuclear Family Was a Mistake." He reports that only a minority of American households are traditional two-parent nuclear families and only one third of American individuals live in this kind of family.

"We're likely living through the most rapid change in family structure in human history," Brooks writes. "The causes are economic, cultural, and institutional all at once. People who grow up in a nuclear family tend to have a more individualistic mind-set than people who grow up in a multi-generational extended clan."[2]

The family is no longer the exclusive source of emotional and financial support, the transmission of values, and a spiritual identity. Several trends underscore the changes. For example, young adults are postponing or repudiating marriage and delaying having children, leading to a decline in birthrates. Another complicating factor is that baby boomers, compared with their parents and grandparents, often live farther away from their sisters and brothers, limiting contact with family members. While previous generations were glued together by lifelong marriages and large families, boomers have more divorces and fewer offspring.

Some of these trends have taken a toll on the feelings siblings have toward one another. In 2015, Michigan's Oakland University conducted a survey of nearly three hundred people ranging in age from eighteen to sixty-five and found that only 26 percent enjoyed a healthy sibling relationship with frequent contact and low competitiveness; however, over a third of those surveyed described their relationship with their sibling as apathetic or openly hostile. The remainder said their siblings were friendly and supportive—terms that the study reports also could capture a relationship that is intensely competitive or one characterized by limited contact. Many used words like "detached" or "antagonistic" to portray their sibling relationships, and they remembered their sibling relationships in childhood as "hurtful" and "competitive."

The Effects of Income, Education, Culture, and Family Expectations on Estrangement

In today's cultural environment, where the family structure has transformed from an interconnected, extended nuclear group into a smaller, decentralized, loose network of relatives, sisters and brothers often lack clear guidelines for their relationships. Siblings are freer than ever to establish their own set of rules. Do they ignore each other and create distance, or do they assist and celebrate each other?

Without cultural mandates that expect families to stay together, siblings who find a brother or sister difficult, disrespectful, or abusive are tempted to release themselves from the relationship. Individuals with more education and higher social standing are likely to be more geographically mobile and less likely to depend upon each other financially. Higher achievers also have a larger social network and are therefore less reliant on siblings.

In his article in *The Atlantic*, Brooks identifies the social and economic implications of the demise of the nuclear family "People with an individualistic mind-set," he writes, "tend to be less willing to sacrifice self for the sake of the family, and the result is more family disruption. People who grow up in disrupted families have more trouble getting the education they need to have prosperous careers. People who don't have prosperous careers have trouble building stable families, because of financial challenges and other stressors. The children in those families become more isolated and more traumatized."[3]

Dr. Stephen Ojiambo Wandera, a lecturer and researcher in the Department of Population Studies at Makerere University in Kampala, Uganda, and the author of dozens of articles on demographics in Uganda, observed some fascinating changes in families in his country as they evolve from large, extended clans into smaller, more urban circles of relations. Dr. Wandera found that estrangement is on the rise in Uganda. Traditionally, extended families were necessary as members cared for orphaned children who had suffered parental losses from civil war or AIDS. Now, Ugandan families are becoming smaller and more nuclear, Wandera explains, and as urbanization increases in the next twenty years, the prevalence of estrangement is likely to rise.

In America, children rooted in families with traditional immigrant cultures tend to feel an obligation to maintain relations with their brothers and sisters to honor their parents. Working-class and poor families, compared with the middle class, also tend to have stronger sibling ties.

Estrangement, however, cuts across all cultures and classes. It would be difficult to imagine a more bitter, high-profile, elite case of sibling estrangement than Britain's own royal family, which ran head-on into the issue when Meghan Markle married Prince Harry. Markle, estranged from both her half-sister and her half-brother, invited neither to the royal wedding. Their estrangement is so contentious that Markle's half-brother, Thomas Markle Jr., sent a handwritten letter to Prince Harry to try to stop the event.

"As more time passes to your royal wedding, it became very clear that this is the biggest mistake in royal wedding history. Meghan Markle is obviously not the right woman for you," Tom warned, adding that she is a "jaded, shallow, conceited woman that will make a joke of you and the royal family heritage."

"To top it all off," he continued, "she doesn't invite her own family and instead invites complete strangers to the wedding. Who does that? You and the royal family should put an end to this fake fairytale wedding before it's too late." In conclusion, Tom wrote, "You would think that a royal wedding would bring a torn family closer together, but I guess we are all distant family to Meg."

Tom's hurtful comments are understandable. Exclusion from a family wedding produces one of the gravest injuries to those who have a fractured relationship with a sibling. A wedding, which celebrates the continuation of the family, brings together relatives who may not see one another often. The happy event serves to knit the family, as members reconnect, dance, and are photographed together. Underlying the merriment, a wedding guest list is a loud public statement of who does and who does not belong in the family.

Chapter 2

Different Types of Estrangement

My mother knows me like no one else.

On the phone again—even when I'm almost yelling my refusal to contact my brother—she somehow hears something. Maybe my throat clearing or my defensive tone, or maybe just my silence: There's a clue here, somewhere, and it betrays me.

Detecting the crack in my fortress, she takes expert aim.

"Somebody has to do something," she sniffs, with an emotional hitch in her voice. "It can't go on like this."

"What makes you think *I* could do anything?" I snap. "What makes you think he'd even want it?"

"He can't go on like this . . ."

"I might make an even bigger mess of things." *Rationalize,* I tell myself. *Step away.*

"And . . ." She stops. Now she's debating whether to ramp up her argument. When it comes to my reconciling with my brother, she often pressures me. More than once, she has told me she's afraid she'll die, and we'll never have anything to do with each other again.

"Well? And?" I'm snapping again; she doesn't respond. "And what?"

"Wellll . . ." She stretches out the word.

"What, Mom? I know you want to say something."

She sighs, then blurts through her tears: "You *are* his sister."

Rattled, I ask myself: *What is my responsibility to my brother? What do I owe him? Especially when we've had no relationship for years?*

"Even if you haven't had much to do with him," she continues, as if she's reading my mind, "you *are* a member of the family."

What she really means is: Even if I'm estranged from my brother, don't I have some obligations to the family? Or to what's left of it—to *her*?

Staring out the window at the budding green of spring, I consider her point: Even if I'm not really his sister, I'm still her daughter.

Outside, the newly lush lawn is a gorgeous comfort after a long, brown, barren winter. In the front yard, the cherry tree's eye-popping pink blossoms are impossibly brilliant. I remember the plum tree in our childhood backyard, where Scott and I always played when the weather finally turned warm. Each year the tree's heavy boughs, thick with pink flowers, offered shade from the bright sun and a promise that the tree would eventually bear fruit.

Maybe—just maybe—things might be different this time. Maybe he's ready to try again.

But I'm afraid to even think like that. This could be another false spring. Another crushing failure.

"Please?" My mother sounds miserable and hopeless, her voice raspy from crying.

Weary from our argument, battered by my own churning thoughts, I weaken. It might be easier just to do what my mother asks than to endure the guilt of defying her.

Besides, I think, *maybe he won't even talk to me.* That would make the whole issue moot. Devastated as I've been with the estrangement, after all these years I can't imagine anything else. Now I'm not sure I have the will, courage, or energy to change things.

So—grudgingly—I'll fulfill my obligation to my mother. Then, I promise myself, I won't have to get involved with him again. *Ever.*

Given our history, I'm ready to bet on that.

"All right, Mom." Heaving a martyr's sigh, I concede. "I'll call him."

Immediately after agreeing to call Scott, I ask myself why I consented to try again when my past efforts have been so disastrous. I'm only minus a family member . . . and one branch of the family. Why is it important to have a relationship with my brother? Why can't I simply experience his absence as a liberation? Why should I be plagued by doubt and guilt if he wants nothing to do with me? Am I the only one to experience this loss so intensely?

Surveying the Estranged

In pursuit of deeper insight, I posted an online survey to my website. I publicized my project and survey on Reddit and other chat rooms where the estranged gather to discuss their painful circumstances. The survey yielded compelling and emotional stories of those who have been shaped by estrangement. About 120 completed it, and the respondents represent a variety of racial, ethnic, and socioeconomic backgrounds, ranging in age from seventeen to seventy-two years old, from a dozen different countries around the world. Having volunteered to fill out my survey, the respondents are self-selected brothers and sisters who chose to answer my questions. To protect their privacy while ensuring maximum openness, I promised respondents that their names and hometowns would be changed in this book.

What follows is the survey I created:

Dear Respondent:

Thank you for taking the time to fill out my survey on sibling estrangement. My interest in this topic is rooted in my personal story; my older brother and I didn't talk to each other for most of my adult life. Over time, we did reconcile, and that journey has prompted many questions. Often, I've wondered about the nature of these relationships and, in particular, when and how they break down, cut off, or enter the territory of estrangement. Do those who experience a break with a sibling feel relieved that they no longer have a troubling presence in their lives or do they suffer from displacement and loss, or a combination? How does the estrangement affect the larger family? Do siblings often reconcile, and under what circumstances? How do siblings bridge their relationship after years of resentment and hurts?

As an author, I often bring my own experiences to my writing. My memoir, Motherland, *explores the difficult relationship I had with my mother, a Holocaust refugee. Recently, I decided to write about the break I experienced with my own brother, and sibling estrangements in general—a condition so common that some researchers say it is an "epidemic." As I've come to understand, it also remains largely unexplored, and often goes undiscussed.* Brothers, Sisters, Strangers *will tell the story of my brother's and my relationship in the context of others, hoping to shine a light on these intimate, often difficult ties. Like me, you may find it helpful to think through these issues; filling out this survey may provide a useful structure to begin to do so.*

For the purposes of generating the broadest range of responses, I have not specifically defined "estrangement." I'm interested in your experience, and why you use that word to describe your sibling relationship.

The information you offer here will remain confidential. You do not need to provide your name unless you would like to continue to explore the topic with me through a personal interview. Should I interview you, I will compensate you for your time. Any stories included in the book will appear only with permission, and with appropriate changes to names and identifying characteristics. I deeply appreciate your responses. Please feel free to contact me prior to responding if you have any questions about the project or the survey.

QUESTIONS FOR RESPONDENTS

How many sisters and brothers do you have and from which sibling(s) are you estranged?

How long have you been estranged? Was there a clear precipitating event that led to your estrangement, or did you just drift apart?

Were/are other family members also estranged from this sibling?

Are there other estrangements in the family (mother is estranged from grandmother, etc.)? If yes, briefly describe.

Please briefly describe the home in which you were raised (for example, peaceful, tumultuous, loving, abusive, disconnected, etc.).

Describe your relationship with your sibling prior to the estrangement.

Do you think about or miss your estranged sibling? If yes, what events or moments bring your sibling to mind?

Does the estrangement affect other relationships (parents, partnership, children, friendships)?

Do you explain the estrangement to your family and friends? If so, what do you say about the relationship?

Do you follow your sibling on social media? If so, how does that affect you?

Have you found sibling substitutes after the estrangement? If yes, please describe.

Please describe a specific experience you have had that illustrates what it has meant for you to be estranged from your sibling.

Please describe your estrangement from your sibling, including what you feel is most important about this experience. (For example: your prior relationship, your feelings about the estrangement, what caused the break, what effect the estrangement has had on parenting or family).

Have you attempted to reconcile? If so, what precipitated the attempt and how did it go?

If there has been a reconciliation, how has it affected other members of your family?

Do you consider your race, gender, sexual orientation, class status, income level, or any other identifier to be a factor in your estrangement from your sibling? If so, please describe.

Just so I have a better understanding of you, I'd appreciate it if you would answer these questions:

What is your age?

How would you describe your racial, ethnic, or socioeconomic background?

What is your gender?

I'm hoping to interview some survey respondents about their experiences. If you would be willing to participate further in my research, please fill out your contact information. I will protect your privacy and will not use your name except to contact you, and if I do follow up with you, you may decline participation in the interview at that time.

I know sibling estrangement is a painful, complicated experience. I deeply appreciate your taking the time to respond to my survey.

Name:

Email:

For a variety of reasons, some people were reluctant to fill out the survey, messaging me privately that they wished they could help, but they were uncomfortable recording their thoughts. Many said that they felt ashamed that they had failed at a primary relationship or they didn't want to see the words on the page, making the abstract too concrete. Some worried about having their private thoughts read by the public, and still others feared that answering the questionnaire would stir up too many negative emotions.

Sixty-year-old Art Stoller emailed me to say that he simply couldn't bring himself to complete the survey. The Chicagoan has been estranged from both of his siblings for most of his adult life, but the situation became especially vicious when his mother died a few years ago. At that time, the three children began to bicker over where their father would live and who would manage his money. It turned out that one brother had drained the father's accounts and spent most of his savings. The siblings' bitter fights grew so petty that, when they visited the father's apartment, each would rearrange the photographs on the bookshelf, hiding pictures of a hated sibling behind their own.

Stoller recognizes that he suffers with PTSD from the fighting and the estrangement. "Sometimes the flashbacks kick in," he writes. "All it takes is a word or fleeting image that might be wholly unrelated, but, for some reason, that triggers bad feelings." The betrayal and constant fighting have taken a bitter toll on him, one he believes he will wrestle with for the rest of his life.

What Is Estrangement?

When a sixty-three-year-old friend, Marcus Lipsky, learned that I was conducting a survey on estrangement, he emailed me to see if he qualified. Ever since he and his older brother had argued over a family business matter twenty-five years ago, the brothers have had little to do with each other. They are cordial when they see each other at family events, but ultimately distant.

> *I hear from my brother once in a while—when someone dies or when our mother is ill in the hospital. Once a year or so, he'll leave me a message on my birthday or for some other reason. But I haven't really talked to him or his wife in years.*

"Is this estrangement?" he asked me.

The answer is yes. Dr. Kristina Scharp, an assistant professor and director of the Family Communication and Relationships Lab at University of Washington, and one of the few researchers on the topic, has created a working definition of estrangement: "It is a process where at least one family member voluntarily and intentionally distances themselves from another family member because of an ongoing (perceived) negative relationship."[1]

Silence sustains sibling cutoffs; it certainly fueled the decades-long divide between my brother and me. At first, withdrawing from a sibling relationship may provide a much-needed respite from distressing contact, but eventually, the silence itself becomes the problem. Behind the exclusion and raw pain often lies a catalyst: an event, a fight, some reason that one sibling turns away from another.

However, some siblings may have no idea why a brother or sister has terminated the relationship. They wonder: Had I done something wrong?

Is there something bad about me? Those unanswered questions mired me in endless speculation. I was tormented by the fact that Scott was very much alive, and yet he wanted nothing to do with me.

Even worse, there is no recourse, no self-defense for the shunned: I couldn't present my side of the story, couldn't ask questions, couldn't apologize. I felt voiceless. The choice to cut off a sibling wields a weighty club of control, denying a sister's or brother's very existence and generating feelings of anxiety, rejection, futility, and powerlessness. As silence continues for months and years, rumination replaces action for the shunned, eroding the urge to attempt to have a productive conversation. In time, the shunned may feel that silence is a deliberate intent to hurt—its own form of betrayal and abuse.

Various Forms of Estrangement

Some sibling relationships, as my friend Marcus discovered, become ambiguous. Even when the relationship limps along, a sibling finds ways to control the thermostat of its intimacy. For example, a brother who wants to avoid feelings of rage and resentment may relocate far away from the family, creating a geographic estrangement.

With or without a geographic estrangement, a sibling might deny family members emotional information—details about his or her feelings or personal life. Siblings who have limited, uncomfortable, obligatory contact at funerals, weddings, and holidays are experiencing an emotional estrangement or a limited relationship. In this situation, siblings often feel anxious when they know they're about to see each other again. When together, they may be pleasant and polite, avoiding contentious topics. In time, the relationship often degenerates into hostility, passive-aggressive behavior, and open conflict. Over the years, emotionally estranged siblings typically spend less and less time in each other's presence, and the relationship sometimes falls away.

Jean Flint, forty-five, who describes herself as a "white, British professional," has been emotionally estranged from her only brother for thirteen years. She idolized him as a child. When they became adults, however, he stopped talking to her and didn't explain his reasons. "I spent years torturing myself as to what I had done," she says. "I sent many apologies and tried everything for him to speak to me again." Nothing changed. She has been so distraught over her loss that she created a Facebook chat room for estranged siblings for support.

"I am a quiet administrator of the group as I am a naturally quiet person," she says, "but I am always in the background. I read all the posts and really empathize with the challenging emotions that members carry on a daily basis."

Flint knows the dread and discomfort of attending family events where one feels unwanted. Five years ago, her brother invited her to his son's wedding—where she again experienced her brother's stinging rejection:

My nephew's wedding was the worst. My brother seated my partner and me with the bride's family! My family all sat together on the opposite side of the room. My brother and his partner ignored me throughout the wedding. They didn't even take a family photo with all of us.

After that scene, Flint might have preferred a physical estrangement, in which siblings choose to avoid each other completely, much like my brother and me. A physical estrangement may be the last straw after decades of unaddressed slights and irritations. Deep issues and resentments, such as different value systems and unfulfilled expectations, build up over time; often they are the true roots of a cutoff.

Recall that Dr. Scharp defined estrangement as "intentionally creating distance," and that distance covers a spectrum. A complete cutoff is the extreme. Instead, many siblings alternate between breaking and resuming contact, and cycling through various types of estrangements and reconciliations in a chronic state of chaos. They push limits and test whether they can tolerate a complete breakdown. Years may go by as the two parties try to find a mutually acceptable level of involvement; in other cases, the siblings simply let time and distance do the work of enforcing an estrangement.

Hannah Ewing, twenty, who grew up in a chaotic, white, lower-middle-class home in Virginia, barely keeps track of whether she is speaking to her older brother. Her only sibling, an older brother, and she have engaged in this tumultuous pattern throughout their adult years.

> *We've been going between estranged and interacting all my life. Our relationship has been on and off, sometimes supporting each other through our parents' disastrous marriage, sometimes ignoring each other, and sometimes leaving the other to fend on their own.*

Some siblings may feel there's little choice but to abandon their involvement when there is an "ongoing negative relationship." In extreme circumstances—such as abuse, neglect, incest, alcoholism, addiction, or criminal behavior—therapists often recommend that a sibling cut off from a family member. If a sibling feels chronically hurt, belittled, or betrayed, they may choose this option so the toxic behavior ceases. Society is quick to judge a sibling who terminates a sibling relationship as "a bad person;" however, those who decide to cut off from a difficult sibling often are protecting themselves from intolerable behaviors.

Marcy Steuben, forty-three, of Pittsburgh, Pennsylvania, has terminated relationships with her three siblings. Her brother is an alcoholic, her half-brother is in prison, and her adoptive brother is violent.

> *If I did something unacceptable, I would expect to be cut off and would do the same in return. My parents are estranged from them, too. All the es-*

trangements were caused by a fundamental unwillingness by myself and my
parents to allow people to use or abuse us.

Recently, Steuben's biological brother asked if he could live with her as he transformed his life. She agreed, under the conditions that he look for a job and that he not drink. For several months, he lived up to her terms. But one day she came home and found him drunk. She had to evict him.

"I would have been okay with cutting him out of my life completely," she says. "I guess I'm unusual in that I don't consider that any kind of emotional hardship. We don't really have much of a relationship anyways."

Severing the connection with a toxic sibling can be necessary and liberating. Forty-six-year-old Janice Stein, who was raised in a Jewish home in New York, hasn't spoken to her brother in three years. "He always detested me," she says. "He told me I was the root of all evil and blamed me for anything that went wrong in his life. He was cruel and sometimes violent. Now I can go whole months without thinking about him. It's lovely and freeing." Stein says she can't mourn what she's never had. For her, the break was a relief, a balm to an ancient wound.

However, maintaining distance can be more difficult than establishing the cutoff in the first place. Families who might encourage a child to leave a relationship with an abusive spouse often pressure the estranged to return and repair rifts with siblings, even when the relationship is abusive. And every time the holidays roll around or a relative gets married or dies, the estranged are forced to reevaluate the cutoff.

Chapter 3

The Grief of Estrangement

⊤

There it is: his cell phone number, listed like everyone else's, right there in my contacts. *How ironic*, I think, gazing at his name: When I first learned cursive as a third grader, I wrote his name and mine over and over on blue-lined, three-holed notebook paper.

My mother gave me his number years ago, hoping I'd use it one day. "Be the bigger person," she would say. Seems to me, the bigger person would delete this hurtful information. Wipe him off my phone. Finalize the eradication of his toxic presence—or lack thereof—in my life.

But I never did. Every time I came upon his name under *S*, the rounded letters seemed to rise up like a serpent to sting me. I kept his number, I told myself, just in case I needed it—if something happened to Mom. But I always scrolled past it quickly, hoping to avoid another dash of salt in my wounds.

Now, for the first time, I search for the name I've avoided so long.

A tap on the screen, and it's done.

One ring . . . two . . . three . . . four. Then that familiar automated voice: "Hello. The person you're trying to reach . . ." He's not answering. Probably avoiding debt collectors, not just me.

My palms are sweaty; I don't know what to say. How can I reach out to him and shield myself at the same time? It's like dipping my toe in water and hoping I won't get wet.

A childish thought pops into my head: *I don't want him to think I caved first!* As if I'm first to look away in a staring contest. *Oh, great! I'm ten years old again, playing stupid games with my brother.*

"Please leave a message." There's the high-pitched beep, my cue to begin speaking. I feel as if I'm standing on stage. Naked, like in a nightmare.

"Umm . . . ummm . . . hi." *I haven't talked to him in years, and that's all I can bring myself to say?* "I . . . I . . ." *Maybe he won't recognize my voice.*

"It's Fern." I spit out the words, to relieve him of the worry that I'm harassing him over a bill. My name echoes in my ears. *It's Fern.* In childhood, I remember, our names were so often said together that they seemed to be combined into one: "ScottandFern."

Suddenly, the gravity of this small, enormous act shuts me down. Surely he doesn't know another Fern. Surely there's no need to identify myself by using the last name we share or—even worse—by saying those two strange, scary words: "your sister."

I gather myself and try again. "Ma . . . Mom . . ." I stumble, not even sure what he calls her now.

"Um . . . Mom just called me, awfully upset." My heart is thumping loudly, overpowering my fitful breathing.

"She says you're . . . you're going through a terrible time. I hated to hear her so upset." I'm still playing the game, as if I'm *really* only making this call for her.

"I know we haven't talked . . ."

In my mind, his adolescent sarcastic voice pipes up: "Ha! That's an understatement!"

"But, well, ummmm . . . if there's something I can do, I hope . . ."

Hope? I stop.

No, not really.

"Well." I pull back, collecting my dignity. "You can call me back."

Just as I'm tapping the red End Call button, the phone startles me with its ring. My brother's name, so familiar yet so foreign, flashes on the screen.

Immediately a pang drills down into my chest; my heartbeat pounds loudly in my ears. *He must be feeling desperate to have called back so fast.*

Suddenly a home movie pops into my mind—so old it's black-and-white—in which he's five and I'm three. We're facing each other, pumping our arms and legs on a double-seated metal swing in the tiny backyard of our childhood home. Just as we find a rhythm and start to gain speed, he jumps off the swing and runs away, out of the frame. Alone on the slowing swing, I'm the picture of disappointment: My little face droops as I realize he's found something he'd rather do than be with me.

"What do you remember most about your brother?" a therapist asked me years ago.

"His back," I answered instantly. "He was always running out the door. Always trying to get away. Always escaping home and family."

Is he finally coming back?

"Hello?" I say, after pressing the phone's green button to answer. I hear thick breathing, but he doesn't say a word.

"Hello?" I prompt, afraid he might hang up before we get a chance to talk. Trying to reel him in, I follow up with another "Hello?" *Too quick. That's bad.*

"Hi." It's a gravelly, elderly man's voice I hear at last—one that sounds as if it's coming from the bottom of a well. He doesn't sound the same, but I don't need the caller ID to recognize him; the quality of his voice is as familiar as the layout of our childhood home.

His "hi" reveals everything I need to know: Sadness oozes from the tiny word that, forty years after he dropped out of my life, still strikes a chord deep within me. Depression, devastation, defeat. Like images whirling in a slot machine, the parts of his misery send my emotions circling and clicking into a new configuration. My anger turns to fear; my wary self-protection melts into empathy; my disappointment gives way to sadness.

"What's going on?" My casual question presumes a closeness and confidentiality we've never shared.

He doesn't say anything, but his laborious wheeze tells me he's there. His breathing, like our father's as he aged, mesmerizes me. Losing myself for a moment, I feel as if I'm listening to Dad.

With a quick head shake, I remind myself of where I am and what I'm doing.

"How are you?" I say gently, trying again.

"Hi," he finally repeats. The word, drenched in grief, triggers a surge of fearful nausea. Waiting for him to say more, I sit stiff and still on the edge of my living room couch, in absolute silence, afraid I'll scare him off. It feels like offering food to a starving, skittish puppy: He needs to come to me on his own terms.

When he doesn't follow up, I finally ask, "You there?" Still, no words. But I hear him organizing himself—swallowing, smacking, sniffling.

Barely tethered to this tenuous connection, I'm already wondering: *What happens when we hang up?*

I try again: "How are you?"

Finally he says something. "Falling apart," he whispers.

I can't stand by and do nothing. I can't jump in to rescue him.

With a deep, deep breath, I drag myself to a single thought: *How* can *I reach him?*

"You know, just because we don't talk," I hear myself say, tipping my hand already, "it doesn't mean I don't care about you."

It's risky to admit after all this time, but what do I have to lose? What's the worst that can happen? He'll stop speaking to me?

No answer.

"You know, things haven't been easy for me either." I rush to engage him. *What am I doing?* Sharing myself with him when I have no idea who he is anymore? All this, just to fill the unbearable silences, hoping I'll get *something* in return?

"I've been through a lot."

Nothing.

"What's going on with you?"

I wait, listening to his heavy breathing. Trying to picture him right this minute—what he looks like, where he's sitting, where he's living—I can't sketch even the barest outline of him and his life.

"You . . . you—" I stumble, then stop when I hear him mutter something.

"I . . . I . . ." A hoarse voice, thick with shame, reaches my ear from far away.

"I'm a mess," he sighs. "A mess."

"In what way?" I fire back and wait.

Another long pause.

"*Every* way," he says finally.

"How?"

Again he swallows and sniffles. Is he drinking? On some kind of drug? Is he anxious? He can't even engage in a conversation anymore?

Impatient, I nudge him, the way I would when we were children and he knew something I wanted to know too.

"Tell me," I say, hearing the little girl in me.

"Where do I begin?" he asks.

I don't need the past forty years right this minute; I just need to know why things are so bad now.

What am I getting into? What if I discover that he's become a patho-logical liar or a gambler? What if he's willing to reconnect with me for some ulterior motive?

"*How* are you a mess?" I press him, looking for an opening. "What's happened recently?"

"It's not all that recent. It's been like this for years."

"Years? How many years?"

"I don't know . . . five or so."

"Five years! How bad is it?"

"Some days, I don't even get out of bed anymore," he mumbles. "I don't do anything. I can't concentrate. Can't make a living. I get anxious around people."

Each of his sentences feels like a body blow to me. When we were children and one of our parents yelled at him, I felt that they were holler-ing at me too. We seemed to share the same skin. Or maybe it was just me—I hurt for him.

Three minutes of reconnection, after decades apart, and now this; it must be bred in the bone.

"So it's hard to be around anyone?"

"Yeah, and my self-esteem is in the toilet." Another punch to my gut. "I feel worthless—like I'm no use to anyone."

I catch my breath and dive back in. "And you're avoiding everyone and everything . . . just so you don't have to feel like that?"

"Yeah." His tone, flat until now, picks up slightly. He's aware enough to be surprised I'd know that. Falling back into his flat tone, he adds, "I feel helpless . . . hopeless."

At least he's talking, I tell myself. He's holding onto enough of life to tell someone. And he's talking to me, of all people, after so many years.

This may be our first honest conversation since high school. *But how bad off is he really? What will happen when we hang up the phone? What will he do?*

"I'm so alone," he goes on, "and I don't know how to handle things anymore."

I flash on when we were nine and eleven, and our parents left us alone in the house at night. We were petrified: too scared to change the television channel from *The Lawrence Welk Show*, fearing even a few notes of the creepy theme music of *The Twilight Zone* or *The Outer Limits*. We wouldn't even go to the bathroom alone; both of us, and the dog, made the excursion together. Once there, one of us would use the toilet while the other faced the pink bathroom tile in the corner, "so you can't see." While watching TV, if we heard the slightest noise in the house, both of us froze and gave each other a terrified, wide-eyed look.

"You scared?" he'd ask me.

"Naaaah," I'd say, shaking inside. "You?"

"Nope!"

Naaaah, I'm not scared now either.

Trying to convince myself that I'm strong, I come up with a controlled, neutral response: "You feel this way often?"

"A lot." I wait for him to say more. Finally—finally—he adds, "More lately, I guess. It's getting worse."

"And you always feel jumpy? Kind of amped up?"

"Yeah." Again he's surprised. "Like I can't calm down. I can't sleep either. And when I finally get to sleep, I have . . ."

"Nightmares," I finish his sentence. "Lots of nightmares."

"Yeah. Lots of nightmares."

"*Every* night at the movies." Maybe I can lighten things up.

"How'd you know?" And in that question I hear him as he once was—a defensive little boy. When I called him a name, he'd snap back, "I know you are, but what am I?"

Then the little boy disappears; the old man returns. "I've got to *do* something. I just can't sit here any longer. I just can't."

"Nobody's asking you to. You don't have to. But what are you willing to do?"

"What do you mean?"

"Are you willing to get help?"

"Fern, I'm desperate! I'll do anything."

The way he says my name—a unique sound signature only he can make—stirs something deep within me, yanking the rope still tied to the girl who loved her brother so deeply.

"Will you do what I say?"

"Anything!"

Stop! I tell myself, though I know I'm already in too deep. How can I trust him? How can I protect myself from getting hurt again? But how can I abandon him now?

Wait! Breathe! Don't give up everything. Set some terms. Take charge.

"I'll help," I say, "but we have to have ground rules."

He doesn't respond.

"I can't get mixed up with you unless you agree to my terms."

"What?"

"Well—you can't disappear on me again."

I realize: He has no idea who I am now. I'm the little sister who followed him around, horning in on his baseball games at the local park when we were kids, wanting to date his friends when we were teenagers. But he doesn't know me as an adult; he has never heard me set boundaries or dictate terms. We're both negotiating a deal with a complete stranger, each of us wondering whether the other is trustworthy.

What if he agrees to whatever I say in this moment—and then, when he feels a little better, reverts to his old, remote self? My brother always was Harry Houdini, the escape artist of the early twentieth century, famous for his ability to free himself from all sorts of impossible physical traps. But with my brother, the challenge wasn't physical. The tight emotional spaces were the ones he squirmed out of effortlessly.

"I'm desperate," he says again, as if he's drowning.

I can't walk away. I wouldn't be able to live with myself if I did. I have to take a chance.

"Here's the deal," I say, taking a deep breath. "You can't bail on me, and you can't lie or hide from me."

Have I covered everything? Just like that? Can it be that simple?

I can't think of anything else, so I repeat: "You can't just disappear on me again, okay?"

"Okay," he quickly agrees. Then he asks, with a trace of eagerness, "When can we meet?"

As soon as possible, he says; he'll come to my house whenever I have time. Luckily, I'm busy for the next few days. That's a good thing because I need time to think.

I can't believe I'm making arrangements to see my brother. I actually *have* a brother.

And, to our mutual astonishment, he still has a sister.

After all these years of separation from Scott, I know all too well how estrangement defies basic assumptions about the family. Relatives expect enduring, predicable, trustworthy relationships; ruptured sibling relationships challenge and destroy the family's required coherence and support. I've learned, too, that few rejections are more powerful than shunning. Humans are hardwired for companionship and community, and they depend upon their families for well-being, identity, and a shared family history. Just the thought of abandonment can evoke feelings of fear and desperation.

The Deep, Devastating Pain of Estrangement

The pain of estrangement can be unimaginable. Survey respondents describe the loss of a sibling relationship as worse than a death in the family. They use vivid words and images to capture their chronic feelings of emptiness.

Estrangement is like a bad tooth that's always pulsating with pain.

Sibling estrangement is a wound that never heals.

After twenty-five years of no contact with my sister, I am still waiting for the hurting to stop.

Death is final, explains one woman who has been estranged from her sister for two years, and, therefore, it is easier to accept. "This is worse," she says. "They're out there, you know where they live, you know their number, but they don't *want* you in their life." In addition, it's difficult to grieve a reality that some feel they simply cannot accept.

In chat rooms, I find that the estranged emerge from their dark hiding places and are especially candid about their losses. While the survey produced direct answers to my questions, in these online conversations, I listen to the shared concerns of the estranged. For example, in one comment after another—and there are hundreds—bereft sisters and brothers list events from which they've been excluded during their years of estrangement. They include the following:

a party to celebrate a sixtieth wedding anniversary

a mother's retirement party, which included a family gathering before the main event a nephew's sixth birthday party

a sister's wedding

a nationwide search for a niece who went missing

These exclusions from family events are devastating, and those who are shunned often are haunted by their hurts and losses. Fifty-nine-year-old Lindy Robbins, for example, dreams about the sisters who refuse to talk to her. She was born into a privileged, white, South African suburban family; but her career as an artist, linguist, and gardener has not been lucrative. Now she lives in a racially mixed part of town, and her family refuses to visit her at her home. Each of the three sisters claims she was bullied by the other two. One sister won't let Lindy see her nieces and nephews. The other sister married a man who has terrorized the family. Lindy says there are plenty of reasons for the cutoffs, but she can't make peace with this reality. She poetically describes her pain in response to a survey question:

> *I had a dream. My sister walked up a mountain, up a wide winding road, and then she disappeared into the mist. I found a ruined house at a bend in the road. I thought, she has left. I felt empty and sad, like I'd lost something out of which life itself is made, and it would be not-life after that. I was so afraid this dream was a premonition of her death; it turned out to be a premonition of her leaving me for good.*

I realize as I read the survey responses and chat room comments that the estranged pass through the same stages of loss identified by Elisabeth Kübler-Ross in her definitive book, *On Death and Dying.* The five stages of grief are denial, anger, bargaining, depression, and acceptance, and the path is not linear. Estrangement is an experience of grief and loss that requires mourning, even for the sibling who made the choice to cut off.

The Crucial Need to Belong

Exclusion can cause pain that cuts deeper and lasts longer than a physical injury, according to Dr. Kipling D. Williams, a distinguished professor of psychological sciences at Purdue University who is noted for his unique studies of ostracism. When someone is shunned—even by a stranger, even if only briefly—Dr. Williams has found that he or she experiences a strong, harmful reaction, activating the same area of the brain that registers physical pain. He reported these findings in a 2014 article in *SAGE Journals*, a collection of publications on policy insights from the behavioral and brain sciences. The difference is that social injuries linger. In his studies of more than five thousand people, Williams used a computer game to show how just two or three minutes of ostracism can produce ongoing negative feelings.

"Our studies indicate that the initial reaction to ostracism is pain," he explains, "which is similarly felt by all individuals regardless of personality or social/situational factors. Ostracism then instigates actions aimed at recovering thwarted needs of belonging, self-esteem, control and meaningful existence."[1]

The eminent psychologist Abraham Maslow identified this crucial need in his "Hierarchy of Needs," a color-coded, weighted pyramid of basic human requirements. The need to belong—whether through family, friendship, shared interests, or sexual intimacy—ranks just after the essentials: food and water, shelter and sleep, physical safety. Like these fundamentals, the human need to belong is lifelong.

Absent a sense of belonging—this feeling of emotional safety and context—people come to fear that their very lives are at risk. They lose the ability to trust and connect with others, instead becoming consumed by the task of surviving alone. The family—that original constellation of relationships—offers an opportunity to belong to a group and a chance to develop deep, lifelong connections that may transcend the transient nature of human existence.

The most definitive long-term study on leading a healthy, happy adult life showed that relationships—especially with a sibling—have a big payoff.[2] The Harvard Study of Adult Development tracked 724 men over seventy-five years. In 1938, researchers interviewed, examined, and surveyed its first group of sophomores at Harvard College and compared the students with a second group of young men from Boston's poorest neighborhood, many of whom lived in tenements lacking such basic necessities as indoor plumbing. The study continues to track the sixty surviving participants and their children, grandchildren, and great-grandchildren. After examining their subjects' work and home lives over the years, the study produced a bounty of data on physical and mental health and concluded that—regardless of location, wealth, or fame—people who are more socially connected to family, friends, and community are happier, healthier, and likely to live longer than those who are less connected.[3]

Dr. Robert Waldinger, a psychiatrist and professor at Harvard Medical School, now the fourth director of the study, says their findings show that the single most reliable indicator of emotional health at age sixty-five was having had a close relationship with a sibling during the college years. The sibling relationship was more predictive of and crucial to well-being than childhood closeness to parents, emotional problems in childhood, parental divorce, or even marriages and careers. The study also found that siblings who lacked a close relationship before the age of twenty had a greater likelihood of suffering from depression later in life.

Other studies corroborate the importance of sibling relationships over the course of a life. For example:

- Adolescents who perceived that their siblings validated their beliefs and feelings reported higher levels of self-esteem.[4]

- Sibling support and a strong sibling relationship are correlated with better academic performance.[5]
- For children at risk of poverty, family discord, parental mental illness or divorce, having an emotionally stable person, like an older sibling, improved their chances of becoming a well-adjusted adult.[6]
- Sibling support and closeness was associated with less loneliness, lower levels of depression, and greater satisfaction later in life.[7]

Given this research, Waldinger recommends people of all ages lean into relationships by "replacing screen time with people time or livening up a stale relationship by doing something new together, long walks or date nights, or reaching out to that family member you haven't spoken to in years, because those all-too common family feuds take a terrible toll on the people who hold the grudges." Even though relationships are complicated, he encourages people to commit to the challenge of sustaining lifelong connections with family and friends.

Chapter 4

Risk Factors for Sibling Estrangement

I 'm always sifting through my mind, trying to tweeze out a possible reason for why my brother and I have had no relationship. A memory from eighteen years ago reveals our divided personalities and perceptions.

I remember calling Scott to tell him that our seventy-three-year-old father was hospitalized after a massive stroke left him paralyzed on his left side and ravaged his ability to speak. The old man immobilized in a hospital bed looked nothing like my vibrant, meticulously groomed, distinguished father. The stroke had altered his face, weakening its muscles and dulling its characteristic intensity and intellect; his flame was flickering. I desperately wanted to lean on my only sibling, hoping we would care for Dad during his last days and mourn his passing together.

"He's not going to make it," I said when Scott picked up the phone. Swallowing hard, whispering into the hospital's wall phone, I tried to keep my voice down so no one in the waiting room would hear what I was saying.

"What do you want me to do?" Scott barked.

"Don't you even want to *see* him before he *dies*?" I hissed incredulously. I knew Scott hadn't spoken to our dad in at least a decade, and they had had only the barest relationship for the past twenty years. But now—surely now—

"I'm not coming," Scott announced.

"What!" I turned to face the wall, hugging the phone. "How can you—Why not?"

"I just can't."

I'd never imagined Scott would go to such an extreme. Refusing to visit his own father's deathbed? Of course, he was still angry now, but wouldn't he be filled with regret later?

Feeling certain he hadn't thought this through, I tried to warn him. "How are you going to feel after he's gone?"

"I'll deal with it," he snapped, shutting me down angrily.

What about me? I thought, dizzy in my isolation. *Do I have to go through this alone? Even if you can't be his son, can't you be my brother?*

Yet I knew I didn't have much of a case. Scott hadn't been a brother to me in years. So instead of taking him on and demanding that he step up for his family, I caved.

"You sure?" I asked meekly.

"Look, Fern," he said calmly, as if he had long anticipated this possibility and figured out exactly how he would handle it.

Then, even though I was in a haze as my father was passing, Scott said something that would always stay with me: "He wasn't there for me in life; I won't be there for him in death."

I couldn't dispute that Scott had every reason to distance himself from our father. Dad's expectations were so boundless, his ego so grandiose, that he had predetermined the trajectory of his son's life before Scott could walk or talk. Viewing Scott as an appendage of himself, he assumed it was his right to set the course of his son's career: Scott would carry on Dad's own lifelong mission by becoming a doctor.

Scott knew what was expected of him at a very early age. Once, as a curious seven-year-old, he rummaged around in the medicine cabinet and found one of Dad's razors. Pretending to shave with it, of course he accidentally cut himself.

"Mom! Mom!" Scott screamed, running into the kitchen. Mom grabbed a dish towel and wrapped it tightly around his small, oozing fingers to stanch the bleeding.

"I don't *want* to be a doctor," Scott wailed. "I *hate* blood!"

Blinded by his ambition, blithely immune to reality, Dad intensified his expectations when Scott entered college. Dad was confident that the medical school where he taught and served on the board would accept Scott's application after the mere formality of four years' undergrad work. His MCAT scores wouldn't matter; all he had to do was pass his premed classes.

Scott knew that he wouldn't—couldn't—be a doctor. But he could never admit that to Dad. Instead, he passively let things play out, starting immediately after he arrived at the University of Illinois in Champaign.

After failing a required course in organic chemistry during his very first semester, Scott was placed on academic probation. During his second semester, he repeated organic chemistry, one of the most difficult courses in the university's premed program. This time he couldn't even bring himself to attend classes—but he knew he had to pass or flunk out of school. The weekend before the final, he crammed, doing the full semester's readings in three days. Remarkably, he passed, with a final grade of C+.

His next challenge, biochemistry, met on Tuesdays, Thursdays, and Saturdays. Given Scott's devotion to the campus party scene, he would never be able to attend Saturday-morning classes after Friday-night revelries. This time, he couldn't pull a rabbit out of a hat. Flunking biochemistry ended Scott's premed path and his college career.

Still, unable to face our father, Scott remained at U of I for what should have been his junior year—though he couldn't even register for classes. Meanwhile Dad, comfortably living in his fantasy, alerted the medical school to his son's upcoming application. He even went so far as to fill out the necessary forms. All Scott had to do was present his transcript.

With dozens of excuses, Scott put Dad off and withheld his college record. Frustrated but undeterred, Dad finally called the university. Angrily intimidating a clerk, he insisted that, having paid his son's tuition, he had every right to see a transcript.

The clerk caved, and Dad finally discovered the scam. There they were: one F after another in premed classes. First probation, final probation, expulsion.

In that instant, everything changed. Scott's fake college career, Dad's fantasy of his son becoming a doctor, their ever-difficult relationship: All came to a crashing, crushing end.

This drama occurred when I was still in my first year of college—and, of course, I was a girl. Dad had never invested in me as he had in his son. He took much less interest in my career and certainly didn't fantasize about my future.

Wasn't I worthy of the same focus, attention, planning, and ambition? I didn't know whether to be insulted or relieved. Either way, over the years and through an endless stream of oversights, slights, and hurts, I chose to maintain a connection—however tenuous—with my father, who made that commitment quite a challenge.

Dad himself rigorously subscribed to a model of coldness and cutoff. For him, all family relationships were expendable. He mastered the practice of estrangement as if it were an art; in fact, it was a cruel means of control, a silent form of abuse he employed to punish relatives who didn't conform to his thinking.

No one escaped his family editing. At various times, he stopped speaking to all three of his brothers, sometimes for decades. He cut off children, siblings, aunts, uncles, nieces, nephews. He even broke off relations with his mother several times during their lives—for the last time, only a few years before she died, in her late eighties.

In all relationships, he kept one hand firmly on the spigot of his affection, turning it on and off at his discretion. He seemed to look for opportunities to terminate contact with family members who demanded too much of his time or inconvenienced him in any way. Often I wondered how he kept track of whom he was speaking to at any given time. Then again, he had a scorecard for everything. Arriving a little late for dinner at his house? Failing to call on Father's Day? Opting out of his Thanksgiving celebration? He was through with you, and he would let you know when—if ever—you were reinstated.

Despite the chaos and turbulence he created, I pursued my father, sacrificing more and more of myself to keep him in my life. I was always tentative around him, always subject to his wrath, always at risk of rejection. But I needed a dad, and I was willing to tolerate almost any abuse to sustain the illusion of a relationship.

After he died, I often said sardonically, "He died. We were still talking. I won."

But I was only kidding myself; there was no winning with Dad. Maintaining a relationship with him was like trying to ride an untamed, unwilling stallion. Over and over, I was thrown; often I was left with invisible but painful injuries. Yet I kept climbing back in the saddle.

Scott, on the other hand, never went anywhere near the horse.

I often envied my brother's choice.

So why didn't he talk to me for decades? Was it our father's model that set us up for a long-standing estrangement? Or has Scott been hiding something shameful—money problems, drug use, alcoholism? Is he trying to avoid uncomfortable feelings like anger or frustration?

Estrangement is not necessarily personal, I try to reassure myself, but it surely feels that way. Our cutoff could be traced to many causes that have nothing to do with me. It could simply be Scott's way of removing complications from his life. It may provide a screen of secrecy, so I can't see or judge his behavior. Or he may be using our relationship as a dumping ground for all his frustrations, especially his disappointments in our family.

The Risk Factors for Estrangement

Many estranged siblings don't know the reasons behind the estrangement. They are searching for some explanation or understanding:

> *I spent years torturing myself as to what I had done, sent apologies, tried everything to restore the relationship, but nothing changed. The only way I can deal with the pain is to disassociate from him, to disconnect from him as my brother.*

> *You never get closure, or answers, or anything neat and tidy.*

> *No one speaks to me. It is numbingly painful, and confusing.*

The results of my survey show that about two thirds of the estranged are aggrieved, and one third relieved, by the cutoff, and 16 percent of respondents—one in six—said they don't know why they are living in this world of pain.

Interestingly, certain risk factors increase the chances of sibling estrangement. Agllias, author of *Family Estrangements*, has identified a number of causes that undermine the childhood relationship, and my survey respondents fall into one or more of the following categories.

Trauma in the Family

Children raised in chaotic, abusive, or neglectful families, according to Agllias, run the greatest risk of estrangement, as many are living with parents who have an authoritarian parenting style. These parents are "demanding, highly critical, and shaming," and they often use scapegoating, favoritism, and name-calling when relating to their children.

"A sense of long-term disconnection in childhood has been described as a precursor to estrangement in adulthood," she writes. "This disconnection may be characterized by a lack of early attachment experiences, a feeling of not 'belonging' to family, and a distinct lack of attention or actual presence by the parent or parents."[1]

Children tend to respond to turmoil with one of two behaviors: They may form a close bond based upon their shared traumas, or, more often, they isolate from the family to take care of themselves. In addition, children who experience or witness trauma in early life may shut down and numb themselves to their emotions, which limits all of their relationships.

Julianna Turner, a fifty-four-year-old woman who describes herself as a white, Scottish Latina from a white-collar, upper-middle-class family, says she hasn't spoken to her sister in five years, and one of her two brothers has cut off their relationship because he can't bear to remember their traumatic childhood.

My brother holds a lot of resentment and anger toward our parents, as we had a very turbulent upbringing. Even though I've always been close to my brother, I've noticed we've drifted apart over the past year. I know in my heart he loves me, but unfortunately, I am part of a past that he just wants to forget. It has nothing to do with me. I give him space and, when he's ready, he'll come around. I don't consider us estranged. I just know he needs a lot of healing.

Melissa Marley, fifty-three, of Calgary, Alberta, considers her difficult childhood a major reason she felt the need to cut off from her brother, who has a gambling addiction. He sees her, she says, as an easy mark, a convenient source of money—and she can't afford, financially or emotionally, to get mixed up with him again. The root of their problems, she recognizes, lies in their rearing. "When there was an insecure upbringing," she says, "the baby definitely gets thrown out with the bathwater. When a sibling distances from a difficult childhood, siblings suffer too."

A 2012 article in the journal *International Sociology* reported on a study of 6,630 Dutch adults that found that people who experienced divorce, addiction, run-ins with the law, financial problems, and other negative life events often had less supportive and more strained sibling ties. A sense of disconnection in childhood, characterized by a feeling of not "belonging" to the family, may result in estrangement in adulthood.

Poor Communication Skills

Poor communication skills can be at the root of estrangements. When parents are unable to express feelings and negotiate differences, they don't model the necessary skills—listening, apologizing, cooling off—to resolve conflicts. As a result, small disagreements can escalate, sometimes exploding into nasty rifts. Those who have poor communication skills may handle stress or strife in a relationship by simply shutting down and cutting off.

Janice Stein, who in chapter 2 described the cutoff with her brother as "freeing," says her parents avoided any confrontations in their white, Jewish, upper-middle-class home in New York. "Most things were swept under the rug and ignored," she says. "Feelings were dismissed, and emotions not tolerated. My older brother, the one who doesn't speak to me, has been on a decades-long downward spiral due to not being able to handle his emotions."

Almost half of those who filled out my survey not only were cut off from one relative but also endured other severed relationships in their family. Four percent of survey respondents identified poor communication in the family—when the connection is superficial, strained, or nonexistent—as a contributing factor to the breakdown.

Even if someone who falls into this category had the opportunity to have a conversation about the estrangement, he or she would likely become defensive instead of listening and trying to understand the estranged sibling's perspective. In blatantly disregarding a sibling's point of view, he or she might argumentatively say things like "That's not true!" or "What about the time you . . . ?" or "You can't blame me for that!" The shunners often see *themselves* as victims, believing that the offending sibling knows exactly what he or she has done wrong. Estranged siblings often judge one another harshly with assessments like "So it's his fault. He started it. I didn't do anything wrong." Each sibling becomes isolated in the silo of his or her own thinking.

Difficulties in a sibling relationship may arise when one has greater expectations and invests more deeply in the relationship than the other. Susanna Garth, thirty-five, who grew up in a loving, lower-middle-class family in Fiji, says she lives in that skewed misery with her only, older sister, and she's frustrated that she has no opportunity to talk about their relationship. She has no idea whether the estrangement is temporary or permanent, and that is its own torment.

I always thought I had a great relationship with my sister. I have loads of happy childhood memories with her. I was the only bridesmaid at her wedding five years ago. I spent lots of time with her and her daughter. I was there for the birth of her son. I always assumed she'd be a very important part of my life.

The estrangement felt very sudden. I not only lost my relationship with my sister, but I have lost contact with my four-year-old niece and five-year-old nephew. My sister said she loves me, but she "just needs to walk away for now." I don't know why.

The grief is overwhelming—suddenly having someone you thought would be there forever completely ripped from your life, not being able to do anything about it, and not knowing whether it will be for a few months or forever.

In the absence of an opportunity to discuss the issues with her sister, Garth speculates that the estrangement could be due to a number of factors: "She could feel uncomfortable about our differing political beliefs," she says. "Or she might feel threatened because the family expressed concern over the treatment of her daughter. Or maybe she's upset with me because I couldn't help her out much when I was in postgraduate school and she was overwhelmed by the needs of her baby daughter." But ultimately, Garth says her head spins with confusion.

Without feedback, each sibling constructs a narrative of what happened and why it happened. Desperate to understand, siblings often come to their own conclusions based upon misperceptions, miscommunications, and their own defensiveness.

Parental Favoritism and Sibling Jealousy

Siblings are especially sensitive to parental favoritism, a factor leading to estrangement. Research by Dr. Karl Pillemer, a sociologist, gerontologist and professor of human development at Cornell University, suggests that between two-thirds and three-quarters of mothers have a favorite child, and their children are keenly aware of a parent's partiality.[2] Six percent of those who completed my survey identify favoritism and pitting children against one another as the roots of a sibling cutoff.

A century ago, the intensity of sibling competition could have devastating consequences, given that significant numbers of children didn't survive childhood. Then, parents with limited resources may have taken only a favored child to the doctor when necessary—a decision that could save an afflicted child's life or sacrifice that of a less fortunate child.

Today, parents with means usually take all their children to the doctor, but they often have other, more subtle ways of showing favoritism. Marco Bertelli, seventy-one, of Sacramento, California, warned his parents when he was a teenager that favorably comparing him with his younger brothers would ultimately damage his relationships with his two brothers. The elder Bertellis, however, didn't listen. Marco, meanwhile, proved himself to be a serious student, serving as a high school class president, attending an Ivy League school, and becoming a prominent lawyer, while his brothers struggled to make a living.

> *My folks would say to my brother who is three years younger, "Why can't you be like Marco?" I kept telling them, "Don't do this." But they laid that on thick, and that created tension between us. One of my brothers resented me so much that at one point in our adult life, he just stopped talking to me.*

On the surface, as children, siblings may wish to be the parents' favorite, but survey respondent Kristin Townsend, forty-three, of Concord, New Hampshire, says no one wins when favoritism is in play. The youngest of five children, she believes that her siblings resent her because their mother spoiled her. She explains that siblings often blame favored children for their status in the family, yet no child asks to be the favorite. In fact, those who are favored often feel guilty, worry about living up to high expectations, and become depressed over small setbacks.

When a parent favors a child, that sibling may become more egotistical, and that could lead to estrangement. The "golden child" places his or her needs above the family, explains psychotherapist Ali-John Chaudhary, who has a bilingual practice in Pembroke, Ontario. "That's where a sense of entitlement grows," he says, "and favored children become hostile towards those who have different needs than them. Parents need to teach that child that the family comes first and individual needs come second."[3]

Survey respondents frequently mentioned sexism in the family as a variable in favoritism. Many sisters said that the boys in the family were always made to feel more important, more intelligent, and more valued. The sexism was subtle but palpable.

Sixty-seven-year-old Elizabeth Volpe, the eldest child and only girl in a Wisconsin family of four children, identifies sexism as one reason she is estranged from a brother who is two years her junior.

I was raised in a male chauvinistic family. For the most part, we were happy, but my dad was very demanding of my mother; she was not allowed to work outside the home. There was a lot of competition between my brother and me. When we were of driving age, even though I was older, I was told to always defer to my brother to drive the car.

My dad was the first son of a first son of a first son. I was the oldest and only girl. I broke the line. My mother always told me that my paternal grandfather sent her a telegram on the day of my birth saying, "A' for effort, but better luck next time!" I now have that telegram, and it actually reads, "Congratulations on the birth of your beautiful daughter." I cried the first time I read that telegram.

Sexism also affected a fifty-three-year-old younger sister and self-described baby boomer who has been estranged from her only brother for five years.

We could have stepped out of a Woody Allen movie or Neil Simon play. He was the firstborn in a middle-class Jewish home in Brooklyn, New York, in the 1950s. Can anything compete with that? The dynamic was created, and it plays into all our family relationships. No matter how hard we tried to change it, we couldn't.

Some adult-sibling divides take root early in life. "My sister hated me since I was a zygote," says Art Stoller, who described in chapter 2 how his siblings and he vied for placement of photographs of themselves on their father's bookshelf. Stoller says the relationship with his sister never really improved much over the course of their lives.

Young children, particularly those who are close in age and in direct competition with each other for parental attention, are extremely sensitive to favoritism. Children are aware and socially sophisticated—sometimes before the age of two, according to research by social developmental psychologist Dr. Judith Dunn. She was on the faculty at King's College in Cambridge and Pennsylvania State University in State College and conducted pioneering studies by observing siblings in their homes instead of a laboratory.

Dr. Dunn observed that the fifteen- to seventeen-month-olds closely monitor how a mother treats an older sibling, and she reports that the greater the difference in maternal affection and attention among children, the more hostility and conflict between siblings. In addition, she says, children know how to comfort, hurt, and intensify each other's pain, and they carry those abilities throughout their lives.[4]

Sibling pairs, ranging in age from three to nine, typically fight roughly every eighteen minutes during play sessions, according to Dr. Laurie Kramer, a professor and psychologist at Northeastern University, Boston, Massachusetts. Parents often find themselves refereeing arguments where one child might insist, "He pushed me!" and the other argues, "I did not!," and it can be nearly impossible to sort out whether one child is too aggressive or the other is too sensitive. Learning to negotiate conflicts is an important developmental achievement for children. When this necessary life skill is never acquired, unresolved issues in childhood may reappear later in life.

Two personality types appear to be particularly vulnerable to estrangement: those who are extremely angry and those who nurse grievances. The issues that divide siblings in adulthood, according to psychologists Joel Milgram, a professor emeritus of education at the University of Cincinnati, and his colleague, the late Professor Helgola Ross, often stem from rivalries over achievement, looks, and intellect. In a 1980 study of sixty-five siblings between the ages of twenty-five and ninety-three, Milgram and Ross found that rivalry continued into adulthood for almost half the brothers and sisters they interviewed.[5]

Some siblings cope better with their less-favored status. The situation becomes problematic when the less-favored child is discontented and disappointed with his or her adult life, explains Dr. Joshua Coleman, a psychologist and author of *Rules of Estrangement: Why Adult Children Cut Ties and How to Heal the Conflict*. "If the sibling remains in the one-down position, the relationship can be more painful because there is nothing to counter it," he says. "But if they are more successful, there's much more psychic ammunition" to overcome resentment and establish a stronger connection in adulthood.[6]

When siblings are more than a few years apart, they often don't share common interests or developmental stages, and they exert less influence on each other. This gap may result in a lack of intimacy, making the relationship more tenuous and easier to terminate.

Raised in a small town in Texas, seventeen-year-old Maddie Blooms is the youngest of five, ten years junior to the family's fourth child, a sister. Blooms says she has always felt like an only child, and now the sister who is closest in age to her has nothing to do with her. "I didn't see much of her growing up," she explains, "because she stayed in her room all the time. I worshipped the ground she walked on, but I never really had a relationship with her. We lived in completely different worlds."

Some elder siblings have ambivalent feelings toward their younger sisters or brothers because they were their caregivers in childhood. When a sibling becomes a caregiver for younger children in the family, he or she sometimes harbors long-standing resentments about that role.

Siblings who never develop a solid, authentic, loving relationship sometimes become apathetic, and they simply stop caring enough to make an effort. Some survey respondents came to realize that they and their siblings are simply different people. Once their parents had passed away, many survey respondents commented, they no longer felt obligated to get together. Many said that they feel they have little in common with their siblings:

> *I feel that I did not truly know my sibling prior to the estrangement. I feel that the relationship we had was never genuine and was only a front to appease our parents.*

> *The "problem" I have with my family is simply indifference. It isn't that we ever had some big argument. There is just* nothing.

> *We don't have much in common. My siblings are constantly analyzing and judging my choices, so I took a break from all of them.*

Some sibling relationships aren't apathetic or competitive; they're abusive. Michael Cavenish of Calgary, Alberta, says he finally cut off his sister after years of sibling rivalry and mistreatment. "Sometimes, when I see that my spouse is close with her siblings, I wish I were closer to mine," he says. "But my sister and I have had I deep issues all of our lives. I can't take her abuse anymore. It's just too painful."

Family Values, Judgments, and Choices

The sense that a sibling has rejected the family's core beliefs may spark estrangement. Thirty-three percent of survey respondents identified this factor as the source of the cutoff, and they reported numerous choices and values that violated their family identity and code:

I'm gay and my sister does not believe in homosexuality because of her alt-right fundamentalist Christian beliefs.

I think the break was related to her choices. I honestly don't have anything in common with her.

I'm trans and my family has nothing to do with me. Estrangement is something many LGBTQ people face.

My brother and sister-in-law prospered. They value money, possessions and status. I don't.

Often a family feels violated by the choice of a sibling's new partner or spouse. This new relationship may present challenging questions: How will this new person fit into the family and affect sibling relations? Is she or he anything like other family members? Can a sister or brother cultivate a warm relationship with this new in-law?

"Our brothers and sisters were our 'first' marriage partners," explains Dr. Karen Gail Lewis, author of *Siblings: The Ghosts of Childhood That Haunt Your Love and Work* and seven other books about sibling relationships. Lewis is also a counseling psychologist in Silver Spring, Maryland, who organizes sibling retreats. "We have a lot of emotional stock invested in them and in the spouses they choose."[7]

If our brothers and sisters are our first marriage partners, the termination of the relationship can be as painful as a bitter divorce. A powerful letter published in *The Guardian* in May 2018 poignantly captures the lacerating wedge her brother's wife created in the writer's sibling relationship. The writer describes how the two fought as children, grew close as they got older, but then became estranged after her brother married. She writes that her brother constantly accommodates his wife, resulting in the loss of lifelong friends and family:

If the genders were reversed, we would be talking about domestic abuse. . . .
Not wanting to damage the one remaining connection you have with our
family, I say nothing. I wait . . . I hope you find the strength to break free . . .
I will be waiting. I will always be your sister.[8]

Why do some spouses choose to divide siblings? A new partner may feel threatened by or jealous of the closeness between brothers and sisters and begin a campaign against the in-laws immediately after the wedding. The sibling dynamic may change quickly—for example, when the couple elects to go to one side's holiday dinner. The new spouse, always in the sibling's ear, is powerfully influential and may speak against the family and, in time, erode the sibling relationship.

In extreme cases, a partner may feel forced to make a choice: your family or your spouse. Often the surrendering sibling harbors festering anger and resentment toward the demanding spouse. Ironically, some siblings actually, if unwittingly, pick a partner who will take on the dirty work of helping to distance or cut off from the family.

A partner exerting pressure to sever his or her spouse from family and friends may be a dangerous sign of abuse. Typically, a controller establishes his or her dominance in a relationship through isolation, requiring the partner to check in often and demanding the partner quit activities that separate the couple. This process gradually enables the controller to gain more power in the relationship and weaken the victim.

By preventing the victim from hearing other people's perspectives, the controller easily intensifies harmful behaviors—such as insults, manipulation, humiliation, intimidation, or physical, sexual, and financial abuse. Ultimately, the abused partner may feel that he or she cannot confide in anyone about these experiences, and he or she has no support system during a time of great need.

Seven percent of my survey respondents attributed the break in their sibling relationship to a new partner or spouse, and many were particularly resentful about this development. Some of their comments are bitter and painful:

> *She met her boyfriend and he slowly started cutting out everything and everyone until he had manipulated her into interacting with him only. I pray I never run into him because I can't be sure I won't pulverize him.*

> *My brother's wife has tons of drama and hate in her life, so I am 100 percent positive she is the precipitating factor—although she is not to be blamed solely.*

> *My brother's wife values status, money, and connections above all else. I have none of these things, so I am not useful.*

Raised in a comfortable, middle-class home on the West Coast, sixty-nine-year-old Sam Goldman now recognizes that his choice in a spouse led to an emotional estrangement from his sister and mother. The death of his beloved father when Sam was only fifteen resulted in an existential loneliness that drove him to marry at twenty-one. Sam's mother and sister didn't accept his wife because she wasn't Jewish. In time, Sam says, his alienation from his family led to a sense of rootlessness and self-eradication.

> *I saw my mother and sister now and then, but our conversations were absolutely superficial and fraught with anxiety. The tension between us was palpable. My first wife did nothing to mitigate that tension; she seemed to feel that if I had a relationship with my mother and sister, it would diminish my relationship with her. The message from my first wife to my children was that my mother was mean, and my sister was disapproving and imperious. It was difficult to visit my mom and sister, especially with my wife. Visits were*

under the cloud of religious judgment, and it seemed we were all looking at
the clock, waiting for the visit to end so we could get back to our own lives.

Some families simply will not tolerate certain behaviors that resist or
defy the family identity. "The 'family myth' is the presumption that every
family member is compatible, possesses the same goals, and loves one another," explains psychologist Mark Sichel, director of the Addiction Recovery Unit at Hebrew Union College, New York. The author of *Healing from
Family Rifts*, Sichel explains that the "family myth," identified by "we" statements, asserts shared values and discourages individual differences. Often,
to keep the family identity intact, members who challenge the myth through
sexual orientation, interracial marriage, religious conversion, political phi-
losophies, unconventional career or lifestyle choices may be cast out.[9]

Politics

Current political polarizations are especially sharp as the Right has gained
power in the United States and other Western nations. Entrenched political divides often split families.

In Poland, two well-known brothers, both political activists, are famed
for their prominent feud. The two once shared similar political views; now
their enmity is public and bitter. Journalist Jaroslaw Kurski runs the larg-
est and most influential liberal opposition newspaper in his country; his
brother, Jacek, chief ideologist for the Polish antiliberal state, heads up the
conservative, nationalist, state-controlled public television station. The two
haven't spoken in years, and Jaroslaw can't even say his brother's name
without deep agitation.

Three percent of respondents to my survey identified politics as the
root of the family divide. Many commented on how politics created a divide in their sibling relationships:

Politics, world views, gun control, differing family priorities caused the cutoff.

Our politics are not similar. When my mother died, his car was ahead of mine in the funeral procession and I recall having to look at an IMPEACH OBAMA bumper sticker on the way to the cemetery.

I couldn't be my authentic self around my brother because we disagree politically. I was always avoiding topics, and eventually we avoided each other.

Deeply entrenched political positions, exacerbated by hateful propaganda, can rip families apart.

Money

Not surprisingly, money issues often rupture sibling relations. Financial questions—why wasn't that loan repaid? who gets the bigger inheritance and why? why did that child get promoted in the family business?—plague many families. In my survey, fifteen percent of respondents said that they are estranged because of money.

Immigration complicated Juanita Hernandez's story of money and sibling estrangement. The sixty-nine-year-old housekeeper came to the Chicago area from Mexico fifty years ago. She no longer speaks to her three sisters who live in Mexico because they continually demand that she send them money. Hernandez's story is not uncommon; she explains the specific challenges of money and immigration:

They are always asking for something. One sister got married at fourteen and had twelve children, and she never has money. When I visited Mexico, the family expected gifts and often complained, "You don't bring us any nice things."

No matter how much money they have, they are always asking me for more. They were using me. They think the streets are paved in gold in

America and I'm rich. We work for every penny. We pay taxes, and it's expensive to live here.

I got mixed up in a pig business with my older sister in Mexico. I sent her seven thousand dollars to buy three mothers and one, you know, who does all the stuff for the ladies. I ended up with forty pigs. My sister said she didn't have room for all my pigs at her place. Then she started calling me and telling me, "Oh, one died . . . then another died . . . then another." She was lying, and I never saw a penny from that business.

I brought my sister to this country years ago, and I spent two weeks at the border fixing her papers so she could come here. But a few years ago, when she bought a mobile home, she used my name to cosign her loan without my permission, and she put other things in my name. When I applied for a credit card at T. J. Maxx for a twenty-five-dollar bill, they wouldn't give it to me. I ended up with bad credit. I feel so ashamed. My sister ruined my life.

I don't talk to my sisters anymore. I don't trust anyone now. If you can't trust family, you can't trust anyone.

Hernandez's feelings of betrayal and resentment are common when money comes between siblings.

Inheritance and Elderly Care

Fights over money may become especially vicious as a parent approaches the last stage of life. Divisive topics—such as health-care decisions and caregiving needs—may reignite old conflicts. Serious parental illness, death, or unresolved estate issues entangle estranged siblings, and suddenly, after years of separation, they have to interact with each other again.

The last months and eventual death of a parent are especially fraught with danger for strained sibling relationships. In my survey, 11 percent experienced estrangement during this time, as siblings fought over care for the elderly parent, inheritance, or personal items.

Eugenie Stanley, a sixty-one-year-old African American teacher in New York City, was blindsided by her only sister's decision to terminate their relationship after their mother died:

I thought we got along okay. But one month after the funeral that we had planned together, she emptied out Mom's bank account and stole my mother's ashes. She tried to take half of the house Mom left me in South Carolina.

Mom was the glue in the family. After her death, my sister disowned me. I haven't seen her in five years. She took my niece and nephew with her. The cousins all sided with her, and they disowned me too.

Estrangement is one of the cruelest forms of power and control. The one who is doing the estranging is trying to control the relationship because they know how desperately you want it. They're saying, "I'll let you know when I'm willing to speak to you." It hurts like hell.

Two years ago, when her father died, Jackie Jenson, sixty-eight, of Columbus, Ohio, learned the truth about her relationship with her younger brother as they went through their parents' possessions. Her brother was to inherit the parents' furnishings, and Jenson wanted her mother's silver. She says resentments between the two have built up over the years, but, during this fight, bitter words escalated and the two called each other terrible names. Eventually, the fight became so vicious that Jenson's brother called the police on her. In the end, she would have gladly forfeited the silver to repair the mess, but now, she says there's no going back. She says the loss of her dad, her brother, and her niece in one afternoon has nearly broken her.

One woman posted in a chat room a desolate picture of a streetlight casting a solitary shadow on a snowy evening to capture her somber mood. She says she is heartbroken because her sister and her beloved nieces, with whom she has enjoyed a close relationship for decades, now want nothing to do with her. The reason for the cutoff, she says, is that her dad has asked her, the eldest child, to take over his financial matters.

It is not uncommon for siblings to vie for position as a parent's life winds down. A rift may occur as parents lose their grip on the family and their ability to manage finances, and one adult child assumes control. As one survey respondent commented, "Now there is a new CEO in the family."

Eighteen percent of respondents said their sibling relationships ended at this life stage. They faced a number of challenges:

My mother is ninety years old, and I am a full-time caregiver. My sister didn't do anything to help.

My mom was diagnosed with breast cancer. She received poor care and not much support from my siblings. Finally, Mom agreed to get treatment at a leading cancer center in my city, but it was too late. My siblings blamed me for Mom's death.

My sister removed valuable items from Mom's home without my permission. She is deceitful and greedy.

The risk of estrangement increases when a parent is diagnosed with Alzheimer's or some other degenerative disease. Two percent of survey respondents indicated that Alzheimer's was a factor in their sibling estrangement; typically, the problem is that primary caregiving falls to one child.

Caring for parents as they decline is a relentless, painful vigil that may cause unprecedented strain and stress. Often the main caregiver feels largely unsupported by other siblings.

Making matters worse, siblings often can't agree on how to care for an ailing parent. Connie Owen, sixty-three, and one of her two sisters have radically different approaches to caring for their father, who suffers from Alzheimer's. As a result, the sisters, who live in Ann Arbor, Michigan, haven't spoken in a year.

She got power of attorney, and then she took it upon herself to put our father into a memory-care facility while I was at work. It devastated me and my father beyond belief. I quit my job to take care of him at home, but she wouldn't let me. He wants to die at home, but she's not going to let that happen. For several months, she even kept me from visiting him. I believe she likes her power.

In some of the most painful cases, some respondents reported that an Alzheimer's diagnosis pulled back the curtain on their sibling's cold-hearted greed. Some siblings used the parent's diminished state to take money from a mother's or father's bank accounts, and some even stopped seeing or caring for the ailing parent.

Finally, a parent's will ultimately validates previously held beliefs that "my parents favored him over me" or "I didn't live up to my parents' expectations" or "Mom thought you were more responsible than I am." A parent's will may be a final statement of love, approval, and power, confirming long-standing perceptions that have haunted siblings.

These end-of-life disputes can become so acrimonious that a new field has emerged to respond to the needs of quarrelling siblings. Elder mediators can help resolve issues such as caregiving, inheritance, living arrangements, and estate planning. A good mediator also can refer families to other professionals, such as a geriatric care manager who can offer guidance on how to care for an elder parent.

Alcoholism, Addictions, and Other Mental Health Issues

Some serious problems—such as mental illness, substance abuse, incest, and violence—may never be discussed in a family setting; however, they may lead to cutoffs. Agllias's research shows that mental illness and addiction (problems that are often related) typically are not the sole cause of estrangements, though drugs and alcohol may fuel abuse and domestic violence. These mental health issues are indicators, and possibly a cause, of broader family problems.

Several survey respondents suspected that their absent sibling had cut them off because of behaviors that the sister or brother felt a need to hide:

Four of my friends have younger siblings who have cut them out of their lives. We don't know for sure, but we suspect drugs or alcohol played a part in the estrangements.

I don't usually acknowledge that I have an older brother. I have been estranged from him for ten years. He was in a gang and his gang friends threatened me. It's a relief that he's no longer in my life.

I keep wondering if my brother is hiding something, and that's why he keeps away from me. Maybe he's embarrassed or ashamed about joblessness, bankruptcy, or an addiction.

Family members who are related to someone who is an addict or mentally ill often feel they must save themselves, rather than fall into the rabbit hole of trying to help an addicted family member. In addition to generating stress, mental health issues drain a family's financial and emotional resources. A sibling may not be able to discern how much of the addict's behavior is his or her personality and how much is due to mental illness. Even when he or she chooses to cut off, a sibling may be plagued by balancing empathy for the addicted brother or sister against his or her own self-care.

Twenty-four percent of survey respondents identified mental health issues as the source of the problem in their relationships with their brothers and sisters.

My brother had a serious drug problem that has ruined our family. He could not be trusted, and he refused treatment. He drained the family emotionally and financially, so I had to cut him out of my life.

I have felt judged, misunderstood, and stigmatized. My various break-downs have given my siblings a handy excuse to shun me. I've felt I have to reach some amazing level of stability and remission of my symptoms before they will accept me.

She is a narcissist who has a bipolar disorder. My therapist recommended I go "no contact" for my own well-being. At first, I had a lot of trouble going "no contact." I wished I had a sister. Not anymore.

Alcoholism and addiction often mask other mental disorders. Many comments in chat rooms and on my survey identify a brother's or sister's narcissism as the reason the commenter had to sever a "toxic" relationship. These siblings are fluent in the psychological language of narcissism, speaking easily of their "narc sisters," "hoovering narcissists" (who suck their victims back into the relationship), and "flying monkeys" (who act on behalf of a narcissist, usually for an abusive purpose.)

In chat rooms, many in narcissistic families complain that as children they competed and were pitted against their siblings. Many experienced narcissistic triangulation when a family member tried to control the flow, interpretation, and nuances of communication. They explore the twisted nature and frustrating effects when a toxic sibling abuses the victim, and then the victim predictably reacts with anger. Cruelly, the toxic person then accuses the victim of being abusive. Children reared in narcissistic homes rarely feel connected to one another as adults.

Narcissism, as described by the Mayo Clinic, is characterized by an exaggerated sense of self-importance and entitlement and a show of arro-gance, haughtiness, and conceitedness by people who monopolize conversations, belittle those they perceive as inferior, and generally fail to recognize the needs and feelings of others.

Karen Martin, a sixty-five-year-old woman from Southern California, is estranged from all three of her older brothers, whom she considers narcissists. She has no contact with two of them and a limited relationship with the third.

It's difficult to sustain sibling relationships with three brothers who are narcissists. They always get upset over trivial things. Underlying every conversation is envy and competition. No matter what subject comes up, they have to be right.

All of them are very bright, and each needs to be better than the other and each needs extreme approbation. Sometimes it shows up in small ways. I'd ask one brother, "What's the weather?" He would answer by telling me about meteorological isotopes. He had to show that he's not inferior. All of them monopolize conversations so they are the center of attention. Life is a game they need to win.

They completely lack empathy. Around others, I feel loved and admired, but around them, I feel unacknowledged. There is no exchange of ideas or validating conversation. I don't get anything out of these relationships.

They were envious of me because I was the only girl and the youngest, and they felt my parents favored me. But they don't realize that, as an adult, I've really worked on maintaining a fulfilling relationship with my parents. They never did.

None of the brothers talk to each other now, and I don't talk to two of them. All are toxic.

When I don't hear from any of them, I'm relieved because I don't worry about when the next earthquake will hit. Also, I really don't like the person I become when I'm with the one brother I still talk to. I'm a strong, assertive woman, but around him, I become frightened and tentative and I succumb to his demands. Sometimes, when he calls and I see his name on my cell phone, I begin to shake. Around him, I lose myself quickly.

Because statistics about sibling estrangement are difficult to come by, it is interesting that a private Facebook chat room poll asking about the reasons members no longer have relationships with their siblings produced similar percentages to my survey. Consider the results of this private survey:

Parental favoritism: 30 percent

Unresolved sibling rivalry: 24 percent

In-laws/spouse/partner: 22 percent

Inheritance/will issues: 20 percent

Never been close/never gotten along: 15 percent

Mental health issues: 15 percent

Abuse: 15 percent

Alcoholism and/or addiction: 11 percent

Different morals/values: 4 percent

Siblings decline to say why: 15 percent

Perilous Turning Points in the Sibling Relationship

Not surprisingly, sibling relationships are most vulnerable to estrangement during certain life stages that require family members to redefine their roles. At such moments, minor clashes may push siblings beyond their ability to cope, prompting a kind of circuit breaker on their emotions. They abandon their familial role as a quick fix to provide immediate relief.

These turning points most prominently include the following:

- Adolescence: In this stage, a teenage sibling, individuating and creating his or her own identity, leaves home for college or a job. He or she may challenge parental authority, changing the established sibling relationships and dynamics in the family.
- Marriage: A new in-law joins the family and may want to control how much time the couple will spend with parents and siblings. The new in-law may have values and beliefs that differ from those of the original family.
- Birth of a baby: As a sibling focuses on his or her new family, some family members may feel abandoned or betrayed. Often sibling rivalry continues into adulthood; siblings may even compete with each other through their children.
- Illness or divorce: Siblings may feel overburdened with the physical, emotional, and financial responsibilities of an ill or divorcing family member.
- Parental illness, death, or inheritance: This stage, during which siblings vie for power, love, and family loyalty one last time, often evokes old family patterns. Difficult conflicts arise over who will make health-care decisions for an elderly parent, who will pay for long-term care, and who will inherit precious family possessions.

No matter what the reason, cutoffs may end the fiery conflict, but estrangement doesn't end the relationship, says Dr. Harriet Lerner, a psychologist and the author of *The Dance of Anger* and other popular works on psychology. "When we cut off from a close family member," Dr. Lerner says, "that person becomes an even bigger presence inside us."[10]

That's especially true when the shunned can't stop ruminating on this incomprehensible situation. Often the rejected sibling analyzes the nuances of an estranged sibling's every comment, searching for clues to explain the betrayal. The silent sibling's final words linger in the mind of the shunned, replaying in a loop.

Survey respondents often referred to this "loop"—the inability to move forward—in their answers:

I think about my sister all the time. I'm shattered that we are not part of each other's lives for so many years.

My head goes round and round about the things that have happened.

I can't stop thinking about the estrangement and the pain is agonizing.

Fifty-five-year-old Marcy Minor of New Haven, Connecticut, last saw her two brothers and one sister at their mother's funeral. She says she has been pulling away from her family for most of her life, due to a tumultuous, competitive upbringing. She claims her parents pitted the children against one another, and she decided as an adult to remove herself from the family so that she wouldn't continue to have those struggles. That choice has given Minor the freedom she needs, but sometimes she carries a terrible emptiness, a feeling that she has no sense of belonging and no one cares about her.

No matter what the reason for the cutoff, few walk away from a sibling relationship free and clear. Those who choose estrangement may feel courageous, exhilarated, and empowered by their decision, but even they, according to survey respondents, often think about their estranged siblings. Still, most do not want to return to the sibling relationship they had before the break.

What happens to a child when those earliest moments—the hours and days in which newborns are programmed to bond with their mothers before facing the world—are squandered? Does love suffer? Is it transformed from immersive salvation to elusive mystery? Will Angela's emotional life be a do-it-yourself project—one she'll have to research and study and construct for herself? Will she have to train herself to feel what should come intuitively in order to learn how to love as a friend, a partner, a mother?

I see myself in Angela.

On Mother's Day a few years ago, my mother asked me the question I had always dreaded: "What kind of mother was I? A good mother or a bad mother?"

"You were . . ." I squirmed. "Well, you were a . . . *troubled* mother."

I had devoted decades to wondering how, or whether, someone who lost everything at a young age—family, language, loyalties, homeland, identity—can grow up to be healthy and functional in the world. In order to survive the loss of her family, my mother unconsciously cut off parts of herself, starting with her capacities for hope and love. How does any survivor of such emotional carnage recover? How can a girl so bereft become a mother capable of giving her children the confidence to believe that the world is a safe place where they can love and trust and make a life?

By avoiding the topic of her early life in Germany, my mother hoped to insulate my brother and me from her sufferings and anxieties. Not long ago, she told me that, in a twisted maternal impulse, she had tried to spare us from loss by not loving us too much. That way, she thought, if we lost everything—as she had—we wouldn't be destroyed and devastated by the experience.

All this, too, had driven me to the Cradle's wooden rocking chairs: an urge to give what I had received only intermittently in childhood.

What I never imagined when I signed on at the Cradle was the emotional support I would get from the staff. I soon recognized that when women of all ages and all walks of life gather and care for infants together, something ancient, elemental, and intimate transpires. We love; we laugh; we drop our defenses and let down our guard.

Every other week, I receive updates: on Susan's off-the-rails sixteen-year-old son, perpetually in and out of rehab; on Rosie's progress in persuading her depressed adult daughter to seek treatment; on Maggie's struggle to lose sixty pounds. Here, women bring to one another what they offer the babies—love, support, empathy. The nursery is a warm, soft-lit den of trust and safety.

I've often wondered about the unique characteristics of the nursery that produce this rare social environment, where women from such a wide range of backgrounds confide in one another and share their lives. We see one another regularly—like, I realized one day, a close, loving, functional family. No subject is off-limits for nurses and cuddlers; after all, we have to discuss the intimate bodily functions of tiny, helpless babies. Regardless of how these babies came into being, we are nonjudgmental toward them, loving them all unconditionally.

Ultimately, we bring the same comfort, compassion, and candor to one another. One night, Susan, a nurse married to a handyman who often doesn't have work, tearfully confided her financial and marital troubles to Rosie, Maggie, and me. "Hard to believe," she admitted, "but I tell all of you more than I tell my own sisters."

Beyond our own concerns, we cluck our tongues and bond over the babies' endless, heartbreaking stories. We, who come from our own dys-functions, gain perspective here, seeing over and over that we are not alone, that many families are much worse off than we can imagine. Story after story after story: Each baby has his or her own uniquely rocky start, each one worthy of an episode in a television series.

One night, I held a baby boy whose mother was only thirteen years old. Her stepfather had raped her, and she had kept the shameful pregnancy secret, giving birth into the toilet all by herself. When the girl's mother learned of the circumstances, she called the police; the stepfather was arrested, and the girl's mother decided to raise her grandson as her own son. After meeting the thirteen-year-old mother, Rosie reported: "Looks like a deer caught in headlights."

Another night, Susan tells me about the East Indian mother of the baby she's holding. Fearing her family would stone her to death for becoming pregnant before marriage, the eighteen-year-old student came up with an ingenious plan: She told her parents she had been accepted at Northwestern University in Evanston. Never asking for proof or paperwork, the family happily paid for her trip to college in late August. Once here, she lived on the tuition money her parents provided until giving birth in December. After the baby's adoption, she told her family she hated Northwestern and wanted to go home.

Another night, the nursery admitted a beautiful, blonde three-day-old. The mother, we learned, couldn't keep her daughter because she is serving a ten-year sentence in the Joliet Correctional Center.

"So what's going on with you?" Rosie asks as a gentle calm settles over us. Sitting side by side in the well-worn white rocking chairs, we gently rock the sleeping babies; Rosie cradles Jordan as I snuggle three-day-old Aiden.

I stare at the paper cutouts of bursting hot-pink flower buds pasted on brown tree branches on the interior window where visitors can view the babies. Rosie—a master gardener whose stunning yard silently commands pedestrians to stop and admire—tells me she loves the budding trees and the promise of spring in this latest installment of the Cradle's handmade seasonal creations. I look at the colorful display, but I don't feel the sense of optimism that the window decorations are trying to evoke.

"Oh, I'm all right," I say quietly, without conviction.

"Not really," she smiles.

I never really talk to anyone—not even my friends at the Cradle—about the cutoff with my brother.

"Tell me," Rosie presses. "What's bothering you?"

I look at Rosie's gentle face; tears fill my eyes as I try to swallow the words and the sadness that lives within me. Suddenly, little Aiden stirs and startles me, and my carefully constructed dam bursts. Through tears, I tell Rosie the long-suppressed story of my estrangement from my brother and its years of hurt and shame. She hangs on every word. Then I fill her in on last week's momentous conversation, her eyes widening and eyebrows arching with each new detail.

Yet I end the story on a low note. "I'm not sure how much I can do." I shrug, backing away from my commitment to help him. "I'm not sure his own family knows how to handle things, so I doubt I can be of much help."

Ever since the call, I explain, my emotional and rational sides have been duking it out. I've been swinging wildly over how to handle this situation.

Rosie's eyebrows jump back up. "What do you mean?"

"Even if he does what I ask of him—and I don't know what that will be—what are the odds, Rosie? He's been suffering for a long time. What are his chances of recovery?"

She knows it's a valid question, and there are others. "Can he and I ever sustain a sibling relationship? Can I trust him? Can I forgive him for all these years—"

"I know all that," Rosie says. "But he's your brother."

"I've lived a long time without him." Even whispering, I sound almost defiant. "Anyway, I've gotten used to it. And . . . well, I'm scared, Rosie. What if—"

"You only have one brother."

"I know." *She's not helping*, I think resentfully.

"You have to do something." Rosie's little Jordan starts to cry; as she shifts him to her other shoulder, her eyes narrow at me behind her red-framed glasses. I meet her burning stare, annoyance rising as I absorb what she's saying without words.

Then, even more emphatically, she says it again: "He *is* your brother!" She's definitely not helping.

Exasperated, I roll my eyes at her and snort, "You sound *just* like my mother."

That's quite a coercion: "He *is* your brother!" But what does it really mean? Of course, biologically, it's an accurate statement. But my brother doesn't act like a brother; he abandoned the role. Doesn't that absolve me of any responsibility? How can I behave like a sister when he wants nothing to do with me? A relationship requires two parties, some sort of correlation and mutual dependence.

For years, I didn't tell Rosie or other friends about the hole that estrangement had opened within my life because I feared I would be judged: Most people project onto others their own notions of what a family *should* look like. Society tends to cherish an idealized version of family in which relationships are indissoluble. It was embarrassing that I couldn't negotiate some sort of relationship with my own brother. How could I explain the experience to someone else when I didn't understand it myself?

The Enduring Shame of Estrangement

Estrangement casts suspicion on everyone involved. No matter whether the relationship simply faded away or if estrangement was a choice, estranged siblings are caught in a swirl of judgments and doubts. For example, the shunner may be haunted by the daunting question: *How could I be so heartless that I would cut off my own sibling?* At the same time, the shunned may be plagued by this question: *What's wrong with me that my sibling doesn't want anything to do with me?*

In a moving essay for thejewishwoman.org, a woman referring to herself only as "Anonymous" wrote about how profoundly disturbed she is by her lack of a relationship with her brother. Anonymous regrets that she can't keep a promise she made to her mother, a Holocaust survivor who was painfully separated from her own siblings. She had told her mother, "I'll stay close to my brother, no matter what." Instead, she writes, "I have lost my brother, my only sibling. Sometimes I truly think my heart will break in two from the pain." Though Anonymous willingly shares her raw emotions, what's most telling is her refusal to attach her name to her powerful words.

The shunned find themselves on high alert to others' perceptions of their possible failings. Their peers may not directly state what they think about an estrangement, but they may subtly communicate their feelings in a rolled eye, averted gaze, or awkward silence. Those nonverbal signals often give the estranged the feeling that they have something dirty to hide. Some survey respondents expressed frustration that nearly all disturbing topics, from divorce to abuse, are openly discussed, yet sibling estrangement is steeped in shame.

An important collaborative study by Stand Alone, a British organization that offers support services to estranged family members, and the University of Cambridge's Centre for Family Research sheds light on the stigma of estrangement. Analysis of 807 members of the Stand Alone community who completed the study's survey showed that 54 percent agreed with the statement that "estrangement or family breakdown is common in our family," and 68 percent of adults estranged from one or more members of their families believe a stigma accompanies family estrangement. The respondents cited the fear of judgment and assumptions of fault or blame as a frequent source of shame.

Shame and stigma can become a source of deep isolation. Sixty-year-old Rebecca Kasin of Chicago, who hasn't spoken to her brother in ten years, commented on my survey that she doesn't discuss her situation with anyone—and she can't wait to read other estranged siblings' stories. "For the longest time," she wrote, "I've thought that there is something wrong with me because of the estrangements in my family, so your project is making me feel that I'm not exactly alone here." It's clear from my interviews and my survey results that Rebecca absolutely is not alone.

The concept of estrangement is so threatening that many people are unprepared to confront, much less discuss, a family model that doesn't conform to their ideals and expectations. Even good friends who have serious conflicts with their own sisters or brothers may scorn someone else's cutoff, fearing —though they are reluctant to admit it—that their brother or sister might stop talking to them.

All sorts of homilies frame a cultural standard of acceptable behavior for siblings. They urge brothers and sisters to maintain a relationship with words like "Love thy family!" "Blood is thicker than water!" and "You can't choose your family!"

Many survey respondents, however, reject the idea of giving brothers or sisters a free pass for bad behavior, just because they are blood related:

Just because someone is related to you does not mean they have the right to be in your life if it is unhealthy. I feel that no one has a right to criticize you constantly.

People can't believe the stories I tell about my family. Some say I should make things work no matter what because it's family. One person even told me that it must be my fault since they've all cut me off.

If she weren't my sister, I'd never be her friend. I'd never allow a friend to treat me the way she does.

For women, a complicated extra layer of responsibility (and failure) often accompanies a fractured family. Women, in general, have been socialized to suppress their own feelings and to "get along" in order to facilitate the family. Traditionally, they are the stewards of the home, hosting holidays, attending ceremonial events, nurturing relationships, organizing social schedules, providing gifts, regularly communicating with relatives, and serving as mediators when necessary. Women carry the family forward. Consequently, a failed relationship with a sibling can be especially incriminating for a sister.

Unacknowledged Estrangement

The estrangement experience is alienating, in part due to a lack of acknowledgment of the griever and scant societal support for the loss. Online chat rooms have provided a new outlet and offer some comfort, but in general, the estranged suffer alone with what's called "disenfranchised grief," which is defined as grief from a loss that is not or cannot be openly acknowledged, socially sanctioned, or publicly mourned. Alone in their suffering, the estranged often experience a simmering sadness as feelings of abandonment boil up with every thought of family loss.

The stigma and shame of estrangement are exquisitely painful for twins, who are perceived as deeply connected. Isabelle Lays, a forty-five-year-old Scottish woman who has been estranged from her twin brother for twenty years, calls herself a "failed twin" or a "twinless twin." She says the two had a deep bond in early childhood, but once they were placed into different classrooms in school, they began to go their separate ways. There was no animosity between the twins; they simply had divergent interests and friends, and they didn't spend a lot of time together. Over time, Lays's brother severed his relationship with her.

Devastated by her loss, Lays created her own ceremony to acknowledge that her twin brother would never be a part of her life again:

In the beginning, when I still had hopes of reconciliation, I couldn't stop talking about my loss to friends. After a while, I became ashamed and stopped discussing it. When new acquaintances asked me if I had any brothers or sisters, I would respond with the vaguest of details.

The day after 9/11, I called my brother but didn't hear back. I made a special card for him for our fortieth birthday but received no response. I have no idea how to reconcile with him.

Finally, in 2015 I conducted a ceremony on our birthday where I "un-twinned" myself from him. That turned out to be a cathartic experience. Since then, I avoid thinking about him, but it's not easy. Estranged twins are very rare, although they do exist. What does it say about me that the person I shared a womb with is someone who wants nothing to do with me?

In the absence of an empathetic community or cultural support, some rejected siblings cope by denying that they have a brother or sister. The shunned also dodge certain questions to avoid social disapproval and redirect conversations as I did, or even lie about their family.

Julianna Turner, whose traumatic childhood in Scotland was mentioned in chapter 4, doesn't like to talk to her friends about her distant relationship with one of her two brothers or her complete cutoff with her sister, so she avoids the topic.

After a physical altercation with my sister in our twenties, I decided to ignore her bad behavior. I've turned the other cheek, accepted empty apologies, ignored, pretended it didn't happen, still hoping for that "sister" relationship. I kept forgiving because society has taught us that family is family and we forgive and get over it.

But I can't take it anymore. She's part of many broken, twisted memories that I want to forget. I mourn the idea of a close family and sibling, but I'm happy without her.

Only a few people know about these estrangements. My friends don't even know I have a sister.

Denial as a coping strategy may be difficult to sustain, especially for those who live in small towns. One woman whose military family lives in rural Arkansas says she doesn't tell anyone in her community about her family estrangements. However, at her children's sporting events, where large extended families gather to cheer on young players, she can't deny or hide her alienation. In the stands, she sits by herself, uncomfortably alone.

What's most shattering to a shunned sibling is the fundamental question that haunts twinless twin Isabelle Lays: whether one is lovable or capable of maintaining any relationship. "What does this say about me as a person?" she asked.

Those who feel stigmatized, socially disenfranchised, and/or isolated often internalize the shame, which leads to feelings of low self-esteem. In other words, the shunned take on the stigma of estrangement as their own personal failing and character flaw, feeling invisible, meaningless, and judged by a culture that expects family cohesion.

Chapter 6

The Possibility of Reconciliation

$\overline{\mathsf{T}}$

I t's nine thirty in the morning, and once again I'm doing the same thing I've done for decades: waiting for my brother.

But this time it's different; my wait isn't figurative anymore. Today, at last, it's literal.

It seems preposterous that Scott's coming over, as if I've landed in some alternate reality. This strange, suspended moment is also a solitary one: My husband, squelching his protective instinct as well as a huge curiosity, has left the house so that my brother and I can be alone.

And I can't sit still. Fifteen minutes before he's due, I throw myself into minor housework: sponge off the kitchen counters, tidy up the mail on the bookshelf, spray and wipe down the glass table. I'm managing my anxiety exactly the way my mother did. When she cleaned frantically, it made me anxious. Yet here I am, moving on to water the plants.

At nine forty-five, our appointed time, I start pacing, glancing every few seconds out the front window, scanning the driveway for a car pulling in. *What kind of car does he drive now? Does he even have a car?*

I look at my watch. A familiar band begins to tighten around my chest. He's ten minutes late. *Typ-i-cal!* his adolescent voice singsongs, taunting me. Then it adds sarcastically, *What did you expect?*

I know I shouldn't expect much. Those rare appearances at family events—an occasional birthday party, a funeral, a wedding—were just enough to remind me that I had a brother. On the rare occasions when he did step back into my life, he immediately began the process of extricating himself. I could feel him shift and practically pinpoint the precise moment he would begin to withdraw again. His pattern was more reliable than he was.

Yet I remember him vividly from the days when he was an important part of my life. Images flash across my mental screen: a chip-toothed first grader with a crew cut; a guitar-strumming eighth grader, his dark frizz slicked down to brush against his eyelashes; a handsome high school senior, long-haired and resplendent in a wide-lapelled sixties black tux, taking his girlfriend to prom; a cocky, grinning college junior smoking a cigarette at the family dinner table, to our parents' utter shock.

But then the slideshow goes blank. I can't really picture him as an adult son, an uncle, a brother; not even as a husband or father.

I look at my watch. He's twenty minutes late.

Nailed! Again I hear his sixteen-year-old self. Rage catches fire beneath my sternum, activated by the anger and hurt from all the times he has disappointed me. Have I fallen into his trap again?

Slow down, I tell myself. *Give him a chance.* He could have a good reason. He sounded genuinely desperate on the phone. Something probably held him up. Maybe he's not sure where I live; he's only been here once or twice.

I could call, but he might be driving. And if he's not on his way, I *really* don't want him to drive while he's on the phone.

Instead, I get out the broom and sweep up a few crumbs from the floor. When I finish that task, I rotate slowly to take in the whole living room. Not a crumb anywhere—but then I notice a thin line of gray dust along the white baseboards. I get down on my hands and knees and run a dust cloth against the edges.

I check my phone. Now he's thirty minutes late.

Okay, that's enough! I'm not waiting any longer.

But what should I do? I know; I'll text him. But I can't think of what to say.

Where are you? No, too annoyed and accusatory.

You still planning to meet me? Too needy, too loaded.

You lost? That's good. I type in the words and hit Send.

Looking at the text, I think, *Well,* that *says it all.*

The question hangs between us. With no response, the screen turns black, a darkened stage. The silent phone rests in my hand.

I wait. No answer. Nothing.

I set the phone on the kitchen counter and walk away to pour myself a cup of coffee. Well, if he's not coming, that saves me a lot of time. A lot of pain. It could take months, even years, to help him rebalance himself, and there's no guarantee of how things would turn out anyway.

Even worse, I could invest in him and he might disappear on me again. How can I trust someone who has let me down time and time again anyway? Would I ever feel comfortable with a brother I hardly know anymore? How could the risk and effort possibly pay off?

From what I've read, reconciliation after a lengthy cutoff is rare. I can see why. During our one recent phone conversation, I felt we'd already reverted to our old childish roles and patterns. Not sure I need another dose of that. What's the old joke? For every day you're with your family, you regress five years—so keep your visit short enough that you're still able to drive away legally.

That's that! I tell myself, briskly wiping my hands on a bright, cheery kitchen towel. I'm not getting mixed up with him again. I'll tell my mother and Rosie I tried. I reached out, but it's impossible to help someone who won't help himself. Obviously, he's not *that* desperate.

So! I'm off the hook.

Suddenly, the phone on the counter buzzes and *briinnnngs* to life. Startled, I lunge for it. The screen lights up.

Five minutes appears beneath the stinging *S*'s of his name. Heart pounding, band tightening again, I fire off a quick response:

OK great thx.

> **Scott:** Construction on Sheridan
>
> **Me:** Oh yeah. New cables.
>
> **Scott:** What time did you think I was coming?
>
> **Me:** 9:45
>
> **Scott:** Had to do errand at 9:45
>
> **Me:** Ah, ok. Mix up.
>
> **Scott:** Sorry
>
> **Me:** No problem. Just glad u will show up
>
> **Scott:** Always was planning to come

Right.

Always planning to leave too.

I have no idea whether Scott will show up, or what will happen when—if—he finally arrives at my door. My feelings about seeing my brother again are wildly ambivalent: I want it, I dread it, I fear it. Hungry for some idea of what to expect, I've been rereading my collection of books on sibling estrangement and googling everything I can find on the chances of a successful reconciliation.

When Reconciliation Becomes Possible

No matter how much time has lapsed or how distant sisters and brothers have grown, a sibling's very presence reintroduces each of us to our former selves. Intricately and inextricably, brothers and sisters—no matter whether or not they speak—are woven into the fabric of each other's lives.

The possibility of reconciliation seems to improve as siblings age. People begin to think more about the past than the future as grown children leave home, careers wind down, and friends move away, become ill, or die. Some brothers and sisters long to reconnect with someone who knew them before they assumed adult roles, before they married, started a family, or entered the workplace. Often a sibling yearns to talk to the only other person on the planet who understands the codes and nuances of their family of origin. My brother must know and still remember how Mom always lost her keys in the black hole of her purse or how that blue vein on Dad's forehead swelled and throbbed when he became enraged.

The bad news, however, is that no matter how hard estranged siblings try to reconcile, about 40 percent simply can't make it work. Most fail because the same patterns of communication that originally caused the estrangement reemerge during reconciliation. Change is difficult; few have awareness about what they did to contribute to sibling tensions and even fewer want to admit they were wrong, to apologize, and to take responsibility for all the hurts and lost years.

To approach reconciliation in a rational, self-protective yet open fashion, it's crucial to assess one's own feelings and prospects for resuming and improving the relationship. Consider the following questions when assessing your feelings:

- Why is this relationship important to me—not to my family or to anyone else but to me?

- Does my sibling want to resume a relationship?
- On what basis would we enter, rebuild, and maintain the relationship? As siblings, as friends, as distant relatives?
- Do my sibling and I have enough in common and a desire to make this effort worthwhile?
- Can I set aside the anger, pain, and/or resentment that led to the break to change our pattern of relating?
- Is it possible to develop a different, better relationship?
- Do I want to resume this relationship if I discover that neither of us has changed?
- Do I have the time, energy, emotional resilience, and support of other loved ones—to reconcile and rebuild this relationship?
- Will I compromise too much of myself if I try to sustain a relationship with my difficult sibling?

My research produced several useful guidelines as to where to begin. Experts who offered strategies include author Laura Davis, whose seven best-selling books include *I Thought We'd Never Speak Again*; Susan Scarf Merrell, author of *The Accidental Bond*; and Dr. Ellen B. Sucov, a psychologist retired from the University of Pittsburgh psychiatry department and author of *Fragmented Families: Patterns of Estrangement and Reconciliation*. In her book, Dr. Sucov describes various stages in the process of resolving an estrangement from her half-sisters and brother that persisted for more than fifty years.

Consider the following list of pointers based upon the suggestions of these experts:

- Put the past in the past; focus on the present and the future. (I'm not there yet, but the experts are obviously right in saying that what's done can't be changed.)

- Start softly. (Though I'm ready to overwhelm my brother with my grievances, it's better to throw out my list. The more calmly I raise a topic during these first meetings, the sources agree, the more likely the conversation will be productive.)

- Be honest but not hurtful. (I'm not sure I can do this either, given the decades of hurts, but the idea is to let my sibling get to know me as I am today.)

- Address differences honestly. Research shows that siblings are most competitive about achievement, looks, and intellect. Use nonconfrontational "I" messages—"I feel so much less accomplished than you"—rather than provocative "you" statements, such as "You always bullied me," which can make a sibling feel defensive. (This is something I've worked on in other relationships, so I think I can follow this advice.)

- Accept your brother or sister as he or she is now. Put away childhood hurts, perceptions, and labels. There are reasons a brother or sister treated a sibling a certain way. Consider that it may be because of how you were parented, rather than anything they did. (For me, it's hard to get over childhood hurts that have carried over into adulthood, but I now understand that my parents have had a role in our estrangement.)

- Withhold judgment in explaining your feelings. To establish a new kind of relationship, give your sibling the benefit of the doubt. Look for the good and avoid trying to prove to yourself that a sibling isn't worth the effort. (At this stage, I have no idea what's tormenting Scott, but whatever it is, I know that judging him will only drive him away.)

- Check your ego. The guides say to take responsibility for any of your own bad behavior that contributed to the estrangement. "Stop trying to prove that you are always right," they say. (My problem here is that, right now, I have no idea what I may have done to contribute to the breakdown in our relationship.)

- Stay in the present. Instead of dredging up your anger from the time your brother's family arrived ninety minutes late for Thanksgiving dinner, simply let him know that you're planning to prepare Thanksgiving dinner at your house, and you hope he and his family will join you. (I'm not sure I can be generous enough to recover the relationship without addressing the things that have hurt me in the past.)

- Be a touchstone. "One of the best ways of remembering who you are is through a sibling," the guides say. Gentle "remember whens" remind siblings of their unique relationship and what they shared long ago. (I remember quite a lot from our shared childhood, and I've often wondered what Scott remembers.)

- Cultivate a friendship. Try to connect with a sibling as if he or she is a friend. Find common ground, even if there isn't much. (Maybe I can do this by mentioning our beloved paternal grandmother, Mama Gussie, who was an important, grounding figure in both of our young lives.)

- Know and avoid triggers. When reestablishing a relationship with a sibling, meet at a comfortable location and limit the time you'll spend together. If the direction of the conversation becomes uncomfortable, don't get drawn in. (Scott has rarely been to my home, so I don't think there is any negative association here. Meeting at my house shouldn't affect our discussion.)

- Manage expectations. One chat room member astutely called expectations "premeditated resentments." A few conversations won't extinguish a lifetime of hurts. Honor small victories and slow progress. (For me, it would be a huge achievement if I could stop dreading the moment I have to see him—although that seems like a *really* low expectation to me.)

- Listen to their stories. (By resolving this long-standing cutoff with my brother, I'm sure both of us could gain insights that would add to our understanding and knowledge of our family.)

Lose the Anger

The biggest hurdle in reconciling with a brother or sister is conquering anger. No matter what other emotions are in the mix, anger is typically a driving force in an estranged relationship. In much the same way that depression often shows itself as anger, fear, too, can manifest as anger. In fact, anger masks many emotions, including hurt, stress, self-consciousness, sadness, guilt, and shame. No matter what's behind it, anger leads to hostility, and hostility erodes relationships.

Reducing anger as much as possible before attempting reconciliation requires a conscious effort. The following questions may guide that effort:

- Can I keep anger out of my attempts to reconcile?
- What benefit is there to holding on to this anger? What is the cost?
- If I constantly feel angry, can I examine what is fueling those feelings? Can I see how it prevents me from successfully reconciling? Can I admit to my feelings and even try again?
- Does anger empower me in a powerless situation? If so, can I find another source of strength?
- Can I set a boundary without becoming enraged or defensive?
- How would I feel if someone discharged the anger I'm experiencing on me?
- How will I feel about myself if I look back on this situation and recognize that I allowed anger to dominate my reaction?

Choose to Repair

What matters in reestablishing a relationship is what we do, what we say, and how we say it. Estrangement makes some siblings feel powerless, but everyone caught in its maze will choose a particular course of action.

Reconciliation requires intent, diligence, and self-agency to achieve the necessary goal of relinquishing the alluring fantasy of a perfect relationship and instead committing to accepting the relationship as it is now and altering the way we relate to one another. We may not have control over our sibling's behavior, but we can control how we see ourselves in relation to them and, ultimately, how we approach them. To achieve reconciliation and change the relationship into one that's functional requires *us* to change.

I tell myself over and over again, *Reconciliation is a choice.* Insightful words attributed to Austrian psychiatrist Viktor Frankl, who wrote *Man's Search for Meaning*, come to mind: "Between stimulus and response there is a space. In that space is our power to choose our response. In our response lies our growth and our freedom."

In that crucial space between stimulus and response, I want to completely reconstruct my relationship with my estranged brother.

PART II

Reconnection

Chapter 7

Estrangement and Self-Esteem

E ver since he was a little boy, my brother has loved cars. It's one of the few passions he shared with our father, though their tastes in vehicles diverged sharply.

Dad, who fell in love with cars as a teenager while working at his father's Sinclair service station, adored the exotics: Lamborghini, Ferrari, Jaguar. Scott, by contrast, was attracted to the flash and speed of American muscle cars: Corvettes, Mustangs, Camaros.

My dad's and my brother's preferences in cars revealed the profound differences in how they saw themselves. Still, as soon as Scott turned sixteen in July of 1968, Dad couldn't wait to bond with his only son over the purchase of his first vehicle. I think they both hoped this would be an exciting pursuit that might, as a bonus, temporarily defuse their seething mutual hostilities. And indeed, after visiting several dealers one Saturday afternoon, they briefly found agreement over a gleaming new Pontiac

Firebird. It was cherry red, with a lustrous black interior, whitewall radial tires, and a factory-installed eight-track tape deck.

Scott's passion for fast, fancy cars never abated. In his late forties, at the height of his extraordinary success as a trader, he actually ran out of garage space for his many vehicles. Though I rarely visited his home and never saw what he owned, he could have stocked a highly selective used-car lot with his fleet of nine pristine new and vintage automobiles.

As for my own taste in cars, Dad and Scott had a rare meeting of minds. Both disdained my pedestrian choices, which sipped gas sparingly and got me from here to there without fanfare. I bought my first car in 1977, scraping together $2,300 for a pale blue Honda Civic hatchback discounted from the previous year.

And now—gazing out my living room window, just five days after my first real conversation with my brother in decades—I get my first glimpse of who he is today. He's pulling into my driveway in a later model of my toy car: a four-door Honda coupe. Beige.

He parks the sedan on my driveway; the driver's-side door creaks open. A ragged, rumpled figure emerges. From the window I can see he's hunched over, head drooping, eyes downcast. He's wearing old, tattered jeans, a tired T-shirt, and gray sneakers that were probably white when they were new.

Slowly he makes his way up the path, and his dark eyes catch mine for a second. Awkwardly, I offer a forced grin and a quick wave, but he abruptly looks away. I'm filled instantly with the fear and dread that have characterized our relationship for decades: I'm always looking for something that he's unwilling to give. *Why am I even trying?*

Opening the front door wide, I move aside to allow him into the foyer. Blinking hard, he looks around the unfamiliar house where I've lived for nearly twenty years. I'm struck by how much he resembles our father—the stocky, compact build, the sharp, dark features—but he lacks Dad's vitality. Colorless and beaten, he squints like someone walking out of a dark theater into daylight. I hear again the words he said on the phone: "Some days I can't even get out of bed."

He follows me down the hallway, his heavy footsteps scraping and dragging behind me. In the living room, we both sit on the couch and eye each other suspiciously but tenderly. He is so familiar, yet a complete stranger. I hardly recognize him. He's older, of course, but what's most striking is that there is so little of him. He's a shell of my brother, hollowed out by life's defeats. Taking in his whole crumpled self, my throat tightens, my stomach clenches, my empathy kicks in.

I know I need to say something, but I don't know where to start. The experts didn't offer advice on exactly which words to use when breaking the ice after decades of silence. I run through the possibilities:

How are you? I already know.

You okay? Obviously not.

It's been a long time. I can hear his sarcastic teenage voice quip, *"No shit, Sherlock!"*

What I'd really like to say is: *About those forty years . . . What happened? Where have you been?* But I know this isn't the time. The experts say to start soft; stay in the present. So I come up with a gentle, neutral opening that's been rolling around in my mind:

"Where do we start?"

"It's terrible," he says without any hesitation. Immediately I see that his desperation dwarfs whatever has divided us for decades. Immediately I push my trust issues aside.

"Just terrible." Distraught, he glances around the room; then his gaze unexpectedly lands on me. His turmoil is frightening; he looks terrified.

"What?" I ask calmly, trying to ground him. "What's happened?"

He looks back at me blankly. But then, suddenly, my question unleashes the swirling emotions he has bottled up and held in for months, maybe years. Anguished sobs rise and gush from deep within. In moments, his unfathomable sadness has demolished my carefully constructed guard.

I reach over and hug him tightly, in a way I never have before. For several minutes we cling together. This is my brother! My heart is cracking, tearing apart. I begin to cry, too, for how much he is suffering, for all we've lost. Wailing into my neck, his howls sound like those of an injured animal.

When he finally catches his breath, he sputters, "I told you on the phone, I don't know what's wrong with me." Eyes red-rimmed and voice raspy, he confesses, "I can't sleep. And when I finally get to sleep, I have terrible nightmares. I sweat all the time. I'm always jumpy. I can't concentrate, can't work, can't even leave the house. I can't even pay my electric bill."

Observing him closely, I study his face and hang on his every word. I feel as if I'm looking at myself in the mirror. Yes, we resemble each other in appearance, but what's eerie is that I, too, have suffered with some of the same symptoms, the same reactions, the same confusion. I've been in this bleak place.

"I think I know."

"Know what?" His sharp tone brings back the way we talked to each other when he was sixteen and I was fourteen.

"What's wrong with you."

"What?" he asks skeptically.

"Well," I say slowly, aware that I'm about to upend his understanding of himself. But then I think of the Chinese proverb that says that the beginning of wisdom is to call things by their proper name. So here goes: "I think you have posttraumatic stress disorder. PTSD."

"What?" His face scrambles as he quickly shakes his head.

"PTSD," I say again. "You have the symptoms."

"But I haven't been to war!"

"Well, you know, you don't have to be a veteran to have it. Sometimes it comes from other things . . . like a traumatic childhood."

He knits his heavy eyebrows, and his dark eyes narrow intensely.

"And," I add, "we both had that."

"That's true," he says. "It was a miserable place." This is what I've been aching to hear: someone to corroborate my own recollections. My brother is the only person on earth who can validate my memories.

"You know, I haven't had an easy life either." I inch toward revealing myself to him, even as I wonder if that's a good idea. He seems too self-absorbed right now to care, and I'm not sure how much he's taking in anyway. After pausing a moment, I choose a different tack.

"I read somewhere that Holocaust survivors and their children are the second-largest group, behind war veterans, to suffer with PTSD. I have it too."

"But you seem so different now." I'm surprised he even noticed. "Not how I remember you."

"Better, I hope."

"Yeah . . . calmer, I guess."

"Well, I've gotten treatment. I understand it and I can manage it now. First thing you need to know is," I say, eyes burning on him as I try to sear this fundamental truth into his brain, "it's not your fault."

That simple fact took me years to absorb. "PTSD is a defense mechanism that saved you when you were a terrorized child," I continue. "But now it's like a stuck thermostat that always runs too hot. And when you're caught up in it, you feel like you can't get it to stop. PTSD owns you."

"Yeah . . . I feel like I have a cancer taking over my brain."

"I get it," I say. "It's like you're walking around with an exposed nerve all the time."

Now I know: We have both suffered with this, and because we were estranged, we couldn't see each other through these dark woods. What else have we missed?

"Several years ago," I continue, "when I was first diagnosed, I suspected you had it too. Given our history, it would be hard to escape. But you and I weren't talking, and I figured it wasn't my business to say anything."

"Even if you had told me then," he admits, "I wouldn't have believed you, and I wasn't ready to do anything about it. I was too stubborn."

"So what about now? Do you believe me? Are you ready?"

"Fern," he says, "I can't live like this anymore. I'm desperate." I think he's telling me that he's hit rock bottom, that things can't get any worse. He's hopeless; he feels alone and doubtful anything will change.

I know that there's great value in hitting this low point. The landing is painful and jarring, but it just may be enough to incite the person to change. Pain can be a powerful motivator.

I ask him: "Are you willing to get treatment?" I can't beg him, shame him, or reason with him. He has to be ready. This is his choice.

"I'll do anything," he says again, repeating the words he used on the phone.

"So . . . I'm willing to help," I continue, staring at his face to see his reaction as I outline my terms again. "But like I told you, you can't lie to me. You need to be honest. And you can't disappear again. Okay?"

Narrowing my eyes in scrutiny, I try to read his countenance, trying to extract an absolute commitment that I won't get hurt again. But it's clear that he's too distraught to give me what I need, even to look at me directly.

There are no guarantees, I tell myself. I'm just going to have to accept this risk. When he finally meets my gaze with his droopy, defeated eyes, I know that, regardless of how he behaves, I can't walk away from him now.

"Okay," he says.

"So let me tell you about the treatment." Now he's listening carefully. "It's called neurofeedback, and it sounds kind of 'out there,' but it works. At least it worked for me."

I try to give him a general explanation of neurofeedback. Now that researchers understand how the brain creates new pathways and connections as needed throughout life, they've identified new treatments for anxiety, depression, PTSD, and ADD. Neurofeedback, a noninvasive technique, uses computers and sensors placed on the head to detect and monitor brain waves that shift constantly with every change in emotions.

Research shows that the brain-wave patterns of someone suffering from depression or PTSD differ from those of a person with a healthy sense of well-being. Neurofeedback allows the patient to retrain his or her brain waves to match the pattern of "normal" individuals, as identified in a data pool. It's a kind of guided meditation that uses music as a reward. When the patient's brain waves match the normal pattern, music plays; when the brain waves are irregular, the music shuts off. With repeated neurofeedback sessions, changes in the brain-wave pattern produce a lasting effect on the person's mood and outlook.

By now we've been talking for over an hour. When Scott realizes how late it is, he tells me he needs to leave. I promise to go with him to his first appointment to meet the neurofeedback clinician.

As we walk toward the door, I can't keep myself from, once again, stating my terms to him. I seem to think if I repeat them often enough, they will penetrate. "No more hiding. No more lies."

Then, with a hug, we say our good-byes. Still stunned by what has transpired, I watch him lumber to the Honda and climb in. But then, as if he has forgotten something, his head pops out of the car again. He climbs back out and shuffles toward the front door.

I look around for something he might have left behind. No, I don't see a thing. Then he opens the door and stands before me, even more agitated than before.

Panicked, I wonder if he's about to tell me he's changed his mind already. Maybe this is more than he can manage. He can't go through with treatment. He's bailing on me again; he'll never reestablish our relationship.

In my mind, the sixteen-year-old Scott jeers at me cruelly: *Juuuust kidding!* That sly, mean joke; that mocking laugh. *Burned!*

"What?" I ask defensively, struggling to shove aside the humiliating "burns" he inflicted on me as a kid. "What's wrong?"

"I have to tell you something."

"What?" I brace myself.

"You said, 'No more hiding, no more lies.'"

"Yeah . . . and?" Quickly sifting through the lines of our conversation today, I try to anticipate what he's about to say. What did I miss?

"So I . . . I'm . . ." He drops his eyes. "I'm going over to Mom's today . . . to pick up a check from her."

This is an old, old issue among the three of us. I figured Mom had been helping support him financially, but they kept this a secret from me. She had so little connection with him that, at times, she used money as a way to maintain contact.

I'm surprised and hopeful at his admission; maybe he is dedicated to change after all. After he leaves, I acknowledge his candor in a text:

Thanks for being honest with me today.

He responds:

Must be honest. It's all I've got right now.

That *is* all he has right now. Honesty is all that's left. It's critical to the success of our reconnection—for that matter, to any relationship. His comment makes me think about how we have to rebuild this relationship from the bottom up. We've lost so much to estrangement, squandering years and forfeiting a sense of our own identities.

Even worse, each of us likely has suffered with low self-esteem resulting from the estrangement. I see it in myself, all sorts of negative thoughts running through my head as I question what I did, why I did it, and how whatever I did led to estrangement.

This negative thinking spilled over into other parts of my life. Even during times of good fortune and joy, I never escaped the painful indictment of my brother's rejection. I couldn't make sense of the loss, couldn't adjust or accept it. The acid of estrangement chronically dripped in my brain, corroding my ability to be happy.

Estrangement Erodes Self-Esteem

Poor self-worth often plagues the estranged—a key distinction between mourning the living and mourning the dead. When a family member dies, the experience perhaps changes but doesn't fundamentally challenge an individual's core sense of self. Death isn't a personal rejection. When a brother or sister terminates a relationship, however, the shunned sibling feels responsible for the situation. The loss leaves a gnawing sense of unlovability and lack of worth.

Those who responded to my survey also noted how their self-esteem suffered from sibling cutoff, even when they weren't to blame:

The "lies" I told myself based on how I was treated by my family really affected my self-esteem. Now I see that the problem was not me; it was them.

I dream about her and wonder if she is okay. I feel terrible about myself and I break out in hives when I have to talk about the estrangement with anyone. I've started therapy for this. I never knew that you could have a physical reaction to this.

The pain I feel has tainted my everyday life. It also has made me try harder to secure and strengthen relationships with other relatives.

I have had streaks where I get very depressed and cry every day several times a day. When this depression overwhelms me, I don't leave my home because I'm afraid of crying in public because it's hard to control.

For any estranged sibling, it's difficult to sort out whether the loss of self-esteem results from the loss of a brother or sister or whether low self-esteem in childhood actually contributes to the cutoff. A child who feels insecure about his or her place in the family and social circles is often unhappy. That childhood unhappiness may lead to sibling rivalry, which results in loneliness, depression, and feelings of low self-worth. As discussed in chapter 4, sibling rivalry in childhood may well be the root of adult estrangement.

The shunned often personalize the experience of being rejected, especially at an early age. That was the case for Rachel Goldman, sixty-seven, the sister of Sam Goldman, who said in chapter 4 that he cut off relations with his family because his former wife discouraged those connections. Rachel, however, claims that her brother's distancing from the family began before his marriage. She has battled low self-esteem for most of her life, in part because of her brother's rejection in their adolescence:

It all started when we were teenagers. I was never good enough to be with him and his friends. He hung around with cool, handsome guys, and he got mad when I talked to them. I felt I didn't have much worth.

When he graduated high school, he didn't want my mother, sister, and me to join him on the field after the ceremony. I felt like we weren't part of his life anymore. I wondered what I'd done to alienate him.

He went to college and then got married at twenty-one. I didn't understand why he was doing this. I didn't go to his wedding. None of us—my mother, my sister, and I—ever felt comfortable around his wife.

Over the years, we didn't see them much, since they lived in another area. They rarely visited, and the rare times we saw them, it was always awkward. I hardly ever talked to my brother on the phone, and when I did, there wasn't much to say.

The years came and went. Decades passed. I felt excluded all the time. I felt there was something wrong with me that my brother didn't want anything to do with me. I carried around that sadness all the time. I often felt worthless and familyless.

As Rachel describes, childhood feelings have a long reach. In adulthood, cutting off from a difficult sister or brother may ultimately produce anxiety and depression. Those symptoms may become so far removed from the estrangement that some may not see the connection between the sibling cutoff and later despair.

I wonder if Scott's current depression has something to do with our years of estrangement. I think I have been caught in what experts call "complicated grief," which is marked by intense yearning, longing, or emotional pain; frequent preoccupying thoughts and memories of the absent person; and an inability to accept the loss. Regardless of the label, I suspect the estrangement has contributed to stress and anxiety in both of our lives.

Estrangement Erodes Trust

Feelings of poor self-worth are not confined to the estranged sibling relationship. The mind perceives information, both consciously and subconsciously, and organizes assessments and sometimes other people's judgments into a belief system about one's character and identity. When an individual perceives incoming information as negative, he or she reinforces feelings of low self-esteem. In turn, a dangerous mix of internal factors (self-esteem) and external factors (stigma) may spill over into other relationships, ultimately limiting one's ability to trust.

Survey respondents reported that they have difficulty trusting others due to an erratic connection with an estranged sibling. Respondents offered the following observations:

> *I am afraid to make friends because I don't trust people. It is hard to trust anyone.*

> *I actually find myself trying not to get too close to anybody because of my experience with the family relationships that have gone bad.*

> *I have major trust issues with everyone now. I worry that those I care about will suddenly leave me with no explanation.*

> *I find it difficult to make friends. I have always been afraid of making long-term committed relationships with men because of my estrangement from my two older brothers. I don't want to repeat the horror of my early life.*

> *When a friend distances themselves from me for good reason (a crisis where they need to be alone), I get triggered and panicked. I feel like I am being taken for granted like my family did.*

These survey respondents recognized that the emotional void of estrangement has handcuffed them, as they find it difficult to be direct and honest with friends and family. Fearing a cutoff, estranged siblings often don't present their authentic selves and forfeit the quality of their relationships.

Several factors unique to sibling estrangement contribute to an inability to establish full relationships outside the family, according to author and researcher Kylie Agllias, who has identified the following three critical challenges:

- The estranged fear others won't understand their severed family re-lationships, particularly if they choose to cut off.
- Those who have initiated the cutoff worry others will identify them as untrustworthy and a poor candidate for friendship.
- With only a few (perhaps no) family members and/or friends to support them, the estranged, who ruminate on their protracted, traumatic loss, often overburden their other relationships, resulting in burnout and yet another ruined association.[1]

Bryn White, thirty-seven, was raised in an "abusive, chaotic, neglect-ful home" in a poor neighborhood in Ireland, and for generations, her family has been carved up by cutoffs. She has been estranged from two of her three older sisters for nearly a decade. She believes the stigma and shame of estrangement have contributed to her lack of self-worth. Bryn doesn't know why her sisters have distanced themselves from her, but she fears the reason might be that she identifies herself as bisexual and poly-amorous while they are what she calls "married homemakers with mort-gages."

"I worry that people will judge and reject me," she says. "I don't talk about my estrangements to anyone except my best friend, as I carry a lot of internalized shame. Estrangements have left me feeling unworthy and somehow defective. I need to stop castigating myself over what might have caused the rifts or what I could have done to prevent them and work on healing. I'm trying to learn to love myself, even if my siblings can't see my value."

Some victims of a cutoff who were desperate to replace the family they had lost sought out enmeshed, dependent relationships to provide reassur-ance and comfort. In those relationships, many felt that they lost their self-agency and became "people pleasers," who constantly yielded to their partner's needs. Some rushed into unsuccessful marriages with the first person who declared love for them, and ultimately, they discovered that their partners were manipulative and exploitive.

The stress of these choices could result in life-changing physiological symptoms. Chronic stress may lead to compromised health and illnesses, including insomnia, muscle pain, high blood pressure, a weakened immune system, and other problems, such as recurrent episodes of depression and anxiety.

"Stress is a killer," says forty-one-year-old Stephanie Bleacher of New Brunswick, Canada, who has been estranged from one of her five sisters for a decade. "There's nothing worse than the stress that comes from family conflict!" Another survey respondent succinctly sums up the profound effect many of the estranged experience: "I feel incredibly lonely, physically sick, and emotionally insecure most of the time."

Healthy Reconciliation Restores Self-Esteem

The hurts of estrangement and the resulting low self-esteem at some point may become a cage. In order to heal and move forward, it's necessary to examine those hurts—but it's also important to release oneself from guilt and old injuries. Because it's impossible to be in two emotional states at the same time—calm and angry, happy and sad, or hateful and loving— those who wish to evolve must overcome the addictive thoughts of bitter estrangements and instead choose to value their own well-being.

Some shunned siblings, however, in their desperation to restore a damaged relationship, submit to the demands or conditions of a domineering brother or sister. When the pain of a cutoff is too great, it's tempting to release oneself from the relentless suffering by simply recanting or apologizing. These shunned siblings who sublimate their own needs back away from who they are and what they know to be true.

Author Laura Davis warns that these behaviors can further damage self-esteem. "When we capitulate in a relationship," she writes in *I Thought We'd Never Speak Again*, "we experience shame, self-doubt, and self-hatred. Anger festers, and we may find ourselves responding to the other person with coldness, jabs, sarcasm, aloofness or with subtle or overt cruelty."[2]

The goal in reconciliation is to bring an autonomous, authentic, whole self to a damaged sibling connection and create a new relationship. "Reconciliation becomes possible as we rebuild ourselves into people who are no longer capable of being hurt in the same way," Davis continues. "As we establish ourselves as separate individuals, we increase our capacity for self-care and gain clarity required to reassess unresolved relationships."

One of the many benefits of reconciliation is improved self-esteem, which enhances other relationships with family and friends. In reestablishing an authentic relationship with an estranged sibling, a brother or sister becomes more adept at self-advocacy, creating reciprocal and fulfilling relationships. Trust can grow in that fertile soil.

Chapter 8

Social Media and the Estranged

S cott asked me to give him a wake-up call on the morning we're scheduled to visit the neurofeedback clinic. Scrolling to his name on my iPhone, I'm pleased to notice things are starting to change: I'm not rushing past *S* to avoid the sting. In fact, I briefly consider adding his name to my list of "favorites." But that seems overly optimistic; before making such a commitment, I want to be sure this reconnection will stick. For now, I'll just take the extra step of scrolling to his name in my full contact list.

Again the robotic voice picks up my call: "Hello. You have reached . . ."

"Hey," I say after the beep. "I'm just calling to make sure you're up and ready to go. Okay? Call me back."

I expect him to call back immediately, as he did last week. But no. Nothing.

So I wait.

Why am I always waiting for him? I wonder. *Is it the same old thing? The power dynamic was established years ago. I wait, constantly wondering what's going on, and neither one of us says anything about it. If we're going to have any relationship, this has got to change.*

Then I shake myself. *Before I tackle the big things*, I think, *I just need to reach him.*

Three minutes pass. Four. I decide to take action and call again.

"Hello. You have reached . . ."

This time I hang up without leaving a message. An uneasiness settles in my stomach. *Where is he?*

I know so little about him, his habits and his routines. I can't begin to speculate about why his phone is going to voice mail. For years, if it weren't for my mother's occasional updates, I wouldn't have known if he were dead or alive.

Four years ago, however, I was stunned to receive a notification from Twitter: Scott Schumer was now following me.

I remember staring, bewildered, at his unfamiliar name. For a moment, I wondered if this was some other Scott Schumer. I went to his Twitter profile to see his picture, but there was only an icon, an empty white oval matted on a green background, marking the spot where his photo should have been.

Puzzled, curious, wary, I finally decided it *had* to be my brother. I was both flattered and insulted that he was following me. The "ping" was a signal that he was still out there, that he had actually had a moment when he thought of me. But it also reminded me that, until then—even though I *was* his sister—I had never made the cut as a social media contact.

Immediately, I looked for other electronic signs of life on the internet— Facebook, Instagram, LinkedIn. But I found him only on Twitter. *At least*, I thought, *he did reach out; I'll reciprocate and follow him back.* True, it was awfully impersonal, but I was hoping to make some sort of safe, if distant, connection.

To my great disappointment, however, he tweeted rarely, and when he did, it was about his favorite sports teams. I never did come up with snappy remarks on the Bears' third pick in the NFL draft.

In time, I realized it was better for me that he didn't post much on social media. These platforms' vivid, irresistible photos of picture-perfect families often add to the pain of estrangement. If I had seen pictures from my nephew's wedding, for example, I'd have reexperienced that miserable exclusion. I'd have had the mortifying sensation that I was snooping, the wretched sense that this was somebody else's family—not my own.

Now, waiting for Scott to call, I grow increasingly agitated. I begin to pace the hallway. My breathing becomes ragged and shallow as my mind fills with horrible images—my worst fears crowding my brain, ramping up my anxiety.

What if . . . ? I think. *Now that we've finally reconnected . . . No, I can't think like that. If he were going to do that, he would have done it before. Now I think he has a little hope.*

Then I stop myself. *Wait . . . wait,* I tell myself. *Slow down!* Am I overreacting? It's hard for me to tell, because my own PTSD can distort my perceptions. When something happens that reminds me of past trauma, I react as though the trauma were happening again now, and anything having to do with Scott always reminds me of past trauma. To determine whether PTSD is duping me, I need to be vigilant, always sifting carefully through my responses and asking myself: *What's the reality here, and what's an overreaction?*

At the moment, though, I'm too agitated to consider that question. Instead, I call Scott again. And again. I keep sitting through the same hollow ringing, fidgeting at the greeting on his voice mail. When I hear his recorded "Hello," I immediately hang up and try again.

Finally, after many attempts, a click breaks into the ringing, and he picks up with a hoarse, gloomy "Hello."

Relieved, I can't stop myself from blurting out, "I've been trying to reach you."

"What? What's wrong?"

"I didn't know what happened to you," I say. My breathing is becoming a little more even.

"What do you mean?"

"Well, you told me to call and wake you up," I say, annoyed but still shaky.

I don't say what's really on my mind: *I'm trying to trust someone I hardly know—someone who's really a stranger to me, who has rejected and burned me so badly, and so often.* The old doubts about whether reconciliation is even possible shudder through me again.

But I don't let on; instead, I grope for a normal response. "It's just that I've been calling and calling, for at least half an hour now—"

With a flash of his old self, Scott cuts me off.

"Fern," he snaps, "I was in the *shower.*"

The day I discovered Scott had followed me on Twitter, I was caught in a confusing swirl of emotions: astonishment, hurt, discomfort. First, I was shocked to see that he had even contacted me. Then I realized reaching out online wasn't exactly contact; it felt more like snooping. Through the act of following me, my estranged brother had gained access to my life without my consent. That made me feel queasy.

Social media, touted as a means of connecting people and facilitating interpersonal relationships can, ironically, exacerbate the misery of the estranged. Facebook and other platforms have created unique opportunities for cruelty, humiliation, and other complications.

The Risks of Social Media

When navigating the world of social media, the estranged need to be cautious and weigh the potential for reconnection against the risk of worsening familiar feelings of grief and anguish. After assuming the risk of "friending" or following distant family members, the aggrieved sibling may be reexposed to the ugliness of relatives' gossip, distortions, false posturing, and exclusions. At any moment, a user could run straight into social media's ultimate slammed door: being blocked. For the estranged, this constitutes yet another hurtful and disturbing rejection.

Even worse, estranged siblings who haven't accepted the severed relationship may find themselves hurt again and again in social media exchanges with relatives. Exposure to an estranged sibling's posts, "likes," comments, and photographs, whether direct or indirect (through a relative's or mutual friend's feed), can be like picking at scabs, preventing emotional wounds from healing and inhibiting the grieving process.

I was spared much of the anguish that social media can generate because Scott was not an avid social media user. However, many who are cut off are repeatedly stung by Facebook entries, "friend" suggestions, Instagram feeds, and tweets that serve as harsh reminders of the family life they are missing. Survey respondents commented on the variety of ways they have been wounded by what they've seen on social media:

My eldest sibling became a grandmother—twice! No one told me. I saw a social media post.

After she had shut me out, my sister recently "friended" me on the game Steam. Sometimes, a notice pops up on my screen telling me that my sister is playing at that moment. It's such a weirdly intimate thing to see when I never see anything else of her.

He and his wife told us that no one would be invited to their wedding cere-
mony, only the reception. The day after the wedding, we found out her whole
family was at the ceremony by seeing pictures posted on social media.

In my survey, a surprising 16 percent of respondents admitted that they follow an estranged sibling on social media. Most of that group said they refused to completely cut off a sibling, hoping that social media would offer remote siblings a unique possibility: Contact via these platforms could crack open the closed door. The medium also provides easy access should an estranged sibling have a change of heart and decide to revisit the relationship. A sister or brother who might not answer a letter or return a phone call would perhaps respond to an instant message.

About 14 percent of respondents said that they or their estranged siblings do not use social media. Seventy percent reported that they simply don't follow an estranged sibling and, of that group, over half reported that their estranged brother or sister has blocked them.

It can be very difficult to resist the temptation, much less the addiction, of glimpsing an estranged sibling who is only a few clicks away in cyberspace. Aggrieved siblings sometimes "creep" on social media for snippets of information, hoping to deepen their sparse present-day understanding of the remote brother or sister with whom they grew up and once knew so well. Above all, they want answers to their burning questions: *Who is my brother or sister now? What is his or her life like? Who are his or her friends? How does he or she spend his or her time? What have I missed in his or her life?*

Brothers and sisters who have experienced long-standing cutoffs often are curious to see what family members now look like. For them, social media provides a window—albeit an opaque and one-sided one—through which to view loved ones. Though they don't have an opportunity to develop these relationships, the estranged may feel some connection from observing relatives in photos or videos.

Helene Pendergast, a British woman in her sixties who hasn't had a relationship with her only brother for nearly fifty years, can't help herself from occasionally looking up her nephew and nieces on social media. She was raised in a chaotic, abusive, and unloving home where the rules were "endless and ever changing," and the three competed with one another for food, clothes, affection, and a place in the family.

In recent years, Pendergast has had health issues. "I face going into old age without the support and love of a family," she says. "It's hard to believe there are people on this earth related to me by blood who don't care a fig about me. It's shocking how people can cut someone entirely out of their lives without so much as a twinge of conscience." But she has not completely cut her brother and his children out of her heart. "On social media," she says, "I am pleased to see all of them doing well, but it is strange to know I have never had a part in their lives."

Almost inevitably, these photographs reinforce the painful reality that family members are physically present, but psychologically absent. This phenomenon is a form of grief called "ambiguous loss." Pauline Boss, author of *Ambiguous Loss: Learning to Live with Unresolved Grief*, explains that those who mourn someone who is still alive often "fluctuate between hope and hopelessness. Suffered too long, these emotions can deaden feeling and make it impossible for people to move on with their lives." She explains that it is difficult to live with what she calls "two truths," such as, for example, my brother, who wants nothing to do with me, is still my brother. This state of limbo thwarts the process, and the solitary pursuit of a sibling relationship on the screen can make the situation worse as the connection may produce an unhealthy sense of attachment. Snooping may keep the user emotionally stuck, freezing the estranged in ambiguous loss.

Anyone snooping on social media also runs the risk of stirring up feelings of jealousy and FOMO (fear of missing out). Many users, after viewing photographs of other "happy" families, feel envious. For the estranged, those images can be particularly unsettling. "My friends post pictures with all their sisters, husbands, and children having a get-together," says

Julianna Turner, who has described her sibling estrangements and tumultuous upbringing in Scotland in previous chapters. "I scroll through the same pictures for hours. It looks so fun and heartwarming. I'm crushed that I will never have that."

No matter how intense their longing, however, the estranged aren't likely to find satisfying or accurate information on social media. Today, Facebook, Instagram, Twitter, and similar "sharing" outlets tend to be more about posturing than connecting, says Dr. Brian A. Primack, Dean of College of Education and Health Professions at the University of Arkansas. He has researched the effects of media messages and technological advances on health.

"Even though it seems like the people you are interacting with are very 'real,'" he says, "their messages and feeds are in fact very highly curated."[1] Users distill their activities into a few words and photos, consciously displaying themselves in the most positive light. Some go so far as to create a carefully designed, "perfect" social media version of their "perfect" lives.

Melissa Marley of Calgary, who described her traumatic upbringing in chapter 4, has encountered her estranged younger brother's "perfect" life on Facebook. She has been distancing herself from him for years "because of his gambling addiction and narcissism." For most of her life, she felt responsible for her brother.

"As the family caretaker," she explains, "it was my job to keep everyone happy." Since her brother had difficulty making friends when they were children, she believed she should help him socially. "As an adult, there were times I would experience extreme guilt when things were going well for me and when I couldn't help him." But eventually she became weary of his lies and his schemes. "Now I know there's nothing I can do for him."

Through the lens of social media, Marley has gotten a clear-eyed view of who her brother really is. "He plays 'Perfect Facebook Daddy.' Barf!" she says. "The truth is that he's a gambling addict and he has spent his daughter's education fund!" For Marley, social media has clearly exposed her brother's "phony posturing" and the ways her estranged brother has manipulated family and friends and "staged" his life.

Reconciliation and the Online Culture

Social media displays an even darker side when feuding relatives use the platforms as another battleground on which to wage war. Aware that a disowned family member is watching, some will intentionally post hurtful entries, consciously heightening bad feelings between themselves and their estranged sibling. Some bail out of this cruel game by blocking all family members from their social media accounts.

The estranged who are hoping for some sort of reconciliation on social media often are disappointed, partly because of the nature of the medium. People treat one another differently online than they might in a face-to-face encounter. Social media has a quality of remove; it is less personal, and users don't worry as much about hurting others' feelings. Social media just isn't conducive to an in-depth conversation, especially the kind of discussion that might lead to healing of a troubled relationship.

Facebook has exacerbated the sibling divide for Diana McCarthy, fifty-eight, of Round Rock, Texas, who hasn't spoken to her three older brothers for more than ten years due to petty jealousies. Born fourteen years after the next-youngest sibling, she says she was raised in a chaotic, alcoholic home. She hasn't spoken to her brothers since their father died in 2008, but recently she decided to give them another chance and messaged them on Facebook. One actually responded and friended her. That's when she discovered the nasty comments her siblings were posting behind her back. "He friended me just because he was nosy," she says. "I found five posts where they were talking about me. It's all made-up crap. They know absolutely nothing about me, my husband, and my kids."

While these platforms may be a space where rifts spread to other family members, social media also may help contain the cancer of estrangement. Parents, nieces, nephews, and others caught in the crossfire may reach out privately on social media to maintain some connection, even if the estranged are no longer attending family events. For those who become collateral damage to sibling estrangement, these contacts may help reduce feelings of isolation.

Need to Step Away from Social Media

Information on social media cuts so deeply that users often question whether it's more painful to sneak views or to stay away from the platforms altogether. Yet Facebook, Twitter, and Instagram are deeply entrenched in our daily lives, and many users aren't comfortable closing their accounts in order to avoid a difficult sibling.

"I kept a social media connection to my eldest sister until last year," says Stacy Browning, forty-nine, of Quebec, Canada. For the last five years, she has been estranged from both of her older sisters, who are eight and ten years her senior. Ever since her birth, Stacy says, her sisters have struggled with jealousy about the "new baby." Her parents anticipated this problem and had the girls name the baby in hopes that they would feel included in the experience. "I loved my sisters dearly," Stacy says, "because they were the only family I had. But they had little to do with me."

Stacy, who has been financially successful, has helped support her sisters by paying their mortgages, their children's private school tuitions, and for their trips to Europe. That ended five years ago when their mother died. The sisters emptied their mother's bank accounts and divided her things between themselves, leaving Stacy completely cut out.

Still, Stacy maintained a Facebook connection to one sister just in case she wanted to restore their relationship. "I thought my connection would serve to refute her claims that I was unreachable," she explains. "The truth is that neither sibling ever returned my calls, emails, texts, or private messages. Finally I decided I didn't want to start the new year with a connection to either of them or their allies. I cut the tie just before 2018."

Susanna Garth of Fiji, who in chapter 4 described her grief over the estranged relationship with her older and only sister, understands the peril of habitually glimpsing her sister and her niece and nephew via social media. Garth doesn't understand why her sister cut her off, and for a long time, she lived with the hope that things would change. Instead, Facebook dealt her another blow. She was shocked and hurt when she discovered one year ago that her sister's husband had blocked her from his page. She then came to recognize that the constant exposure to her estranged sister through the stream of family pictures and posts on Facebook was taking a terrible toll.

"I need space to grieve," she says. "I have decided to block my sister so she can't find my profile. Hanging on to what was is not healthy for me."

For Susanna and others who are estranged, social media may seem like an opportunity to recapture some of what has been lost. Yet its use may keep the wound open and raw, perpetuating the unending turmoil and relentless sadness of mourning the living.

Estranged siblings need to carefully weigh the risks and rewards of social media. If an estranged sibling is aggressive, it might be best to avoid these platforms, which can become another battleground. But if users can tolerate feelings of exclusion and jealousy that might result from seeing an estranged sibling's posts, social media may offer a thread of a connection to that branch of the family.

Users who are deciding whether to stay connected on social media may ask themselves these questions: How hostile is my estranged sister or brother? Is he or she likely to lash out at me on these platforms? How well adjusted am I to the estrangement? Can I stand to have some exposure to my sibling's life, or will those encounters disturb my ability to accept the cutoff?

Chapter 9

Reconnection and Reestablishment of a Sibling Relationship

With a warm smile and an outstretched hand, Dr. Elsa Baehr offers Scott and me the two tan upholstered chairs in her office. Only when we're seated does she settle into her sleek black chair. The early-morning sunlight streams in through her floor-to-ceiling windows, casting a mesmerizing kaleidoscope of triangles on the brown carpet.

"I'm glad you came in today. Nice to meet you, Scott." Elsa, a tiny, attractive woman, is nearing the end of an illustrious sixty-year career, during which she established herself as a maverick, then a leader, in the emerging field of neurofeedback.

It's been months since Elsa and I last met, so she asks me a few general questions about how I'm doing and what I've been working on recently. "Really good to see you again," she says, her dark eyes shining with kindness.

Then she turns her attention to Scott. "Before we talk about neurofeed-back," she says softly, looking directly at him, "I'd like to know a little bit more about you."

I glance over at my brother, who has never been comfortable talking about himself or his feelings. Yet he looks relaxed with Elsa, whose strikingly serene presence suggests a nurturing, nonjudgmental grandmother. I've always appreciated her gift for creating a safe space in her cozy office, which is lined with bookshelves providing not quite enough space for her sprawling collection of professional psychology books and a smattering of family pictures. Entering her soothing space, even the most distressed soul can feel valued and validated.

"I know from my work with Fern that you two haven't always . . . How should I put it?" She smiles a little. "Haven't always sustained your relationship."

"Yeah," Scott volunteers, "you could say that."

"That's surprising," Elsa says, "because the two of you seem comfortable in each other's company today." I squirm and shift in my chair. *Well, sort of.*

"When did you reconnect?" she continues.

We exchange a quick glance; I narrow my eyes and respond, "Last Monday? Tuesday?" So much has happened, I can hardly remember.

"Really!" She looks at both of us, trying to absorb the suddenness of this dramatic change. "I would have never guessed."

In this moment, I observe the two of us through her eyes. She sees two compatible middle-aged siblings. What she can't imagine is the agonizing years of estrangement that divide us, or the distressing personal history that draws us together. At the very least, I realize, I should fill her in on the developments since that frantic phone call from my mother, now more than a week ago.

"Things have happened pretty quickly," I begin. Then I dive into the

story: the long drought in our relationship, Scott's recent crisis, our fledgling reconnection.

When I finish, she turns to my brother. "If you don't mind, Scott," she
says, gently but directly, "I'd like to ask you a few questions. I'd like to
understand a bit more about you."

"Okay." I'm struck by his willingness to discuss our problems here. He
seems so different from how I remember him. Maybe it's just another in-
dication of how desperate he is to change.

"Can you explain why . . . why you didn't talk to your sister for all those
years?"

There it is: the question I've wanted to ask him for decades—the core
issue that plagues many abandoned siblings. Yet her question triggers every
one of my inner alarms. She has just violated, flagrantly, the approach to
reconciliation that all the experts outlined:

Take it slowly.

Don't bomb him with old hurts.

Put the past in the past.

But I didn't ask the question; she did. And the experts didn't mention
any rules for an outside mediator.

Scott stares silently at Elsa. I can't read him. Watching him shift uncomfortably in his chair, I wonder, is he angry that she posed the question
or just unsure of how to answer? Is he thinking about getting up and
walking out?

Then I remember: We came to Elsa's office together—in *my* car. He
can't leave. We're stuck with each other, and he has to endure the next
hour of truth-telling in Elsa's den.

His heavy breathing sounds labored; he pulls a tissue from the pocket of his jeans to blot the sweat dribbling down his forehead. His eyes shift back and forth as he runs through his thoughts. He's the living picture of anxiety. The question hangs between us; the wait for his answer grows uncomfortably long.

My old sisterly instinct, to come to his aid, kicks in. I could brush off Elsa's question by rationalizing, *We were always very different*, or *Our lives took different directions as adults*, or *We were busy with our families and careers*.

No, I tell myself, *I'm not giving him any excuses. I'm not rescuing him*. If we're ever going to build any kind of relationship, I need to hear *his* answer. And so does Elsa.

"What was it?" she nudges him.

"I . . . I'm not really sure," he says. "I don't know."

Really! After all these years, after that excruciating silence—he doesn't know! I'd like to chime in with something like *Well, you certainly know more than I do*.

But I remind myself to let Elsa direct this conversation. Unlike me, she's not emotionally invested, and unlike me, she's an expert at encouraging people to talk about things they'd rather avoid.

"Was there some argument, a catalyst?" she asks. Scott's silence buzzes like a live electrical wire. Listening to nothing, I almost feel as if I've disappeared from the room. Maybe that's part of her strategy.

"No . . . not really. It's been so long, I hardly remember. It's just always been this way."

"But you must have some feelings that drove you to distance yourself from your sister?"

"I . . . I can't really explain it." Ashamed, he drops his head. Then he looks back up at Elsa. "I just couldn't be around her," he says simply.

Elsa persists. "What kind of emotions did you experience on the rare occasions when you saw your sister at family events?"

"My dad either," he adds, giving Elsa a little something to work with. "I wasn't ever comfortable with either of them."

"What was it about them that made you uncomfortable?" Unrelenting, she presses.

I suddenly hear in my mind a snippet of a conversation Scott and I had with Dad many years ago. It was one of the few times we talked openly. When it's clear that Scott can't come up with an answer, I try to help him remember what I could never forget.

"Well, you know we discussed all this a long time ago," I say. They both turn toward me. "You, Dad, and me.

"It was 1990, I think." Hard to believe, nearly thirty years ago now! "It was the only time Dad tried to talk to you about your estrangement from him. He wanted me there, too, to hear what he had to say. You know he was never nervous or unsure of himself—but that day, he could barely get out a complete sentence. The gist of what he was trying to say, Scott, was that he wanted you in his life."

Scott slowly nods; I can see that he remembers. "He invited us to his house," I continue, "and he tried to explain his marriage to Mom. And the divorce. He talked about the choices he made, the way he lived his life, the kind of doctor and dad he was. I remember he was pretty defensive. Really unwilling to listen or hear anything we had to say."

"Wasn't he always that way?" Scott rolls his eyes and shakes his head in disgust.

"Well, anyhow." I can't stop now. "The conversation seemed to lapse into the same old pattern, and it got pretty heated. You know, he kept saying: 'I did the best I could. . . . I had a busy life with lots of demands. . . . I can't change the past.' It was frustrating, and after listening for a while, you got angry and walked out without saying good-bye."

I take a deep breath. "And that was it! That was the moment you swore off any relationship with Dad and me."

"Yeah." He gazes off into the distance, as if we were back in Dad's living room. "I was so sick of his excuses for why he wasn't a better dad . . . why he was never around," he says. "It was all such bullshit." Then he mimics Dad's voice with a mocking, deadeye authenticity: "'I am a doctor. I have a big career. I have things to accomplish and contributions to make.'"

"I *know!*" I can't restrain my anger. "But *I'm not Dad!*"

There it is. At last I've articulated what I've always felt.

And there's one more thing I say almost breathlessly: "I don't want to be *lumped in* with him."

Silence hangs between us. Scott could never see me apart from the unit that was our family. In creating his own identity, he had rejected *everything* he associated with Dad.

I had taken a different approach, trying to make peace with Dad in part by ignoring his many flaws and selecting some of his better qualities to emulate: his intellectual curiosity, his ability to focus, his drive.

Scott distanced himself from me in part, I suspect, because I shared some of Dad's characteristics. He couldn't differentiate between Dad and me. I was a casualty of Scott's need to separate from—and, finally, to reject—our father.

If we're to have any hope for reconciliation, he first needs to understand that I am not Dad.

So I dive back in. "Do you remember what I told you that day?"

"Not really."

And then I say what I know Dad never would have said: "I said then, 'You don't have to talk to me, but that's not going to stop me from loving you.'"

Scott's eyes glitter with tears as he stares at me, unblinking.

"Though I gotta say"—I swallow the lump in my throat—"you haven't made it easy to keep that promise."

The three of us sit quietly for a moment, absorbed in our own thoughts, soaking in a mixture of intense emotions. That old conversation in Dad's living room rings in my ears, like a meme on endless replay.

"And do you remember what Dad said?" I break the silence. "Actually, he was pretty insightful."

"No." Scott shakes his head. "What?"

"He told you why you couldn't stand to be around us."

"What did he say?"

"He said we brought back memories of the past that you didn't want to remember."

"I suspect he's right," Elsa jumps in. "That's a pretty typical response to a traumatic childhood. Sometimes we cope by avoiding anything that reminds us of painful experiences—people, places, thoughts, activities, or even objects. Your father and your sister probably brought back things you were trying to forget. They were triggers. When that happens, you're not reacting to what's happening in the moment; you're reacting to the things you haven't processed or grieved."

"Makes sense," Scott says.

"But I think there's more to the estrangement than that," she says. "Families are complicated, and sibling relationships are even more complicated."

She goes on to explain that siblings often displace and "dump" their rage—about their parents, their upbringing, even their own feelings of failure—on a sister or brother. "A brother or sister can become the repository of all those things we don't want to acknowledge in ourselves," she says. "In most cases, children need their parents in order to survive, and that need, while it changes over a lifetime, doesn't just disappear. Most children—though this was not exactly your story, Scott—avoid risking their relationships with their parents, but a brother or sister is more expendable."

What often comes between siblings, she continues, is the limited availability of their parents' love. "Earlier, you actually identified that your dad didn't love you enough. It is easier to blame a brother or sister—not necessarily consciously—for taking whatever love was available and leaving you with nothing. In your case, you cut off both your father *and* your sister. Sometimes separating is the only way to get some distance from a dysfunctional family, and it probably gave you the space to begin to create a sense of self."

Cutting off a loved one doesn't mean you've shut off your emotional involvement, Elsa says, confirming what I've read about estrangement. "It doesn't mean you are indifferent to each other," she says. "It's really just a sign of intense, unresolved animosity and guilt. And that's what I'm seeing here."

Elsa looks from Scott to me. Then, gesturing toward us with both hands, she says, "So I'm glad you came in today."

By now Scott is slumped deep in his chair, his head sunk onto his chest, the muscles in his face loose and sagging. He squeezes his eyes tightly, trying to hold back the tears.

"I feel terrible about things. . . ." His effort failing, he begins to sob quietly. Maybe by naming his feelings of animosity and guilt, Elsa shook him beyond composure and into raw emotion.

Again I'm tempted to let him off the hook. To be his nice sister, to say, *Oh, it's okay; it's over now.* Instead, I press my lips together hard. I stare at him. Steeling myself against his tears, I wait.

"Talk to your sister, not me," Elsa says gently.

"I . . . I . . . was a terrible brother." He turns toward me, still sobbing. "I feel so bad. . . . I'm *so* sorry that I didn't invite you to my son's wedding." Now he's looking directly at me. "What I did to you was unconscionable. I felt so terrible, it was hard for me to even enjoy the evening. I knew I was wrong. I'll never forgive myself for what I did."

There were so many slights over the years, but we both know that exclusion from his son's wedding crushed me. "I'm done," I told my mother when she called after the wedding to tell me all about their family celebration. I knew my words would cut her deeply, but for once, my injury trumped hers. I couldn't bear to be hurt any more, and I stated my position to her in no uncertain terms: "I'll never have anything to do with him again."

But Scott continues. "I . . . I'm so sorry." Coming from my brother, these words sound like a foreign language. I can't remember a single time he has apologized to me for anything.

"I will have to live with this for the rest of my life."

Still refusing to bail him out, I let his words hang between us.

"I hope you can forgive me," he sobs into his shredded tissue. "Can . . . can you forgive me?"

I *want* to trust him. I *want* to believe he'll never wound me so deeply again. However, I can't erase the decades of hurts and silence.

But—well, I'm willing to try. I want to see where all this goes, and in this moment, I decide to grant him some relief.

"I . . . I will," I say, choosing my words carefully.

"That's a good start," Elsa says, sparing us from having to press further.

My body crumples with exhaustion, as if I've been tossed by an emotional tsunami. Scott looks drained and weary too.

It's a huge relief to both of us when Elsa slips into a practical discussion about how she uses neurofeedback to treat PTSD, anxiety, and depression, and how she believes the therapy can be beneficial.

"It sounds like you have suffered for some time now," she says to Scott. "So how have you been dealing with the problem?"

"I haven't done much," he shrugs. "Which is why I'm in this mess."

"Well, the reason I ask is that some people come to me after years of using drugs or alcohol to self-medicate," she says with clinical detachment. "I tell all my patients that the treatment will be far less effective if you are disturbing your brain waves with other substances."

I know Scott used plenty of drugs and alcohol over the years—drinking at the beach routinely in high school, partying nonstop through college. During his years as a commodities broker, downtown Chicago's trading pit was notorious for members' drinking and drugging. It was one way to cope with the exuberant highs and shattering lows when fortunes could be made or lost in seconds, on one trade.

For years I worried about Scott and substance abuse, but I have no idea if he actually became dependent on anything. Again I wonder: *Is he hiding some sort of behavior—from the family? Is that another reason he has distanced himself?*

Scott doesn't answer Elsa's question. Like a good poker player, he maintains a blank expression, revealing nothing.

That difficult conversation in Elsa's office gave me a greater understanding of the roots of my brother's and my long-standing estrangement. Early on, our family split into two distinct camps—Dad and me, Mom and Scott. Many families fracture into competing factions when parents can't negotiate a healthy, mutually satisfying relationship. Our parents' contentious twenty-seven-year marriage ended in divorce, but while they were married, Scott and I became entangled in their arguments. As our parents struggled, Scott became protective of our mother and got angry when Dad mistreated her. I felt torn between both parents. The sharp divide in the family may have contributed to our split.

Scott and I were fortunate to have Elsa jump-start our relationship by posing difficult questions and directing our first serious conversations about estrangement. But how do others have this type of dialogue without a mediator or someone to guide them? Is it even necessary to explore what led to the estrangement, or can siblings avoid these uncomfortable, unpredictable discussions and simply pick up where they left off?

To figure out how to move forward, I call Elsa a week after our meeting in her office. "I don't know where to go from here," I tell her.

"What kind of relationship are you looking for with Scott?" she asks me. "What kind of contact would be best for you? Do you want a fully restored or limited relationship with your brother? Maybe, if all this is too difficult, you might clean up the unfinished business between the two of you so you can let him go."

Elsa encourages me to have an open discussion with Scott about our estrangement. "He seemed pretty receptive to a renewed relationship," she says. "Though I'm not sure he's aware of all the psychological forces that drove him to cut off from the family, so he may not be able to give you the answers you're seeking."

Then she advises me to focus on my own reactions to him and the estrangement. "If you are looking for an authentic relationship with your brother," she says, "take the crucial first step of releasing your resentments. That won't be easy. Keep in mind that releasing anger doesn't mean the hurts didn't happen." She presses me to consider my brother's perspective, to understand what motivated him to cut me off, and to reflect on how my own behavior may have prompted his actions.

I don't think I can ignore all the hurts. I want to know what happened and what he was thinking during all those years. Did he miss a sibling connection? What is his side of the story? I fear that if I don't get some answers, I will feel mired in the same isolation I experienced when we were estranged.

Reconnecting After Estrangement

There are simply no rules on how to reconcile. Some people simply pick up a relationship without having a conversation about the past or the events that drove them apart. Other estranged siblings fear that they will continue to harbor resentments if they never discuss the source of their problems.

When they were in their twenties, Leah Barr of Naples, Florida, and her older brother stopped talking to each other. The two, now in their sixties, have never discussed the issues that fueled the estrangement.

At the time of the cutoff, both had young children, and the families would alternate having Christmas and Thanksgiving dinners at each other's houses. Suddenly, one year, Leah's brother didn't invite her family to the holiday dinner at his home. That seemed to be the catalyst. When they attended a family gathering, the two would avoid each other by staying in different rooms in the house. In time, the divide spread to other family members.

After six years, the two finally spoke to each other again at their mother's funeral:

> *My brother and I looked at one another over her casket and said to each other that it was horrible our mother went to her grave thinking that two of her children were not talking. Mom was only fifty-nine when she died. I swore I would never have another divide, even if it meant eating crow. I never want to hurt others in that way.*

Yet because the two haven't addressed the cause of their split, Leah says she never feels fully reconciled. When she asked her brother if he would like to be interviewed for this book, he refused. He said the estrangement was in the past, and there's nothing to talk about now. Without an understanding of the causes, Leah says she never feels close to him:

> *I don't know if I fully trust him because I don't understand what the issue was then. How can I correct my own actions if I don't know what I did wrong? And it's hard to fully commit to someone when they've betrayed you in a fundamental way.*

Leah describes their current relationship as an amicable cease-fire, but she has no sense of peace.

The Hicks Dignity Model

How should feuding siblings address the issues between them? Dr. Donna Hicks, an associate at the Weatherhead Center for International Affairs at Harvard University, has worked as a third-party facilitator in some of the world's most intractable conflicts. She has drawn upon her experiences mediating international disputes to create a model for communication that applies to families as well as to nations. In her book *Dignity: Its Essential Role in Resolving Conflict*, she outlines her approach, which aims to rebuild relationships by requiring a mutual honoring of human dignity.

Dignity, she explains, invests each of us with an inherent value and worth. When individuals are denied their dignity, they feel inconsequential and irrelevant, and they become enraged and resentful that they are not seen or heard. They ask the following questions:

How can you treat me like this?

Can't you see we are human beings?

Can't you see we are suffering?

She outlines the four necessary steps to begin the process of resolving disputes as follows:

1. Sit down together.
2. Listen without interrupting or challenging each other's stories, and listen to seek understanding. (All experts agree that true listening—where one person genuinely takes in what the other person is saying—is crucial to reconciliation.)

3. Acknowledge and recognize what the other has been through. (When each party hears the other's experiences, neither party can dehumanize or exclude the other from the moral community.)

4. Honor and acknowledge each other's integrity and, in doing so, create a mutual bond.

For this process to succeed, Dr. Hicks lists the following ten essential elements of dignity that must be honored:

1. Acceptance of identity—Accept others as their authentic selves, without fear of judgment, regardless of their race, religion, ethnicity, gender, class, sexual orientation, age, or disability. Any or all of these characteristics may be at the core of an individual's identity.

2. Inclusion—Make others feel they belong to a family, community, organization, or nation.

3. Safety—Make people feel safe from bodily harm and safe from humiliation and retribution.

4. Acknowledgment—Listen, hear, and validate other people's feelings and experiences.

5. Recognition—Validate others for their contributions, talents, hard work, and compassion.

6. Fairness—Treat people justly and with equality.

7. Benefit of the doubt—Assume people have good motives and are trustworthy.

8. Understanding—Give others the opportunity to explain and express themselves while actively listening.

9. Independence—Give people hope and a sense of control over their lives by encouraging them to act on their own behalf.

10. Accountability—Take responsibility for your actions and, if necessary, apologize and change your behavior.

Those who follow the Hicks Dignity Model eventually will have to talk about their shame. In general, Hicks explains, people tend to deny shame rather than discuss it. In our session with Elsa, I was impressed that Scott took the crucial first step in releasing himself from the grip of shame by speaking the truth: He recognized that he had been a terrible brother and that I had suffered for it.

In Dr. Hicks's experience, the Dignity Model reveals that the truth is larger than the separate stories: Crying out for change, both parties are part of a larger dysfunction. "The biggest lesson I learned from these encounters is that vulnerability is where the power lies," Dr. Hicks writes. "The magic happens when we expose the truth to ourselves and others and are ultimately set free by it. . . . When we honor others' dignity, we strengthen our own."[1]

Chapter 10

Estrangement and Mental Illness or Addiction

For years, I was my mother's point person. This involved tasks and challenges of all sorts, one being that I did whatever was necessary to give Mom some sense of family. She had married my stepfather in her late sixties, some fifteen years after she and Dad divorced, and they had a companionable relationship. Still, Mom continued to count on me for support, family connection, and holiday gatherings. Zealously over-compensating for her family losses, I tried to fill in for her sister, who had died in her fifties; her parents, who were murdered by the Nazis; and her son, who had a limited relationship with her. But no matter how much I did, I remained, as I often joked, a paltry "Committee of One."

This singular status did have an enormous advantage: I never had to fight with a sibling about any issue that fell my way. With no one to dispute my judgment, I successfully leaned on Mom to cut back her work hours. I encouraged her to buy a new car and helped her with personal finance decisions and estate planning. I persuaded her to cull some belongings from her overstuffed house, found a good doctor to manage her health and monitor her care, and pitched in on chores—even some modest renovation projects—around the house.

It was a lot of work, but some people found my autonomy enviable. Friends pointed out that I was spared the miseries of acrimonious sibling conflicts. One friend claimed she would give anything to get some relief from her three belligerent sisters, who engulfed her life—with hours on the phone and dozens of texts each day—as they debated every detail of their ailing mother's care.

But as I always reminded this friend, being the "Committee of One" had its drawbacks. I wasn't just the only voting member; I was the sole proprietor. No one shared my investment in the family; no one shouldered the work of maintaining Mom, of hashing out practical solutions to countless dilemmas. At times, I wondered if I was doing the right thing. Often I felt abandoned and resentful that I had to carry these responsibilities alone.

So alone, in fact, that my family name gradually became a source of disconnection and detachment. "Schumer" started to echo not with pride but with pain; it spoke of the tumultuous relationship I had with my dad and the shameful shunning I endured from my brother. Disrupting my fundamental identity and familial context, my last name turned into a troubling reminder of what felt like failures. More and more, I tried to use only my first name whenever possible. If someone called me by my last name, I would ask, without explanation, that they just call me Fern. It was the only name that truly belonged to me.

I was surprised to learn from some survey respondents that they, too, have had difficult and ambivalent feelings about their own names. Some say they took on a husband's name to avoid the association with their original, dysfunctional family. One woman answered a survey question with the comment that "The hardest thing about being estranged from all of my family is that no one who carries my maiden-name gives a hoot about me."

Now that Scott and I are speaking again, though, the family name doesn't sting in the same way. Other possibilities quickly emerge from our reconnected status. Back home after our appointment with Elsa, I receive a call from Mom: She needs a ride tomorrow evening to pick up her husband at the airport on the South Side of Chicago, a 120-mile round trip from my home.

This is an instant logistical nightmare, because I'm already picking up my daughter at the same airport much later in the evening. Then I recognize it: the perfect opportunity to call on the new member of our reconstituted family. Surely Scott can drive Mom to the airport to meet her husband at his returning Honor Flight, a daylong trip to Washington, DC, that offers military veterans the opportunity to meet other vets while visiting the city's war memorials.

But my brainstorm isn't quite as simple as it sounds. The airport lobby will be crowded with jubilant families greeting their loved ones, along with others celebrating the veterans' service. Scott's anxieties intensify in crowds; he has repeatedly told me that he has dodged panic attacks by avoiding people. I debate with myself whether I should even ask him to drive Mom but then decide that he needs to make his own choices. When asked, he insists without any hesitation that he's happy to take on the chore, assuring me that he'll be just fine.

When Mom and Scott arrive at the airport lobby, it's a mass of excited families, friends, and well-wishers, singing and chanting, waving WEL-COME HOME signs and banners and flags—there's even a boisterous brass band. The brouhaha prompts a series of worrisome texts from Scott:

> You wouldn't believe what's going on here!
>
> Really crowded!
>
> It's wild here, like a July 4th parade!

Very loud and uncomfortable!

Sweating!

With each text, I feel his growing anxiety. I hang on every comment; my own breathing becomes shallow; my heart races. Only now do I see how difficult his life has become. I wish I hadn't asked him to do this.

Then comes a familiar feeling that has struck me repeatedly since we reconnected: I've taken on way more than I can manage here. Yet there's no turning back.

I text him: Can you leave Mom in the lobby and go back to the car to wait for them?

He takes his time answering. Is it so noisy that he can't even hear a text notification? Finally he responds:

It's okay. Mom went off on her own.

So, where are you? I ask. Again I wait. At last he sends me a cryptic text:

Standing away from all the chaos.

A few days later, we meet for coffee at a place near my house.

"Thanks for taking Mom on Wednesday," I say as I pull out a chair and set my coffee down on a wobbly little table.

"It's okay." He looks agitated today, his eyes darting around the room. Only one other table is occupied this early morning. A half dozen students from a nearby medical school, all wearing their white coats, are slumped over books and calculators, studying together.

"I know it wasn't easy," I say, trying to acknowledge his discomfort without directly addressing it. "I guess I didn't really understand what things have been like for you. Hope it wasn't too much to ask."

"I managed," he grunts, not looking me in the eye. *What's bothering him today?* He seems more distant and distracted than usual. Normally I would pretend nothing is wrong—but that never did work, and I'm trying to establish new patterns of relating here.

So instead I do something different: I ask a direct question.

"Is something bothering you today?"

He doesn't respond, so I rush to fill the awkward silence. "You know, you need to tell me when you can't do something. I need you to be up front with me—"

"I was okay . . . on Wednesday." He sips his coffee, its steam fogging the bottom of his glasses.

Acknowledge the good. That's what the experts on reconciliation recommend. "Well, I really did appreciate the help," I say. "I don't know what I would have done if—"

Scott cuts me off. "But I . . . I guess I need to be direct with you about something else."

Taken aback, I mutter, "Oh, okay."

For some reason, without any sense of where this is going, my heart starts ticking faster. Unsure about our relationship, I tumble back into my most basic fears: that I'll be rejected again, that he simply can't manage a relationship with me, that reconciliation just isn't feasible.

With dread, I ask, "What is it?"

"You know, when we talked to Elsa . . ."

"Yeah." I narrow my eyes at him. I'm really confused.

"And she asked how I cope. . . . Well, I think it's only fair to tell you . . ."

Casting his eyes downward, he quietly says, "I drink so I can fall asleep."

"Oh!" I'm relieved and disturbed at the same time. *Well, maybe that's not so terrible. Lots of people use some sort of sedative to help them get to sleep.* But then a darker thought creeps into my mind: *If he's bringing this up, maybe it's a serious problem.*

"So . . . how much do you drink?" I ask, bracing myself.

"Well, I never let myself have a drink before four in the afternoon."

I guess it's good he's able to impose some limitation. But it's not much comfort. He could down a lot of booze in six or seven hours.

"So what does that mean?"

"You know, I have a lot of trouble sleeping." I get that, but the way he's dodging my questions makes me even more worried. *I don't want to judge him for his coping skills.*

"Yeah," I say with my best poker face, "that's probably from the PTSD."

"And it's a lot easier to get to sleep if I have a few drinks before bedtime."

"Oh, so how many is a few?" I press, trying not to sound alarmed.

"I've known for a long time that I needed to do something about it," he continues.

And there it is: as close as he'll get to acknowledging that he has a drinking problem. Then I remember his last text from the airport: He said he was "standing away from all the chaos." I assume he uses drinking for the same purpose—to distance himself from feelings and events he can't tolerate.

That won't work anymore—and yet I know I sometimes get on his nerves with my calls to action. "Not everyone is as assertive and aggressive as you," he has said several times during the past few weeks. I don't really see myself that way, but I'm trying to be mindful of how he perceives me.

Still, right now we need action. I can't stop myself from asking, "So what are you going to do about it?"

I'm afraid he'll tell me to back off. It's a relief when he shrugs and says, "Not sure."

"I mean, I don't think it's worth doing neurofeedback unless you stop." This is not just my opinion; I'm reminding him of what Elsa said.

"I know. I'm not going to do that."

What is "that," I wonder—neurofeedback or drinking?

I don't want to even consider that he might not go through with neurofeedback, so I press forward on his drinking. "Have you thought about AA?"

"I'm not doing that either." He sounds gruff and inflexible. And to make sure I got the message, he adds, "I'm not going to AA."

"Why not?"

This could be a deal breaker. He's got to address his drinking problem. Period. Otherwise there's little hope for his recovery and even less for our relationship.

"That's just not how I do things," he says. *I don't care how you do things,* I think. *This is how it needs to get done. How else can you stop?*

"I don't want to join a group," he adds. *Really! That's going to get in the way of addressing this problem?*

"Okay," I say, trying to conceal my irritation. "Then how will you quit?"

"On my own," he says confidently.

"Just cold turkey?" My eyebrows shoot up.

"Yeah."

I give up. He might as well know that I think this is absolutely unworkable. "You know how hard *that* is?"

"Yeah," he says. "But that's how I'm going to do it. That's how I did it with smoking."

It was true; he had smoked at least a pack of Marlboros daily for nearly ten years. Then, one day, he decided he'd had enough. No tapering off. No nicotine patches or gum. He just stopped.

"I remember I was driving, and something just came over me," he continues. "And I thought to myself, *This is so disgusting. I smell. It's a terrible habit.* I whipped the pack of cigarettes out the car window and never smoked again."

"But this is even harder," I warn him. I don't know anyone who simply stopped drinking on his or her own, as if it were as easy as avoiding a certain street corner.

"I know what you think, Fern," he says impatiently. "But I have a plan. I know what I'm doing. I'm going to ask someone who quit to be my buddy—you know, my sponsor. To keep me on track."

"Okay, but—"

"It'll work," he cuts me off, unwilling to listen to any more of my objections. "And I can always join AA," he concedes. "And I will, *if* I can't quit on my own."

I guess I always knew . . . but I didn't want to believe it.

Observing him from the other side of banquet halls at family weddings or bar mitzvahs, I'd watch my brother down Crown Royal, one after another. I'd wonder if he had a drinking problem, but then I'd tell myself that *everyone* was drinking on these special occasions. *This is just celebratory behavior*, I thought, *not a daily routine*.

When I made that first call to him a month ago, I still held on to an old image of my big brother from our childhood days, when I would tag along after him and his posse of friends. On a good day, he might be charitable and play games or set up a lemonade stand with me. And on a really good day, I could count on him for comfort when Mom or Dad would become irrationally angry.

That's the brother I missed during our years apart. When he became a teenager and spent less time at home, I knew he was experimenting with drugs and alcohol. Back then, I thought it was just a passing high school stage. As an adult, I wanted to believe those days were behind him. Now I see that I was always finding explanations and excuses for his behavior.

With Scott's admission of his addiction, reconciliation is the least of our problems. I don't know how to support him as he attempts to quit drinking.

Addiction and Estrangement

Addiction can roil relationships with abuse, betrayal, and domestic violence, placing great stress on a family. Typically, parents and siblings who try to help or manage a family member's addiction find themselves sapped of emotional energy and drained of financial resources. My survey shows as many as 10 percent of respondents suspect that a sibling is hiding an addiction.

I wonder: Does the addiction produce family problems, or do a dysfunctional family's issues result in addiction? It sounds like a chicken-and-egg question. I suppose at this moment the sequence of events doesn't really matter to me. What I need is guidance on helping my brother conquer his alcoholism.

Typically, when it comes to addiction, many experts advise using "tough love" to change behavior—promoting someone's welfare by enforcing certain constraints on them or requiring them to take responsibility for their actions. The family uses relationships as leverage, threatening to expel the member who is addicted. The message of this model is explicit: "If you don't shape up, we will cut you off."

Tough love relies on solid, established relationships; otherwise, the family member at risk may feel he or she has nothing to lose. My relationship with Scott is tenuous, anything but solid. He has lived without me for decades, and if I try tough love, he could easily revert to our former state of estrangement.

I wonder if there might be another way.

Possible Causes of Addiction

Addiction is a complex phenomenon involving physiological, sociological, and psychological variables, and each user reflects some combination of these factors. In Scott's case, because alcoholism doesn't run in our family, I don't think he has a biological predisposition to drink. I suspect my brother's drinking results from other origins.

Current research identifies unexpected influences that also may be at the root of addictive behavior, including emotional trauma, a hostile environment, and a lack of sufficient emotional connections. Addictive behavior may be closely tied to isolation and estrangement. Human beings have a natural and innate need to bond with others and belong to a social circle. When trauma disturbs the ability to attach and connect, a victim often seeks relief from pain through drugs, gambling, pornography, or some other vice.

Canadian psychologist Dr. Bruce Alexander conducted a controversial study in the 1970s and 1980s that challenged earlier conclusions on the fundamental nature of addiction. Users, his research suggests, may be trying to address the absence of connection in their lives by drinking and/or using drugs. Working with rats, he found that isolated animals had nothing better to do than use drugs; rats placed in a more engaging environment avoided drug use.[1]

Similar results emerged when veterans of the war in Vietnam returned home. Some 20 percent of American troops were using heroin while in Vietnam, and psychologists feared that hundreds of thousands of soldiers would resume their lives in the United States as junkies. However, a study in the *Archives of General Psychiatry* reported that 95 percent simply stopped using, without rehab or agonizing withdrawal, when they returned home.[2]

These studies indicate that addiction is not just about brain chemistry. The environment in which the user lives is a factor. Addiction may, in part, be an adaptation to a lonely, disconnected, or dangerous life. Remarkably, a tense relationship with a sister or brother in adolescence may contribute to substance abuse. A 2012 study reported in the *Journal of Marriage and Family* entitled "Sibling Relationships and Influences in

Childhood and Adolescence" found that tense sibling relationships make people more likely to use substances and to be depressed and anxious as teenagers.[3]

Those who grow up in homes where loving care is inconsistent, unstable, or absent do not develop the crucial neural wiring for emotional resilience, according to Dr. Gabor Maté, author of *In the Realm of Hungry Ghosts*, who is an expert in childhood development and trauma and has conducted extensive research in a medical practice for the underserved in downtown Vancouver. Children who are not consistently loved in their young lives often develop a sense that the world is an unsafe place and that people cannot be trusted. Maté suggests that emotional trauma and loss may lie at the core of addiction.

A loving family fosters resilience in children, immunizing them from whatever challenges the world may bring. Dr. Maté has found high rates of childhood trauma among the addicts with whom he works, leading him to conclude that emotional damage in childhood may drive some people to use drugs to correct their dysregulated brain waves. "When you don't have love and connection in your life when you are very, very young," he explains, "then those important brain circuits just don't develop properly. And under conditions of abuse, things just don't develop properly and their brains then are susceptible then when they do the drugs." He explains that drugs make these people with dysregulated brain waves feel normal, and even loved. "As one patient said to me," he says, "when she did heroin for the first time, 'it felt like a warm soft hug, just like a mother hugging a baby.'"

Dr. Maté defines addiction broadly, having seen a wide variety of addicted behaviors among his patients. Substance abuse and pornography, for example, are widely accepted as addictions. For people damaged in childhood, he suggests that shopping, chronic overeating or dieting, incessantly checking the cell phone, amassing wealth or power or ultramarathon medals are ways of coping with pain.

In a TED Talk, Dr. Maté, who was born to Jewish parents in Budapest just before the Germans occupied Hungary, identifies his own childhood traumas as a source of his addiction: spending thousands of dollars on a collection of classical CDs. He admits to having ignored his family—even neglecting patients in labor—when preoccupied with buying music. His obsessions with work and music, which he characterizes as addictions, have affected his children. "My kids get the same message that they're not wanted," he explains. "We pass on the trauma and we pass on the suffering, unconsciously, from one generation to the next. There are many, many ways to fill this emptiness . . . but the emptiness always goes back to what we didn't get when we were very small."[4]

That statement hits home. Though my brother and I didn't live as Jews in a Nazi-occupied country, we derivatively experienced the pain our mother suffered after her expulsion from Germany and the murder of her parents. Our mother's childhood traumas resulted in her depression and absorption in the past and inhibited her ability to nurture her children.

Still, in the end, it's impossible to determine precisely the source of an addiction problem. Maybe it doesn't matter anyway. The real question is, What can I do about it?

An Untraditional, Hopeful Approach to Addiction

A nationwide program in Portugal provides a unique way of treating addiction. In the 1990s, Lisbon was known as the "heroin capital" of Europe, but an innovative program went into effect in 2001 in Portugal that halted the crisis. Addicts, the Portuguese discovered, do remarkably well when they feel valued by their community. When these people found a purpose, they also established new bonds and relationships with the larger society—and rates of addiction dropped significantly.

Consequently, Portugal decriminalized all drugs, from cannabis to crack cocaine to heroin. The country then redirected funds formerly dedicated to punishing addicts, which inevitably disconnected them from society, and instead devoted those resources to helping addicts find a larger sense of purpose. Along with offering rehab and talk therapy, Portugal created a massive jobs program and made loans available to addicts who wanted to start small businesses. The Portuguese model values addicts, allowing them to learn to value themselves.

The program shifted the drug problem from a criminal issue to a public health challenge, and that change helped to drop the drug death rate in Portugal to the lowest in Western Europe. Consequently, according to a 2017 *New York Times* analysis, the number of heroin users in Portugal declined from about 100,000 to 25,000. In addition, the program has seen a significant drop in clients who are HIV-positive—a measure of drug use. Three decades ago, that figure was 55 percent; in 2018, it was only 13 percent.[5]

This humane approach, which shows how recovery requires connection, makes sense to me. *I* want to be like the Portuguese! I want to support my brother in whatever productive ways he chooses, to be part of a larger support network that compassionately helps him overcome his addiction, to focus on his strengths and value him for who he is.

This is an opportunity to give him what neither of us received consistently in childhood: unconditional love and support. I don't want to judge him for how he coped. I want to love him, and, when he sees himself the way I see him, I'm hoping he learns to love himself.

As it happens, Father's Day is approaching. Given what I now know about this new way of addressing addiction, I realize I have a moment to strengthen our connection. For years, even from a distance, I have admired how well Scott has fathered his children. He recently told me that he used our father as a cautionary tale: "Whatever he did," Scott said, "I *didn't* do as a dad."

I decide to send him a Father's Day card that includes my own encouraging message.

Dear Scott,

I want you to know that, over the years, I've observed you and marveled at how you always knew just what to do as a dad. Even when you've struggled yourself, I know you have insulated your sons from your pain. You have been a constant, loving presence in their lives. It's hard to give what you didn't get, and I know—probably better than anyone—that you didn't have a strong role model. I hope you are well-celebrated today. You deserve it!

I'm also impressed with what you are trying to do with your life now. It's difficult to change course in your 60s, yet, somehow, you have dug deep and discovered the strength to tackle this challenge. I know you have the determination and discipline to be successful. And if you falter, I am here for you.

I am behind you and ahead of you.

Love,
Fern

Chapter 11

Estrangement's Ripple Effect in the Family

THE CRADLE NURSERY

Summer 2014

The first thing I notice when I walk into the Cradle on a summer Sunday evening is a change in the front window's colorful construction-paper decorations. The pastel budding trees of springtime have given way to gaudy summer: tall, eye-popping yellow-and-brown sunflowers, lively orange-and-black monarch butterflies. The new display does a lot to brighten the drab pink decor.

The next thing I notice is that the place is nearly deserted.

"It's so *quiet*," I say to Rosie, before I even say hello.

Usually when I walk in, I find Rosie and the other nurses sitting in the white rocking chairs, everyone holding a baby while rhythmically tapping their feet on bouncy seats on the floor to gently bob two other infants. They always make me think of a multi-instrumental one-man band. Today Rosie is alone, standing at the counter, carefully folding laundered baby blankets, onesies, and small spit-up towels. Looking around, I see through the slats of the twenty cribs that most are empty.

"Where is everybody?" I ask.

"Oh, hi!" she says. "Only four babies today. Hard to believe. I think the last time you were here we had a sorority—seventeen girls!"

"Yeah, what happened to all of them?"

"They all found a family and a home," she says.

I offer to help Rosie with chores, but she says there isn't much to do tonight. When she finishes the laundry, she says, we can sit in the rockers and catch up.

I take the first rocker in a line of five and wait for her. The eerie silence makes the nursery feel like an empty nest. When I first started cuddling six years ago, the cacophony of infant cries was so unnerving that I would leap to attend any baby who whimpered. The nurses would laugh at me.

"He's fine," someone would call out. But I couldn't help myself. When I was a young mother, I would tell them, I never let my babies cry.

"Not here," they'd say. "We can't jump and attend to them every time they moan a little."

The demands of caring for dozens of infants at a time are so great, and the nurses have trained themselves to read baby cues with exquisite accuracy. The babies develop a distinct response to whoever eventually appears to take care of them. They never attach to any one caregiver because they have so many; they calm down not when they see the face they're waiting for but when they see the white smock all of us wear.

The Cradle nurses have all sorts of tricks to comfort an inconsolable baby. Sometimes, Rosie holds the infant facedown, like a football. She'll gently tuck a diaper over a baby's mouth to prevent the pacifier from falling out. (I wish I had known that trick when my children were infants.) The Cradle staff never seems to get flustered. I, on the other hand, am often unnerved by baby howls—so much so that when I drive home from my shift, needy cries ricochet in my head.

Sitting down at last to join me on the rockers, Rosie cuts to the chase. "So how's your quest for family going?"

"Okay . . . not great," I tell her. "There are so many things I didn't think about when I started all this . . ."

"How's your brother doing?"

"Actually, okay," I tell her. "He's doing everything he said he would. He's taking responsibility for himself. He's been honest with me, and he's committed to the treatment."

"That's huge!" Her eyes widen at this good news.

"Yeah, you're right," I say, glad to be reminded of what really matters. "But there are lots of complications."

"Like what?"

"Like my children!" I explain. "*I* might want to reconcile with my brother, but my kids aren't exactly on board. I didn't realize how this change would ripple through the rest of the family."

"Really!" she says, eyebrows up. Obviously, this is a twist Rosie hadn't anticipated either. "What's happened?"

With most people—especially when it comes to estrangement—I often dodge an incisive question that makes me uncomfortable. But with Rosie, I'm candid. I suspect it's part of the nursery culture, where a secure, loving blanket envelops everyone here. The only other place I see a similar openness is on an airplane, when a seatmate tells all to a perfect stranger.

I pull out my phone and scan to find a message to show Rosie. "Here, look at this," I say. "Scott emailed this to one of my sons. He sent a similar message to my other son and daughter." Rosie takes my phone and carefully reads the email:

I know this email is coming out of deep left field. I feel I had to explain myself to you. We haven't spoken in many years, and I have been completely out of your life for most of it. I am writing you because as you know I have been in contact with your Mom as she heard of my issues with depression through Oma. ["Oma," the German word for "grandma," is what my mother's five grandchildren call her. Until now, she was the only family member they had in common.] We talked for many hours and she knew how to help me.

Without going into too much detail, I have been sort of a recluse for the past five years. I have detached myself from the outside world, which of course is very life threatening and dangerous. Fern realized that I was headed down a road of no return and told me I needed help. She put me in touch with people who helped her. She and I have been in contact every day and have rekindled our relationship.

I know this is very foreign to you, as I have been an asshole to her in the past as I treated her with an on and off relationship. Also, I know you are very distrustful of me. You probably worry that I might be gone again tomorrow.

I hope you can understand that this is not just a peace offering to you. I am still in a very bad way and your Mom is helping me find a way out.

Also, I would like to get together with all of you in September, if that is okay with you. (My son, who lives on the West Coast, will visit then.) I know that a short email can't make up for years of a wasted relationship, but I needed to give you some insight into what is going on. Remember what they say: "You can't choose your family."

Scott

"Well, that couldn't have been easy to write." Rosie hands the phone back to me.

"Yeah, it took guts," I say. "I told him that my children were worried about our reconnection, and he knew he needed to do something. I was really happy about my daughter's reaction to his email. She said, 'It's all in the past now, and let's move forward.' But my sons are another story."

I call up a message my middle son wrote in response and read it aloud to Rosie:

I'm glad you're getting help with your issues, but I hope you are not taking advantage of my Mom's generosity and forgiving nature.

I'll have to think about September.

"Well, at least he acknowledged your generosity and forgiving nature." Rosie grins.

"My other son completely ignored the message!"

"He acknowledged nothing." She smiles at me; then a baby starts crying, and Rosie walks over to the crib, swaddles the baby, picks him up, and coos into his ear, "Ooooh, Patrick." Rocking him in her arms, she goes to the counter where nurses store enough formula to survive a major weather event. Rosie picks up a bottle of formula, shakes it, and screws a rubber nipple onto it, practically with one hand. Returning to her rocker, she neatly tucks a small white towel under Patrick's chin. Patrick grunts and coos, eagerly sucking on the bottle.

"You act like you haven't eaten in weeks, Patrick!" Rosie locks eyes with the infant.

Then, without looking up from the baby, she asks me, "When was the last time your children saw their uncle?"

For a moment, I have to think about whom she means when she says "their uncle." Scott has never been in their lives long enough to actually have a familial title. It's a little like my maternal grandmother, Frieda, who was murdered in the Holocaust. Scott and I never knew her, so we never gave her an endearing name.

"Can't remember," I say. "He's only made a few cameo appearances."

"So this is a big change for them." She turns to look at me directly.

"I know. So where do I begin?"

"You need to talk to your sons," she advises. "They're adults now, and they're going to make their own decisions. But you need to make them understand how important the relationship with your brother is to you. They need to understand—he's the only sibling you have."

Heeding Rosie's advice, I make a call the following evening to my most resistant child. As the eldest, he often sets the tone for his younger brother and sister. Even before I press his name on my iPhone, I brace myself. He can be intransigent, so I'm not expecting this to go well. Still, I need to have this conversation because the underlying issue isn't going away. Besides, sometimes, after a first rancorous reaction, he softens.

"Hello," he says, and I try to sound as if this will be a routine conversation. I ask about our usual topics: How's work? His girlfriend? Plans for the weekend?

Then I try to smoothly slip into the purpose of my call.

"I . . . I have something I want to discuss with you. Something that's important to me." An icy tension instantly sets in, dividing us. He seems to know exactly where this is going. I imagine he and his siblings, who text each other constantly, have upgraded this dramatic subject to phone discussions, for commiserating and bolstering one another's arguments. I can almost hear their conversations: "Now he wants to be an uncle!" "Where the hell has he been all of our lives?" "There's no way!"

But I have to try. "It's . . . it's about my brother. I'd like you to give him a—"

"Forget it, Mom." Already edgy, he cuts me off.

"I need you to do this for me." My anger spikes, and I regret what I just said instantly. After promising myself to stay on topic by only discussing my brother's difficulties and the meaning of family, I've already made it about me.

And my son isn't having any of it. "I'm not getting behind you on this one."

"But I need you to—"

"Don't put this on me." His tone sharpens. "I'm not willing to support you in a situation where I think you're going to get hurt."

Taking a deep breath, I try to recalibrate and change the tone of the conversation. Softer and calmer, I say, "I can decide if I'm going to get hurt. I'll take care of myself. You need to let me make my own choices here."

"And you need to let me make mine," he lashes back. Fair enough: I should have known I was setting him up for that cogent response.

Entrenched, these two lines summarize the rub. I should stop right here. Often I'm on the losing end of his lawyerly reasoning as he uses my points to solidify his own. Meanwhile, he's probably not hearing anything I'm saying.

I know all this—but I don't have the discipline to stop myself. "You can't just give up on people. Especially family!" I say. "You have to give him a chance. People can change. They're not fixed, no matter how badly they behave."

"Here's my advice: Don't get mixed up with him again," he fumes. "Shit's going to happen. He will betray you. And you're going to be right back where you started . . . only worse."

"You're right about that last point," I storm back at him. "I may get hurt again. Don't you think I've given all this a lot of thought? But I have to live with myself. It would be worse for me if I turned my back on him. Just like I wouldn't ever turn my back on you."

That must have caught his attention, because he doesn't fire back immediately. My tiny triumph creates enough of a break in the argument to allow me to come up with one final punch line: "And I hope you wouldn't turn your back on your brother or sister either!"

"Well, they're different," he seethes. "They wouldn't do that to me."

"I hope not, but you just don't know," I say, thinking that no one ever expects or imagines that they will become estranged from a family member.

"He's always been this way, Mom," he insists. "This is a pattern, and you're just going to get hurt again."

The argument has become repetitive and circular. "Maybe we should discuss this on another day," I offer, "when we are both a little calmer."

"There's nothing more to talk about," he says dismissively. "*You* can do what you want, Mom. But *I'm* not willing to do anything. I don't want to see you get hurt again, and I'm not getting involved."

Now that, finally, I'm no longer cut off from my brother, I have a whole new kind of shunning: Two of my children are essentially limiting my family experience by blockading him. Their intractable position acknowledges my right to have a relationship with my brother—but if it's up to my children, he and I won't be allowed to benefit from the broader family connections that should provide *all* of us with a sense of belonging.

"So what you're really saying is that I'm not entitled to have a family?" I say. "What am I supposed to do when we want to celebrate Oma's birthday? Or Thanksgiving?"

"This is not on me," he snaps. "I didn't create this. He did."

"So I have to pick and choose who I can have at my table at every event?"

"Sorry, Mom." He digs in deeper.

"So what you're saying is that I can either have you or my brother, but not both? I'm not going to balance the guest list according to who doesn't like whom. That goes against the whole concept of family."

"That's your problem, Mom. Not mine."

It's a big request to expect my children to open their hearts to my brother. Even though I don't like what they said, my sons' reactions are completely understandable. Their feelings toward him have ranged from ambivalence to deep resentment, and they are not about to reconsider their position just because he has suddenly reappeared in my life.

To build a solid relationship, family members routinely visit the youngest members as soon as they are born. The role of aunt or uncle is somewhat ambiguous and largely voluntary, as each adult relative determines how much involvement he or she wants to have in a niece or nephew's life. Now that my children are grown, is it possible for my brother to cultivate a relationship with his nieces and nephews? Maybe it's simply too late.

Estrangement: the Ripple Effect

The lack of connection between my brother and me not only affected my children, but it also shaped nearly every relationship in the family. Often, when there's a sibling cutoff in the family, cousins never see each other, and some may even be unaware that there's another branch of the family. Holiday celebrations—a roll call for family members—are underpopulated. Parents may throw out birthday cards sent to a niece or nephew to avoid answering inevitable questions. Questions like, "Who is Aunt Mary, Uncle Jack and Casey, and why don't we see them?"

Marjorie Watson, sixty-four, of Bangor, Maine, who has little to do with several of her relatives, told a revealing story about the ripple effect of estrangement. She illustrates how removed her children have become from an estranged uncle. Marjorie's husband hasn't spoken to his sister and brother-in-law in over sixteen years:

> *My adult son, who hadn't seen his uncle since he was a child, sat down next to a familiar-looking man on a train. Discreetly, he used his iPhone to take a photo of his seatmate. Then he sent the photo and this text to me: "Mom, is this Uncle Michael?" I looked at the picture and, even though I hadn't seen him in years, I was sure it was him. But my son didn't introduce himself. It made me sad that my son couldn't even recognize his uncle on a train.*

Survey respondents describe the tidal wave of estrangement that can sweep into the next generation, destroying those relationships as well:

> *My children absolutely adored my brother and his wife. They are too young to understand, but they are losing out, too. I am so sad for them.*

> *When I watch my three sons playing, I see my little brother, too, as he used to be. Remembering how he played in the same way with the same toys, my*

heart aches that he is missing out on these three beautiful boys that he will never know.

Our entire extended family has been affected by my estrangement with my only brother.

In some families where estrangement has occurred, the number of cut-offs seems to multiply exponentially. Long-standing estrangements may become an acceptable model, replicated by generations that follow. In these families, when stressful situations arise, siblings easily justify cutting off from one another, given that their parents didn't maintain relations with their own brothers or sisters.

Survey respondent Helene Pendergast, who described in chapter 8 her heartache of fifty years due to the lack of any relationship with her only brother, sees estrangement as a product of family history. "Those who come from well-adjusted, happy families are most fortunate," she says. "If those who are estranged were to track their family histories for two or three hundred years, I am sure they would find that brokenness stretching way back."

Several survey respondents concur with Pendergast's point, as they witness more and more cutoffs in their own families:

My stepmom was the only grandmother my children and grandchildren knew. She has not seen or attempted to see them in three years. How painful for my granddaughter, who remembers her Nona. The others were not born yet. She's never acknowledged they are on this earth. My sisters also act like my adult children don't exist, and they have also never met my grandchildren.

First, I became estranged from my sister, and then, my only daughter. All I have left is my 96-year-old mother. Once she's gone, I'll have no family, and I'm not sure I want to remain in this world.

I miss my idea of her, but that is not the reality of her. I have no one to talk to. I wish I could call her and discuss other family events. With the loss of contact with her, I've also lost contact with her children and grandchildren.

Marjorie Watson says she can't keep track of who is speaking to whom in her family without a scorecard:

My four children have contentious relationships and little to do with each other. My two daughters are completely estranged now for almost five years. My husband has a sister we haven't talked to in over a decade, and another sister who only returned to the family when my mother-in-law was dying. My grandmother didn't speak to one of her ten sisters. I don't speak to my own sister and have little contact with her children.

After filling out my survey, Marjorie, who says my questionnaire caused her to reflect on the state of her family, sent me a private email, elaborating on why various members terminated their relationships. Bickerings, slights, and childhood traumas, Marjorie says, all factored into the cutoffs. After her long, painful summary, she concludes her email with these exasperating words: "Families are SO complicated."

Reconciling for the Sake of the Family

Sustaining any type of estrangement may take considerable time, effort, and determination, as family members often exert considerable pressure on the estranged to reconcile. "Parents sometimes see sibling estrangement as their failing, but it's not," explains psychotherapist Ali-John Chaudhary. "We're all human and we have distinct personalities and sometimes we clash. You don't get along with every single person in the world, it's just unfortunate when it happens in the family unit. What you think you can live with will dictate your behaviors and actions."

Consequently, every family event presents a crisis of conscience over what to do and how to answer implicit questions that arise:

- Do I have to go to the party or family event?
- Do I have to invite them?
- What do I tell the children or stepchildren?
- How do I get relatives to stop talking about my estranged sibling or pressuring me to reconnect?

Before siblings reach the point of no return, nonestranged family members often insist that brother and sisters stay connected to avoid the stigma of estrangement and to maintain the appearance of a "functional" family. To promote relationships, some family members go as far as making excuses to mitigate a sibling's bad behavior, a strategy that can be even more divisive. Some estranged siblings succumb to the pressure, and, to appease others, they minimize hurts, exaggerate the level of intimacy or contact with a sister or a brother, and even interact with them at a family event to cover the cutoff.

Twenty-year-old Hannah Ewing, who described her on-again, off-again relationship with her only brother in chapter 2, says that her parents have pressured the two into having some sort of connection. "Our parents told me that he is the only brother I have, so we need to make up," she recalls. "So we did. We just avoid any land mines in the conversation that would bring up the past." However, some estranged siblings complain that when they are forced into a relationship, they feel a sense of inauthenticity.

Terminally ill parents may even go as far as begging their children to maintain some kind of relationship on their deathbeds. Helene Pendergast's mother expressed a desire just before her death in 2011 that her two children stay in touch. "But you can't make something out of nothing," says Pendergast. "Our parents didn't do much to create a nice family atmosphere. We grew up in fear and chaos. I did try to stay connected, but I was met with this complete indifference. So I have given up."

Even if family members don't actively lobby for reconciliation, they often are grossly insensitive to hurt feelings. For two years, thirty-five-year-old Cassie Brady of Tucson, Arizona, says her older brother had given her the silent treatment. Cassie's family seems to fall into several risk categories for estrangement: She describes her brother as an angry, manipulative, alcoholic man who always envied Cassie because she was the favorite child. Recently, Cassie was furious at her mother for exposing her young daughter to the family hurts and losses. While babysitting for her granddaughter, Cassie's mother helped the five-year-old make a gift for her cousin whom she has never met.

Sometimes a family member will go to extremes, attempting to reunite estranged siblings without their consultation or consent. The estranged often complain about those who push too hard, concluding that it produces more resentment. "I mourn the *idea* of a close family and sibling," says Julianna Turner, who has discussed her estrangement with her sister and tenuous relationship with one of her two brothers in earlier chapters, "but I'm happy without her. Recently my mom guilted me because my sister has cancer. Laying guilt trips doesn't change or improve the situation. Actually, it makes things worse."

Several survey respondents commented that family members guilted and gaslighted them into maintaining relationships with siblings. Using shame and guilt as weapons, family members may manipulate the estranged, but these damaging behaviors often result in unintended consequences, sweeping more members into the vortex of the original estrangement.

When Family Members Take Sides

Estrangement often places family members in the discomfiting, virtually impossible position of having to choose sides. The situation may become so polarizing as to incite a familial civil war. Sometimes the estranged—who desperately want to hold tight to nonestranged relationships for fear of also losing them—aggressively recruit and lobby nonestranged family members to take sides by bullying, accusing, and attacking. In their desperation, the estranged may demand loyalty or threaten to end relationships with family members who refuse to take their side.

Survey respondent Jill Pressin, sixty-four, of Manchester, England, says that family members took sides when she and her bullying brother and sister-in-law became estranged five years ago. Now, she says, she has become isolated from all twenty of her relatives. When she turned sixty, no one acknowledged her birthday with a card, message, or email.

In an attempt to neutralize the situation and protect others from additional fallout, some family members avoid any discussion of the cutoff, shrouding the subject in secrecy. Consequently, others in the family who have no information about the situation try to imagine what's going on and why is there so much tension. When they don't understand the reasons, they often grow suspicious, and distrustful. They may even choose to distance themselves from the family.

Isabelle Lays, forty-five, of Scotland, who describes herself in chapter 5 as a "twinless twin," came from a solidly middle-class family. She says her estrangement from her twin brother and her only younger sister has completely upset the equilibrium of her nuclear family. Isabelle has suffered with mental illness, and she says her sister wants nothing to do with her and her problems. "My mother refused to take sides or discuss the situation with any of us," she explains, "and established distinct, separate relationships with each of us. There have been no family gatherings at all for many years."

Avoiding the problem may backfire, as that tactic may make the estranged feel even more isolated, as family members refuse to "get involved." Stephanie Bleacher, who commented in chapter 7 on her estrangement with one of her five sisters, resents her father for tolerating the long-standing cutoff.

My dad texts me today to share good news about the sister I'm estranged from. My response: "Good for her and thanks but I'd rather not receive any info about her in the future." Then he said, "Forget about it and be happy." It's easy for my family to say "accept it." They aren't the ones cut out. How can they believe I would do something to warrant this kind of treatment? How do I have a relationship with the rest of my family without feeling guilty, responsible, and like I'm a bad person? How do I get over the pain and betrayal I feel from no one defending me or seeing my side?

When the estranged do not feel seen, heard, or validated, the fallout may spread to other family members.

How Estrangement Affected My Mother's Relationship with Her Children

My own mother, Edith Schumer, felt her relationships with both her children suffered because Scott and I didn't speak. Here my mother describes the dilemmas she faced during those decades:

It was always in the back of my mind—I have a son and daughter who have nothing to do with each other. I was always thinking, What can I do? How can we get together? How can I get my family back? I felt hurt and embarrassed that my children didn't have anything to do with each other. I never talked to anyone about it. I felt ashamed, so I carried the pain alone.

At times, I was furious about the situation: I would get invited to a family party that excluded one of my children. I never knew what to do.—Should I attend or not? Should I insist that I will only go to an event if both my children are invited? Whatever choice I made, I was going to hurt one of my children.

For years, I resented my mother for her choices. I felt she hadn't done enough to prevent the family breakdown, and that she tacitly accepted my brother's behavior by attending events that excluded me. In my mind, she was voting with her feet, and her actions revealed that she wasn't willing to protect me or act in the best interest of our entire family. In time, my anger over the estrangement disturbed my relationship with her as well.

The Legacy of Estrangement in the Next Generations

The hurts and deep divisions of estrangement may result in other complications for families. Those siblings who don't talk, for example, lack the ability to address important issues together: Is it time to sell the family business? What kind of care does our ailing father need? Should we move Mom out of the family home?

At the same time, when estrangement ripples through the family, important historical and health-related information stretching back generations may be lost. No one may know, for example, that a great-uncle suffered with an illness that now plagues a descendant—or that the condition was successfully treated with an unexpectedly effective medication.

Survey respondents and countless posts in estrangement chat rooms describe how cutoffs hurt children, stepchildren, and grandchildren, as these young family members feel like they are lone stars in the universe who are not part of a recognized constellation. Young people typically crave a sense of belonging that a functioning family provides. Often, they will search elsewhere when those needs are unmet. They may find surrogate grandparents, aunts, uncles, and cousins, substituting unrelated people for their own missing relatives.

That sense of disconnection may carry its own risks, as some young family members may turn to more ominous alternatives. "The gang has quite a bit to offer the very young," explains Dr. Zina McGee, professor of sociology at Hampton University in Hampton, Virginia, and author of *Silenced Voices: Readings in Violence and Victimization.* "There is that sense of acceptance, there is that sense of value that comes from being a member of that gang. [The young] gain their sense of self from that group." [1]

A 2010 survey found that many gang-involved youth feel cut off from their families. The survey, sponsored by the Alfred P. Sloan Foundation (a nonprofit that does original research) and conducted by psychologists at the Emory Center for Myth and Ritual in American Life, asked adolescents about their family histories and if they knew stories of their ancestors. Those adolescents who had personal knowledge about their family history, according to this research, had a greater sense of well-being, and they tended to be higher achievers. Typically, they came from stable and more functional families. [2]

It's not just young people who benefit from family connection. Family identity provides the foundation for crucial aspects of human development: a sense of self, a stage, a platform, a safety net. Who we are, regardless of age, is shaped by the stories, memories, and narratives about the past and present. Families promulgate a set of collective values, common expectations, and a shared culture—all of which are tragically and irreplaceably lost when relatives have nothing to do with one another.

Chapter 12

A Balance Between
the Individual and the Family

SEPARATING AND MAINTAINING
FAMILY RELATIONS

I n rebuilding any relationship, it's important to manage those first awkward face-to-face encounters, which all too easily can underscore the distance and discomfort that have set in after bitter arguments or years of silence. When reestablishing contact—whether in a broken marriage, a shattered friendship, or a sibling cutoff—experts say that sharing an activity may pave a path to connection. It could be anything: planting a garden for a parent, working side by side in a neighborhood cleanup campaign, creating a family website. What's important is that it facilitates friendly, constructive communication, allowing both parties to step back into the relationship in a relaxed setting and reduce the potential for confrontation. Estranged siblings may have a small advantage, as they can choose an activity they shared in childhood.

I sift through my memory, searching for who Scott and I were as children and what we liked to do together. During our teenage years, we occasionally played Ping-Pong when we should have been doing homework. We competed intensely, but he usually won. Ping-Pong might be an ideal activity to restart the relationship, but I don't have a table anymore.

I consider what other activities might offer us a chance to bond as adults. We rarely rode bikes together as kids, except for the few times when fall weather made it pleasant to wheel our way to school. On those trips we rode single file, with no opportunity to talk, and I probably lagged far behind him. Still, I happen to have a spare bike in my garage, and I decide that we should try what we *could* have done as children, picking up where we left off.

When I call Scott to ask if he'd like to use my extra bike for a ten-mile ride through a nearby nature preserve, he surprises me by jumping at the chance.

"When can we go?" he asks. "I used to love to ride!"

"Really?" Maybe I just don't remember riding bikes together. I'm picturing our girls' and boys' Schwinns leaning against the brick wall in the carport. Is he talking about some other time?

So I ask. "You did? When?"

"In my thirties and forties."

"Oh!"

The tiny syllable is freighted with all I don't know about my brother.

On a sunny June morning, Scott and I take our first bike ride together as adults. First we stop at a sporting-goods store to buy him a bike helmet. While he's debating whether he wants lime green or black, a woman our age grabs his elbow and exclaims, "Scott!"

Startled, he looks up; his face brightens, and he greets her with a warm hug.

"What are you doing here?" she asks. "Where have you been? I haven't seen you in such a long time."

The two catch up, laughing about the coincidence of running into each other at a store so far from their neighborhood. They ask about spouses, kids, mutual friends. They seem to know each other well.

"Did you hear about Howie?" the woman asks.

"Yeah," Scott says. "I heard he should be done with treatments in several weeks. Hopefully he'll be better by Rosh Hashanah, so he can come to our dinner."

"Yeah," she nods, "it wouldn't be the same without him."

They toss out the names of a few other friends, sharing what they know. After five minutes, when Scott realizes that I've been standing on the periphery—left out of the conversation—he turns to face me. "Robin is a good friend of ours. We know her from the synagogue."

"Oh, hi," I say, extending my hand in greeting. "Nice to meet you."

Placing his hand on my back, Scott turns to her and says, "This is my sister."

"Oh!" she says, her features scrambling in confusion. She carefully scrutinizes my face, maybe looking to see if we resemble each other. Nobody says anything for a few moments, and an awkward silence sets in.

Finally Robin sputters, "I . . . I didn't know you *had* a sister!"

The old knife—the one that cut every time someone asked about my brother—slices me again. I feel completely removed and eradicated, but when I look at Scott, he shows no reaction.

After saying good-bye to Robin and settling on the lime-green helmet, we get back on our bikes and ride on the path to the nature preserve. Along the way, we stop and start at intersections and traffic lights. Sometimes we ride single file, to make way for pedestrians or other bicyclists, and that inhibits our ability to talk.

Once we reach the nature preserve, though, we have the path and the place to ourselves. We chat easily, catching up on the safe subject of where aunts, uncles, and distant cousins are now and what they're doing.

Then the conversation wanes, and I look at him, remarking that he looks a little better today. He has lost some weight; the dark circles under his eyes are less pronounced, and he has some color in his face.

"I stopped drinking," he says. I'm glad he volunteered this information, because I haven't wanted to ask.

"Oh! How do you feel?"

"Better, but it's only been three weeks or so."

"Is it hard to do?"

"No, not really. I just drink water instead of alcohol at night."

"Did you throw out all the old bottles of Crown Royal?" I ask.

"No, my sponsor says I shouldn't. I need to have the discipline to have alcohol in the house and not be tempted to drink it."

"Sounds tough."

"So far it's okay," he says. "And I think neurofeedback helps too." He has been doing the treatments for a month or so, probably having had about a dozen sessions. Elsa told us that in just three, the patient typically experiences changes.

In the last few weeks, he *has* seemed a little less depressed. A couple of weeks ago, he laughed for the first time since we reconnected. It sounded foreign; I don't think I'd heard his rich cackle since childhood. Then, in a text a few days later, he unexpectedly cracked a joke about his new glasses, which led to a clumsy exchange:

> **Scott:** Takes getting used to my new bifocals. I might need more sessions, he wrote.
>
> **Me:** ??? Sessions with Elsa? Is that what she suggested?
>
> **Scott:** I'm joking!
>
> **Me:** Oh! Since we reconnected, u haven't made too many jokes. Now that your old sense of humor is coming back, you caught me off guard.

I saw another sign of recovery when he stopped by my house to pick something up. Before now, he was always on guard, scanning the environment for anything that might make him anxious or stressed. This vigilance seemed to demand so much of his attention that he hardly noticed his actual surroundings. This day, though, as we stood in my living room, he gazed at the large flower boxes outdoors, lush and overflowing with purple and white petunias. "Those flowers are really pretty," he said, to my great surprise.

I wonder what changes he has noticed. "How do you think neurofeedback is helping?" I ask.

"Well, for one thing, I never used to put on the radio when I was driving," he says. "I didn't want to get the news that forty-nine people were shot today. I didn't even want to hear oldies."

As a kid, he loved Aretha Franklin, Otis Redding, Smokey Robinson and the Miracles—all the Motown and soul artists. It was a constant soundtrack to his teenage years, and to mine.

"I was scared the music might make me feel something," he continues. "But lately I've been putting on the oldies station, and I enjoy driving around now and listening to music.

"Another thing I noticed last week is how I reacted to a movie," he continues. "I used to be able to watch the most gruesome, violent scenes, and nothing ever bothered me. But I was trying to watch *Gangs of New York*, where these gangsters murder this guy, and I just couldn't stomach it. I had to turn it off. I think I'm starting to feel things again."

If he couldn't feel anything before, I guess it wasn't hard to sever himself from the family. Without empathy, he had no awareness of how his behavior might affect others. Slowly, I'm putting the pieces together, and I tell myself that if the moment arises today, I'm going to ask him more about the drought in our relationship.

"Did you see that red Ferrari just before we turned into the nature preserve?" Scott asks me, as we roll past an old farmhouse, the only building in the woods. "It makes me think of when . . ." That shifts the conversation to our memories. We fire questions at each other, resurrecting the amusing family lore that only he and I know: Remember when we all went to New Jersey in our Corvette Stingray, and you and I had to lie flat on our backs the whole way because the car didn't have a backseat? Remember when Dad told the neighborhood kids that he painted his car when he actually bought a new one that was the same model in a different color? How about the time Dad and I went to a Bears game in January, Scott recalls, and I didn't have any warm winter boots, so I wore Mom's high-heeled, fur-lined boots?

Then I go way back in time and ask about a vivid memory featuring our beloved grandmother.

"Remember Mama Gussie's purse?" Her metal-clasped handbags always held the candies her grandchildren craved: a bag of M&Ms for me, a box of Good & Plenty for Scott.

"No," he says. "'Mama Gussie's purse'? What are you talking about?"

"Don't you remember how as soon as she came through the door, we used to dive for her purse?"

"Not really."

"But you *have* to remember!" I fill in the details in hopes it will all come back to him. "We were probably three and six years old. Dad told her he didn't want her to bring us candy anymore. He told Mama Gussie he wanted us to love her for her, not her candy."

He looks at me blankly. "What can I tell you . . . ?"

When we weren't speaking, I took small comfort in knowing that at least we carried some of the same moments from our childhood. His poor memory feels like a betrayal, as if he has broken a trust. But then, I remind myself, my perceptions are my own, and sharing an experience doesn't guarantee that we derived the same meaning from it.

We continue gliding along the path through the woods, rolling over sun-speckled patches on the ground. Scott hasn't been on a bike in years, but he has no trouble keeping up with me. Still, after riding several miles in the hot sun, both of us feel overheated and tired. We travel from the woods into a clearing, and when Scott sees a bench in the distance, he asks if we can sit for a while.

When we get off the bikes, I scan the abundant prairie wildflowers—carpetweed, sundrops, forget-me-nots—all in full bloom. It's a pinch-worthy moment when I look at Scott and tell myself: *This is real! I'm not dreaming. On this glorious day, I am riding bikes with my brother in a nature preserve!* It feels ordinary and extraordinary at the same time.

On the bench, the sun bakes our faces as our conversation turns to what we've missed in each other's lives.

"Did I tell you I went to Alaska?"

"Did you know my son got an MBA?"

"Did you know I lived in Northfield for a few years?"

After we've run through these topics, a comfortable silence settles in. I hate to disturb our sense of well-being, but I yearn for answers and this seems like the moment to dig deeper. I remind myself of the elements of the Dignity Model, especially understanding, accountability, and acknowledgment.

I dive into choppy waters.

"So, I need to ask you." I chew my bottom lip. "How . . . how did you feel about our not talking for all those years? I mean, did it bother you?"

He looks off into the distance. I'm sure he wishes I would just put all this behind us. But he must sense my needs, and without looking at me, he admits, "I was never comfortable with it."

"Did you think about it a lot?"

"Yeah. Sure I did."

I had thought it weighed only on me, given that he had cut me off. "You know, it was really hard on me. Everything was so messed up when we were kids, and I felt isolated because I had no one to help me sort things out. At times I felt like Mom, with no living relatives at all."

"I know," he says. "But I didn't know what to do. I didn't know how to start talking when we hadn't talked for so many years."

"Yeah." I think about how stuck I felt. I couldn't figure out a way to change my relationship with him either. The estrangement had its own momentum along a relentless trajectory that only a dramatic intervention could have changed. Paralyzed by anger, resentment, and dread, I did nothing for days, months, years—and, finally, decades.

"I'm sure you had no idea how I would react if you did contact me," I say, "so you probably were afraid to even try. Maybe you thought I didn't want you back in my life."

"It had been so long since we had anything to do with each other. I had no idea what would happen if I reached out to you. I hardly knew you anymore."

"I know." Sadness washes over me. I look at him and notice his crow's feet and the creases in his face. "So why do you think the cutoff happened?"

He takes his time in answering. At last, he begins, "I talked to Elsa about it. . . ."

"Oh?"

"And . . ." his words slowly unwind, "she thinks I did to you what Dad did to me."

"So he didn't talk to you," I say, absorbing this idea, "and then you didn't talk to me. I never really thought of that. Though now it seems pretty obvious."

"What bothers me," says Scott, "is that Dad never got to know me."

"That's because he didn't let you be you," I say. "You were supposed to be an extension of him."

"I know," he says. "If I didn't become a doctor, then I was a failure."

"But I don't think this was ever really about you," I say, telling him what I've been thinking for a while. "It was about *him*. He was never up to fathering two children. He was a workaholic, and his career came first. So, in his twisted way, he made you into a hopeless disappointment, and since I was a girl, I didn't count. That's how he got himself off the hook of being a good parent."

"I never thought of that," he says. "But you're probably right."

"And you and I," I continue, "by not speaking for all those years, we re-created exactly what we experienced in childhood with our parents—not being seen or heard."

"That's true," he nods. Then he volunteers: "But cutting off from the family really cost me. I paid a huge price."

"What do you mean?"

"I lost . . . myself."

"How?"

"By abandoning you, I abandoned myself."

His words hang between us; we both feel the weight of what he is saying.

The blistering sun bakes the wooden slats of the bench where we're sitting. Now both of us are really sweating. "We really picked the day to ride," Scott says, wiping his brow with his shirtsleeve. "It's gotta be over ninety degrees out here."

He turns to me and holds up a plastic water bottle, offering me a drink. I take his bottle and swig the lukewarm liquid.

"You *are* changing!" I tell him, handing his bottle back to him.

"Oh!" His eyes widen. "How's that?"

"Well, before you were always so quiet," I tell him. "I never knew what to say to you, and in the old days, I always felt awkward and self-conscious around you. But now you talk!"

"Yeah, I guess so."

"And you seem to like it," I say, teasingly.

"I do," he admits. "It's engaging."

"Yeah." I smile at him sardonically. "That's why people do it."

In six words, "By abandoning you, I abandoned myself," Scott has captured how siblings anchor each other. Siblings often look alike, and share the same beginnings. They know one another intimately. Yet they don't understand what shaped each others' lives, and in some ways, they know little about one another.

Other factors complicate our understanding of siblings. We remember our sisters and brothers as they were when they, or we, left the family home. We tend to freeze our siblings as younger versions of themselves. As siblings transition from childhood to adulthood and embark upon their own lives, they grow and change through their unique experiences.

Each sibling must navigate—sometimes unconsciously—their own crucial psychological challenges. Every sibling, for example, must negotiate on his or her own how to maintain a place in the family and, at the same time, separate, differentiate, and individuate from parents and siblings. When a sibling is unable to individuate, he or she may become mired in the dysfunctional relationships of childhood, running the risk of repeating unhealthy patterns in adult relationships. When family members are so close that they don't individuate, they may become enmeshed, depending on each other to fulfill their emotional needs. It is not functional or healthy for a family member to rely on a relative—or for that matter, anyone—for a sense of well-being.

Separating from Family:
A Necessary Step into Adulthood

Dr. Murray Bowen, a psychiatrist and pioneer in family therapy, hypothesized that each brother or sister must become autonomous and learn to separate his or her own emotions from those of their parents and siblings. Children who have not differentiated, for example, might blame themselves for the ills in the family, such as their parents' divorce, their siblings' emotional problems, or family feuds. By contrast, the differentiated individual, Dr. Bowen explained, responds to the world independently and logically.

Those who are deeply enmeshed with family, Dr. Bowen reasoned, are likely to be insecure and anxious. For example, a sister or brother who turns to a sibling for care, protection, or confirmation of his or her identity may feel agitated and deprived when those needs and expectations are not met. This could lead to a cutoff, Dr. Bowen explained, because, ironically, as psychologist and author Dr. Lerner identified in chapter 4, estrangement indicates that an individual is not less but *more* involved in a relationship. In fact, Dr. Bowen theorized that those who are deeply fused to the family often address their inability to effectively separate themselves by going to an extreme and limiting or terminating family contact to reduce their anxiety.

How does a sister or brother develop an autonomous identity while sustaining connections with other family members? "It's a strange, hard thing to pull away from family, to create yourself, and still try to stay close to them," writes Kaitlyn Greenidge, author of *We Love You, Charlie Freeman*, in a 2018 article in *The New York Times*, "I'm still not sure how to do it." In her late teens and twenties, she pulled away from her family by moving to another city and creating a circle of friends who know nothing of her origins. But this approach, according to Greenidge has resulted in a false self—one she says "is as shaky and unknown as the stunted self that comes from sublimating your desires for those of your family."[1]

Ideally, an individual learns to balance his or her independence while maintaining family relationships, but each of us falls on a spectrum somewhere between successful differentiation and an unhealthy degree of fusion. It's necessary to establish clear boundaries in *all* relationships; however, the practice of distancing oneself or cutting off whenever differences arise may become dangerous, especially when it is used to avoid closeness, to isolate from relatives, or to punish them.

Sam Goldman, whom we met in chapter 4, admits he chose an unhealthy approach to individuating by moving to another city and marrying a partner who promoted distance from his family. His younger sister, Rachel, who discussed in chapter 7 how she has suffered from low self-esteem due to her brother's rejection, explains that Sam's choice to cut off from the family ultimately was devastating to Sam himself:

It's difficult to comprehend how deeply Dad's death when we were children affected my brother. When Dad died, I recall hearing him wailing in his room, and I often said that he never stopped crying. Sometimes I wondered if his pain was so great that he wanted nothing to do with those of us who reminded him of the loss. Now he struggles with the guilt of his choices. He can't seem to forgive himself.

Immediately after he left his marriage, the first person Sam called for counsel and comfort was his only living sister, whom he hadn't been close to in decades. Now that the two have finally developed a satisfying relationship, they are able to support each other in their daily lives, reflect upon the sad circumstances of their shared childhood, and discuss what they lost to estrangement.

The Consequences when a Sibling
Can't Separate from Family

Family interactions in childhood create a blueprint for how an individual will relate to others in the future. Adults from troubled homes often hope that a romantic relationship will offer a convenient escape from their difficult family life. However, Dr. Bowen, whose family-systems therapy claimed individuals are inseparable from their network of relationships, suggested that the damaging effects of difficult family relationships and estrangement may spread to a romantic relationship.

First, sibling difficulties and troubled family relations may lead to a poor choice of a partner. A woman who has not spoken to her brother in decades, for example, may react to all men, especially a partner, as if they were her brother, expecting every man in her life to treat her badly and/or abandon her. Even though she has no contact with her brother, she remains emotionally embroiled in her relationship with him.

Second, an individual will bring unresolved issues into new relationships, often re-creating the same patterns from the family of origin. One study, conducted at the University at Albany, State University of New York, and reported in the *Journal of Counseling Psychology,* found that differentiation of self can predict the quality of a marriage.[2] The study concluded that individuals bring the same level of differentiation they've established from their family of origin into a partner relationship. In other words, partners with a history of family strife will likely reenact the anxiety and overreactions they experienced in their original families in their romantic relationships.

Third, children who feel their parents and/or siblings rejected them are not necessarily self-aware and often misread emotional cues. This pattern of relating may be disastrous in a romantic relationship, as a partner may perceive hostility and rejection from their partners where none is intended. In addition, the partner often lacks self-worth—even when others reassure them that they are loved and loveable.

Finally, those who come from difficult, dysfunctional families may never have learned the skills needed to build healthy relationships and repair damaged ones. "Their response to stress or strife may be to end the relationship," explains Dr. Linda Stern, a clinical psychologist who practices in Highland Park, Illinois, "rather than confront, address, and resolve divisive issues. When one cuts off from a sibling or parent, the result is estrangement; when one cuts off from a spouse, the result is divorce."[3]

Family estrangement also can place more stress on a marriage, which can lead to other worrisome outcomes. If one or both members of a couple are estranged from family, the couple will have less external support when their marriage becomes strained, intensifying their dependence upon each other. A 2003 study by Douglas Murphy, director of postgraduate training at the Georgetown University Family Center, suggested that these overly interdependent couples may be at higher risk for domestic violence and even child abuse.[4]

Ultimately, spouses in tumultuous relationships may find themselves transmitting their psychological issues to their own children and grandchildren. Connie Owen, whom we met in chapter 4, said that she stopped speaking to one of her two sisters when she placed their father in a memory-care unit without Owen's or her father's permission. Now the estrangements have created tension and distance in her relationships with her children and grandchildren.

"When I tried to explain the reason for the cutoff to my daughter," she says, "she and my granddaughter immediately took my sister's side. It broke my heart. It's just been hell on earth for my father and myself. It's changed my life completely; it's changed me entirely."

For other survey respondents, sibling estrangement is so painful that they have factored this reality into their major life choices. Some say they chose not to have children to avoid the pain of another estrangement. Others said they had only one child so that he or she wouldn't have a life-long sibling bully. Still others had children with the hope of creating the family they never had. But sadly, that often doesn't succeed. One woman whose motivation was to give to her children the family she wanted says her effort backfired. When the children left home at eighteen, they never returned, and now her children have nothing to do with her and her husband.

Ultimately, however, those who forsake family often relinquish a part of themselves and bury feelings that may resurface later in their lives. In time, many of the estranged recognize the hole within themselves. Cutting off family, ancestors, and history is a form of eradication, and estrangement can be a kind of self-exile.

PART III

Reconciliation

Chapter 13

A Limited Relationship
with a Difficult Sibling

The old wooden door at my mother's house, the 1950s beige split-level where I grew up, slams behind me with the same hollow timbre I've known intimately for five decades. The door, with its single, stingy top window where my mother pasted a now-faded U.S. flag decal, always seemed to have a voice of its own. When the four of us lived there, it announced who was passing through its frame countless times every day. I became so attuned to each family member's sound signature that I not only knew who was there but also could identify his or her mood, much the way some people can read footsteps on stairs.

The door punctuated the frequent arguments my father had with all of us. After booming the last word, he would storm out, violently jerking the old brass doorknob. The slam amplified the door's voice as the whole house rattled, right down to the basement—a noisy exclamation point on his wrath. A few times, I feared his thundering rage might bring down the roof.

The warped, chipped door, its bottom shredded by water damage, also spoke of my mother's frugality and resistance to change. Even though the door has needed replacement for at least two decades, its deterioration perpetually escaped my mother's notice.

Now, as I enter the house, the wind grabs the door and slams it hard, shoving me inside. Mom has insisted Scott and I come to lunch today to meet distant German relatives who are in town. As we debated whether we *had* to go, he said, "I hate going there. But I know it's important to Mom, so I guess I'll just tough it out." If he was going, I felt I had to go too.

Scott and I rarely come here. We share a dread of this place and its painful memories. When I hear the door's heavy, echoing thud, I immediately feel trapped: the doomed sound of a prison gate shutting.

Nothing has changed since we lived here. When I walk into the living room, Scott is sitting in the same tan leather chair he preferred as a teenager. Mom, as always, is scurrying around, clanging silverware and dishes in the kitchen.

Fifty years drop away as I see both of them in their familiar spots. I half expect my father to lumber down the stairs and ask in his deep, rebuking tone, "Why aren't you two doing your homework?"

"When will they be here?" I call to Mom as I enter the small foyer, already looking for my escape.

"Not soon enough," Scott mutters, just loud enough so only I can hear.

The guests arrive, and we readily chat, eat, and laugh. But a completely separate drama is playing out in me, as flashbacks from this theatrical stage of my childhood loop in my mind. No matter how far I go from this house, those terrorizing scenes never leave me. Sometimes they creep into my daily life without my awareness.

After scarcely more than an hour, before we've even eaten dessert, Scott abruptly announces that he has to leave, creating some lame excuse about a delivery at his house. I'm not surprised; for the past fifteen minutes, I've watched him grow more and more agitated. Clearly, the people and the place are getting to him. I feel the same way, and shortly after dessert, I make my getaway too.

Later in the day, I check in by text to see how he survived the harrowing event:

> **Me:** Had a big PTSD slide after going to Mom's today. Did u?

> **Scott:** Yes, I felt terrible. We have to talk. Worst feeling since I started all this.

> **Me:** Sorry to hear, but I guess it was to be expected. Want to meet for breakfast tomorrow?

The next morning, I head for Sandy's, the small diner where Scott and I got together a few weeks ago. The place has kept the same menu and decor for fifty years: chipped Formica tables, black-and-white tile floor, swiveling barstools at the counter. Arriving before Scott, I take a seat in one of the old booths next to the window. The elderly owner comes over to my table, pours a cup of coffee, and hands me a menu. "Your brother coming today?" Sandy asks casually.

I'm still rattled by those two words—"your brother"—but quickly remind myself that there's nothing extraordinary about her recognizing a brother and sister who occasionally visit her diner. "Yes," I say, with a smile. "I think so."

The moment I spot him coming through the door, his slumped, shambling gait and gray face announce that he's struggling again.

"Hey," I say softly, as he slides into the booth and Sandy returns to pour him a cup of coffee. "I'm still getting over yesterday," I say as she walks away. "It feels like that visit to Mom's put a drag on every cell in my body."

"Me too." Hunched over, he shakes his head. "I didn't think it would be that bad, but I could barely get out of bed this morning."

"Well, I'm glad you made it." I'm both alarmed and comforted that I'm not alone in my reaction.

"I just can't stand it. I'm not doing that again. I can't go there."

"Me either," I say. "What got to you most?"

"Everything. The light coming in the front window. The way the stairs creak. The rumble of the garage door opening."

"The worst for me is the front door. That hollow slam—it's so creepy."

"And I can't *stand* those Heritage House books."

Oh, the books! In the 1960s, my father decided that the home of an intellectual like himself required a distinguished library. So he splurged by subscribing to a monthly book club, amassing a large collection of literary tomes, many of which he never cracked open.

"And I *never* should have sat in Dad's old chair at the head of the dining room table," Scott goes on. "I kept hearing him criticize Mom."

Imitating Dad with startling accuracy, he lists a cascade of complaints: "'I can't eat this. You know I hate overcooked meat. This is no good. Why did you make this? I don't like it.' At one point, I looked over at Mom and she had that same expression she had when we lived there—sad, lost, old."

"Same for me," I say, and then add, "but different too. When I go there, I'm always angry at Mom."

"Mom?" Scott's eyebrows knot in confusion. "Why Mom?"

"Because I always got the brunt of Dad's bad mood, and she didn't do anything to stop him. She didn't protect me." I've surprised myself by confessing what has burned within me for decades.

"Protect *you*? How could you expect her to protect you?"

"What do you mean? Is it unreasonable to expect that a mother would protect her child?"

Narrowing his dark eyes, he shakes his head. "She couldn't even protect herself!"

For years, I've harbored resentments toward both of my parents—Dad for his temper, Mom for her silent tolerance of his cruel behavior. I carefully consider what Scott has just said: *She couldn't even protect herself!*

Our mother's early life—fleeing the Holocaust alone, losing her parents and grandmother, growing up in a dark well of loneliness—left her voiceless and helpless. Her own sense of self was so diminished, that she was incapable of articulating or advocating for her own needs, let alone anyone else's.

His words shift my understanding of my mother. Only a sibling could offer me this insight. I'm flooded with gratitude and a sense of connection: I have a brother who understands.

Sandy brings our breakfast. I watch as he pours maple syrup, picks up his fork, and slowly pokes at his pancakes.

"I'm worried about you," I say, suddenly losing my own appetite.

"I hate the summer solstice," he says, squinting at the bright sun pouring through the window. "Too many hours of daylight. I prefer the cold, short days in winter."

Elsa told us that his progress would not be linear. Clearly, he has slipped into depression. I worry he might go back to drinking.

"I feel so down," he says. As if reading my mind, he adds, "Last night was the first time since I quit that I was tempted to drink again."

"That's not a solution," I say calmly, hoping to shut down this option.

"I know." He pushes the soggy pancakes to a corner of his plate. "But that's what I always did when I felt bad." Thinking for a moment, he then adds, "You know, I've been escaping my whole life. Everything I ever did was a way to avoid feeling like this."

"You feel terrible right now," I say, "but you won't always feel this way. You need to step back and take the long view. You've done so much over the last few months. You stopped drinking. You're going to therapy. You're changing all of your relationships."

"Yeah, everything's different now." I'm relieved to hear that. "I'm not living the way I did for years—drinking and trading. When I went out with my old friends, all we did together was drink. Now I'm trying not to be around that, so what am I supposed to do—make all new friends? And what am I going to do with myself? How am I going to make a living?"

"I know this is a lot," I say. "You're changing everything—your friends, your family, your work."

"You have no idea."

Maybe it's too much for him to change everything at once. I guess it's time to make a suggestion I've been thinking about—though I'm hoping he'll turn me down.

"I . . . I know you feel bombed by all this change," I begin. "And I know it's not easy for you to be around Mom and me. As Elsa said, we bring back your painful past."

"Yeah."

"You know, if it's too much, if we make things harder for you and . . . you need to step off the path for a while, I understand."

As if on cue, Sandy appears to clear our dishes and give me a moment to breathe. When she asks Scott if he's finished with his barely touched pancakes, he nods and she removes the plates.

"What?" he asks. "If what's too much?"

"If . . . if you can't manage it all right now," I offer reluctantly, "we can go our separate ways for a while."

He looks more confused than comforted at the idea.

"I have a better understanding now of why we were estranged," I continue. "It won't eat me up this time. If you need a break, I won't take it personally."

If we stop seeing each other now, I'll miss him terribly. But I want to help him find the most expedient path out of his misery—even if it means sacrificing our fledgling reconciliation.

He narrows his eyes at me. "I don't even *think* about that!"

"Oh! Ohhh, good!" I sigh, my tension dropping away. "Because I don't think it's natural or healthy not to talk to someone who you were raised with, but—"

"Fern!" he says with a familiar ring of irritation. It's exactly how he said my name when we were kids and I got on his nerves. "I've lived without family long enough. I don't want to do it again."

Then, to underscore his point, he adds, "I'm *not* going back."

Fine. Neither am I.

What a relief that Scott refused to even consider my offer to take a break. It seems to me that if he had wanted to reduce our relationship, we would have a couple of options: We could cut off completely again and agree to a temporary suspension of contact, or we could negotiate some sort of limited connection, which some therapists actually recommend. Siblings in that kind of relationship engage in a superficial, casual relationship to protect themselves from getting hurt.

Neither of these choices appeals to me; I prefer to continue on our faltering path—trying to re-create a relationship in the wake of all the anger, betrayal, and mistrust of estrangement. As difficult as reconciliation is at times, I know I'm fortunate to sit across from Scott and tackle uncomfortable topics. I remind myself that encounters with a brother or sister—even those siblings who were never estranged—can be loaded with love and hate, adulation and jealousy, empathy and exasperation. The connection we're building—slowly and tentatively—will, with our continuing commitment, progress from our old state of exile to one of equilibrium as siblings. Our relationship is under construction—but after our last conversation, I know it's not about to collapse—at least, not right now.

Maintaining a Limited Relationship

When siblings don't get along and constantly teeter on the brink of estrangement, the best they may hope for is a limited relationship—consisting, for example, of occasional emails, infrequent phone calls, or seeing each other at annual family gatherings. This kind of superficial connection focuses on harm reduction and contains the hurt that a deeply contentious relationship can inflict on an individual.

A limited sibling relationship insulates antagonistic siblings from the devastating fallout that may result from a complete estrangement. This option placates family members, balancing the collective good against a sister or brother's need for dignity, authenticity, and autonomy. With a limited relationship, siblings are comforted with the knowledge that he or she has done everything possible to keep the peace.

"What you think you can live with will dictate your behaviors and actions," explains Ali-John Chaudhary, the Ontario psychotherapist who often counsels his clients on how to manage a limited sibling relationship. "Some clients decide to reinvent their relationship with a difficult sibling. Others may decide to have a more superficial connection. And others may decide they don't want a part in the family anymore. Each sibling must determine his or her values and decide what works best."

Chaudhary, who has had a strained relationship with his younger sister, has chosen a limited relationship. For years, his connection to his only sibling has been what he calls a "surface relationship."

Why maintain a limited connection? "I have only one sister," Chaudhary explains. "This is my only family. If it's a choice between having no sibling relationship and having a relationship on some level where I can have contact with her, I'll take the limited relationship. I keep things superficial purposely, and I buy peace. Sometimes, I have to put on blinders, so I'm not psychologically affected, which requires effort."

Chaudhary has specific recommendations for his clients who want to maintain a connection with a difficult sibling and, at the same time, protect themselves from potential hurts. First, he says visualization can be effective, so he asks a client to identify the difficult family member as a specific animal. "Then I ask them, 'What does it mean when you come in contact with that creature?'" he says. "'How do you protect yourself?'" Another visualization technique he recommends is to imagine that you are wearing thick, full-body armor when you are about to encounter your difficult sibling.

Chaudhary also offers the following suggestions on how to negotiate a limited sibling relationship:

- Avoid contentious topics. Chaudhary advises clients to stay away from issues that are known hot buttons. "You can make jokes," he says. "You can start singing. Do something, anything that cuts the tension. Only discuss the weather, work, or talk to the sibling about his or her interests. Those are safe topics."
- Have an exit strategy. "If things become tense," he says, "help out with food or go into another room. If you are ambushed, you want to know how you can get out of the situation."
- Be careful not to regress to childhood roles. Preparing in advance for an upcoming family event—by anticipating, visualizing, and planning for the encounter—may significantly reduce conflict and explosions. "This is where the work on yourself becomes especially important," Chaudhary explains." You want to make sure you're not squeezed into old roles by someone else. If an old identity is forced upon you, you will become defensive."
- Maintain boundaries—physical or psychological. "You have to be your own shield to protect yourself," Chaudhary says. "That way, you're in control, and you aren't allowing the toxicity to get to you."

- Find a neutral ground for meetings. "If you meet at a coffee shop or in a public place," Chaudhary suggests, "there's less likelihood of an outburst."[1]

Several survey respondents have discovered Chaudhary's strategies on their own. They keep encounters with their estranged siblings courteous and brief. Several say that the relationship with their difficult brother or sister is superficial, even fake. When the relationship has been fraught with arguments and betrayal, siblings cannot trust each other and there is no potential for growth and, therefore, a superficial relationship may be the only option.

Even with the knowledge that their relationship is limited, hopeful siblings often bring loaded expectations—fantasies of the perfect family, the idealized relationship—to every encounter with a challenging brother or sister. To avoid repeating the same mistakes, it's important to remember the history and limitations of the relationship.

In challenging relationships, it's best to anticipate how to defuse a tense situation. For example, when a distant sibling asks a prying question, it might be best to answer: "How would you feel if I asked you that?" This unexpected response forces each party to think before speaking, and it could result in avoiding a brewing rift. Asking a question also provides some control over the direction of the conversation.

At the same time, a sibling who is trying to keep peace should not ignore hurtful comments or acts, especially when these are intentionally cruel. Pointing out provocative actions may cause a defensive sister or brother to take umbrage—but sometimes it's necessary. When calling out offensive comments or hurtful behavior, a calm, gentle approach, which frames statements with "I" messages that address an individual's feelings, works best. An example of an "I" message is "When you exclude me from a guest list, I feel hurt and dismissed. I feel I am not a family member."

A sibling in a strained relationship might try to change the pattern of the relationship by changing their reactions and choosing a different approach. To become more assertive, *act* more assertive. With consistent practice, "acting" becomes "being."

Set Boundaries and Limits

Sixty-year-old Avery Benjamin, who has served as a second mother to her six younger siblings for most of her life, is employing these strategies to maintain a minimal but functional connection with her siblings. However, caring for their ailing mother strains family relationships, and at times Avery feels stuck in her dispiriting family narrative:

I grew up in an East Coast urban area, in what I thought was a healthy, model family unit. We went to church, had nice clothes, maintained lots of family traditions. On the outside, we looked perfect; but inside, the family was chaotic.

As the eldest, I was more of my mother's assistant than her daughter. It was my responsibility to help my mother care for her four other children. When my mother became pregnant again when I was twelve, I was furious. I didn't feel I could handle another child. I felt unseen and unimportant.

Starting in first grade, I was repeatedly sexually assaulted by a teenage cousin. I never said a word because I didn't want to make waves, and I'm not sure my mother would have believed me anyway. After several years, I finally told the cousin to stop, which he did. That's when I realized that I had to resolve my own problems. When you're eight or nine, that's empowering and devastating at the same time.

Alcoholism runs in my family, which I didn't realize until I was older. Two siblings became alcoholics. We would develop a plan to help them, but there wasn't any follow-through because my mother was so invested in maintaining the illusion of the perfect family.

Now my mother is old and ill, and my sisters expect me to take care of everything. My mother set this up, always referring to me as "my staff." When I don't meet their expectations, my sisters scream and yell, just as they did when we were growing up.

It's difficult to maintain any relationship with them. I don't have the energy to give and give anymore, and the stress has resulted in numbness in my face, heart arrhythmia, and constant fatigue.

My siblings can be so abusive that I've finally realized I can't live like this. Still, I'm reluctant to set boundaries because I worry they might cut me off; I feel they just aren't that interested in me—much like my mother.

I've have had to force myself to create distance, set limits, and place value on my time. Just as I did when I was little, I've had to stop the abuse and take care of myself.

Avery is learning that setting boundaries—whether they are verbal, physical, or emotional—is not an unloving act; it's self-preserving and protective. Verbal boundaries deem certain topics off-limits and steer the conversation toward safer subject matters. Physical boundaries limit the amount of time one spends with a difficult sibling by determining when to meet and how to interact. Emotional boundaries help control the narrative of what has happened, as a sibling assertively identifies his or her own feelings and experiences. In the absence of boundaries, resentment festers, further reducing the chances of any healthy sibling relationship.

When all else fails, the parameters of a strained relationship might be established in a "terms of engagement" agreement, especially for siblings who are attempting to reestablish a relationship after a long cutoff. "If the estrangement was due to a conflict," explains psychotherapist Alexandra Butler, who practices in Chicago, "it's inevitable that some uncomfortable memories and feelings will resurface as you resume interactions."[2]

Feuding siblings may be able to decide on specific rules and conditions for peaceful interactions in limited circumstances. Certain topics, jokes, or stories may be off-limits. The place, circumstances, and ground rules of any encounter may be determined beforehand. Sometimes an unbiased mediator is necessary to negotiate these terms, especially when the issues involved, such as sexual abuse, may be awkward and sensitive. "When historical relational injuries are provoked," Butler adds, "give yourself permission to process these in a safe environment, preferably with an unbiased professional."

A popular saying of unknown origin asserts that "if you don't heal what hurt you, you'll bleed on people who didn't cut you." Even the most tenuous sibling connection lessens the chance that chronic hurts will psychologically intrude upon other ongoing adult relationships—in other words, bleeding on people who didn't cut you. A limited relationship—if one can be established and maintained—may create a space to live with the past and thrive in the present.

Chapter 14

An Irreparable Sibling Relationship

T he commodities-trading world of fuel, foods, metals, and money, which Scott entered in 1975, was a daily exercise in extremes. Fortunes were made and lost in moments by men and a few women who spent their working hours screaming at one another.

The trading pits in those days promised people like Scott—many of them barely past adolescence—a daredevil life of fiscal thrills fueled by turbocharged profits. As one leader of a large trading company put it, the exchanges offered any kid "with perseverance, and a little native ability," a solid career and the potential to become the next multimillionaire.[1] Scott, a smart but directionless college dropout, made a deal with our father, who was forever trying to buy his way into his son's heart: Dad would set Scott up to do business by purchasing a seat on the exchange if Scott returned to school and completed his degree. Dad upheld his end of the bargain, but Scott did not. My brother's refusal to finish his degree was a betrayal of our father's trust and a loud rejection of our accomplished father's principles and the high value Dad placed on education.

Hanging in Scott's home office is a black-and-white picture from his early days in the trading pit of Chicago's MidAmerica Commodity Exchange. Standing shoulder to shoulder with several other young, competitive, ambitious brokers, he is wearing a traditional trading jacket with his ID badge, "SXS," pinned above the left breast pocket.

In the picture, Scott is only twenty-one years old. His dark-brown eyes blaze with the same vitality and intensity as our father's. His mouth is open as he yells to someone unseen, though I doubt anyone could hear him. The pit typically was as loud as a pro sports arena, and the only way to communicate clearly was through hand signals. Both of Scott's hands are high above his head, like a football referee calling a successful field goal attempt. Flashing three fingers on his right hand, he's indicating the price and contract terms for the trade he's attempting to place. In his left hand, he's holding a card to scribble notes of his trades and match them with those of other buyers and sellers at the end of the day.

He is playing what some called the world's highest-stakes poker game. Pit trading was awash in all the sweat, stench, and testosterone of a contact sport. To sustain performance in a job so arduous, some traders pumped iron daily. Others, like Scott, relied on superstition. Believing that some sacred article of clothing might sway his fortunes, he would wear the same shirt every day for months. He was careful to always take the same number of steps into the elevator up to the trading floor, a gesture made to Ceres, the Roman goddess of grain—whose golden statue stands atop the Chicago Board of Trade building—in hopes of attracting her favor in the day's work.

Yet no matter how traders dealt with their occupational hazards, inevitably the risks would catch up with them. Scott once described coming home from a crushing day in the market and curling up in the fetal position for hours. "You felt like the biggest loser," he says. He remembers that alcoholism, overdoses, and suicides were common at the board.

For centuries, face-to-face trading as practiced in the pit was standard, and its adrenalized brokers always gambled on high-risk trades. During the past forty years, however, technology has transformed the exchanges. When the Chicago Mercantile Exchange (where Scott was then trading) introduced computerized trading in 1992, Scott understood the seismic nature of the shift that soon would transform the industry. He seized the opportunity to make some changes of his own. At forty, he could see that the traders' lifestyle—partying, drinking, drugs—was killing him. This was a place where phone clerks made more money dealing drugs from their desks than in their biweekly paychecks.

Recognizing that the new technology could be his ticket out of a decadent environment, Scott eagerly embraced the computer as it revolutionized the financial world. He was one of the first to trade remotely from his home office, thereby removing himself from the pit. What he didn't foresee was that computers would eventually cut out the middlemen—the traders themselves. Electronic trading became faster, cheaper, and less error-prone than skilled floor brokers. In the old days, it took five minutes to fill a trade in the pit; on a computer, it takes five thousandths of a second.

Consequently, by the middle of the nineties, neither Scott nor the brokers he rubbed shoulders with in the pit were trading anymore. Some who owned seats invested wisely, leaving the business with millions of dollars and a secure future. Others were crushed by the changes and had to find alternative, less satisfying—and certainly less lucrative—lines of work. However, Scott refused: He continued to dabble in the markets as long as possible, sometimes trading on margin, where someone can lose much more money than he or she initially invested. Scott's refusal to leave the trading world led to his financial disaster and deep depression.

"I don't know what to do with myself," Scott tells me over coffee on a blustery fall day. Now that he's had a clearer head for a good five months, time weighs heavily on him. Often he beats himself up for not having invested more wisely. "I was a terrible businessman," he has said repeatedly. Had he been a prudent investor, he always tells me, he could be retired now, spending his days golfing in Arizona without any money worries.

"What about getting a job?" I ask, while fidgeting with the cardboard sleeve on my coffee cup. I'm remembering all the times he and I tackled a problem or schemed together. Sometimes, as children, we would collaborate on a cover-up for one of the many misdeeds we didn't want our parents to discover. Other times we occupied ourselves with an experiment from his Gilbert chemistry set—a dangerous venture, given that we never followed the directions. Impatient when we didn't get the predicted outcome, we would mix all the open chemicals in one flask and shake, hoping for a volcanic explosion. Occasionally we would get out the big atlas and huddle over it together, looking for the tiny German town where our mother was born. It's not on most maps, but we were convinced that if we could locate it, we would somehow get a glimpse of our mother's childhood, her lost family.

This time, it's a future we're chasing.

"I don't have any skills," Scott says grimly. We've had this conversation before; he admits that he's angry with himself for not having sought some kind of training, somewhere along the line, so he would now be able to support himself. One rhetorical question I've heard often: "Why didn't I take flying lessons or something?"

"No skills!" I say. Once again I'm in the position of having to correct his thinking. "You traded for decades. You know a lot about finance and money."

Just hearing the word "trading" seems to set off alarms in him; he shifts uncomfortably in his chair as his face turns gray. "I can't trade anymore." He shakes his head. "I don't have that kind of confidence, and I can't take the stress."

"I understand, but there must be other places you can apply your knowledge."

"Who's going to hire a sixty-two-year-old?" he comes back at me, edging toward anger. "And I don't even have a college degree."

He has a point—but at the same time, he needs something, some sense of purpose, to continue on the path of recovery. I remember how the Portuguese solution focuses on the importance of substance abusers finding purpose and value in the community and therefore has created massive jobs programs and offered loans so clients could start their own small businesses. Suddenly it hits me. Given his age, Scott would have more opportunity if he were to start his own business. But what kind?

"What did you do all those years when you were home and couldn't trade anymore?" I ask, hoping to uncover some unknown marketable skill.

"Not much." He stares out the window blankly.

"Did you read?"

"Yeah."

"What kind of books?"

"You know: legal thrillers, mysteries, sports biographies."

"And what else did you do?" Somehow, he filled the endless hours when he was alone in his house. "Those were long days."

"Slept a lot." He picks up a paper napkin, rolling its edge.

"I know that, but you couldn't have slept all day and all night."

"No." His napkin is fraying into little shreds. "I played with the computer."

"Doing what?"

"You know," he says matter-of-factly. "I took it apart."

"What?!" This could be just what I'm looking for! "You can take apart a computer?"

"Yeah."

"Can you put it back together?" I try to sound measured. Every conversation with Scott lately feels like a strategic game of chess. If I'm too enthusiastic, he'll put me in check. Typically, the more excited I get, the more guarded he becomes—so I tamp down the tone of my response.

"Yeah. I'm actually pretty good at that sort of thing." Scott never admits to being good at anything, so he must have strong computer skills.

"How did you learn that?" I ask.

"I just kept taking apart different computers and putting them back together until I figured it all out," he explains. "You know, when I was trading, I was always having to fix something on the network or the computer."

As much as Scott has tried to distance himself from our father, this was also Dad's skill. He eagerly assembled and disassembled anything mechanical: cars, radios, clocks, watches, computers. Dad was fascinated by all systems, including the human body.

When I was writing my first book in 1998, I complained to my father that my computer screen kept freezing. One day after work, he stopped by my house unexpectedly to repair it. I wasn't home, but the front door was unlocked, and he let himself in and began taking apart the motherboard. When I arrived home from the grocery store, I found him sitting on the floor of my home office, surrounded by large, mysterious pieces of metal: the guts of my computer.

"Dad!" I shrieked, nearly dropping three bags of groceries. That computer's hard drive contained more than a hundred pages and thousands of hours of work. "What are you doing? My book!"

"You have a backup, I'm sure," he said nonchalantly.

"Actually . . . I *don't*!"

"What?" he said, alarmed. "Why not?"

"I didn't know you were going to come over and take the thing apart."

"You have to back up your work every day!" he said sharply.

"Can you put my computer back together . . . with . . . without losing anything?"

"I don't know," he said, barely looking up at me as he continued to work on the computer's pieces. "We'll see."

I couldn't bear to watch what he was doing. I left him alone and tried to dispel my agitation by doing kitchen chores. All I could think of, as I clanked the silverware into the drawer, was how much could I remember of those pages and how could I possibly write them again. After an hour or so, he called me into the office; he was ready to fire up the computer. Both of us were annoyed, and we looked at each other warily. I quietly prayed to the computer gods that I hadn't lost everything.

"Don't worry," he said dismissively. "It'll be fine."

"Easy for you to say," I muttered.

He held his finger on the power button and the screen popped to life. Incredibly, Dad was right. He had fixed the problem—*and* my book was completely intact.

"Well, that's a skill," I say to Scott without telling him this story. I don't want him to sour on the idea just because it was something Dad loved to do too. "Maybe you could do something with computers. Maybe start a service to help people when their computers break. Like a tech rescue."

"Who's going to hire me? I don't have any credentials. Not even a college degree." He's so defensive that I don't know how to break through his fortress of negativity.

"It's a *possibility*," I say, trying to buoy him. "What else might you do?"

"Well, Elsa did say I should go back and finish my degree," he says. "But I don't know. I'm not sure if I could get through college now."

"How long would it take you to finish?" I ask, trying to sound neutral.

"Don't know. I think I'd have to take classes for a year and a half or so."

"Where would you go?" I ask.

He takes a sip of coffee and then adds, "But I doubt I have what it takes."

"You have what it takes," I blurt out. I just can't let his negative thoughts have their way. "I have no doubt."

"I don't have the focus," he snaps, "and I'm old now."

I recall an advice column I read long ago about education and aging.

"Remember what Ann Landers [the old syndicated advice columnist] used to say?

"What?"

"Years ago, some guy wrote her asking if he should enroll in medical school after getting his bachelor's degree as an older student. He told her, 'In four years, I'll be fifty-two. Should I go?' She gave him a great answer: 'And how old will you be in four years if you *don't* go to medical school?'"

He snorts at the story and then becomes quiet. For the first time in decades, he may be giving serious consideration to college.

Possibly for the first time ever.

Every so often, when I read some of my journal entries from those early days, I'm struck by how little I knew about my brother, how skeptical I was that we could establish any relationship, and how scared I was to try. I never imagined that we might develop a relationship where he would consult me on an important life decision, such as returning to college.

Before the fateful voice mail from my mother, I had reached the devastating conclusion that I needed to give up on my brother, and make peace with the fact that he did not want me in his life. I felt I had no other option.

Thankfully, I didn't need to come to terms with this bleak reality.

However, many estranged siblings are not so fortunate. They must accept their cutoff as permanent, find a way to grieve the loss of a brother or sister, and mourn the relationship they might have had.

But how? I wonder. How does a sibling accept this heartbreaking reality and live the best possible life without a brother or sister?

Letting Go of an Estranged Sibling

As difficult as it is to adjust to life without a sister or brother, many say it's even more difficult to maintain a tenuous relationship with them. Some survey respondents report that it's simply not worth the effort; they are tired of getting hurt, and they have no desire to reconcile.

However, that decision does not give them peace, as many survey respondents find themselves stuck in grief. One respondent asked, "How does one accept that their sibling doesn't love them or care enough to maintain a relationship? How can I move forward without rumination and resentment?"

Taking conscious steps toward accepting the reality of the estrangement may ease the grief. The relationship may not be salvageable, but the estranged can—and must—save themselves.

Necessary Steps toward Accepting the Loss of a Sibling Relationship

The first step in accepting the loss of a sibling relationship is to identify it and call it by its name. Simply stating, "We don't speak" or "He's never around" or "We don't get along," blurs the relationship status and reinforces denial of the situation. Instead, Dr. Agllias says it's important to confirm reality by admitting, "We are estranged," and to tell the story of what has happened. This benefits the individual and, at the same time, it helps to reduce societal stigma as more people talk about this underacknowledged phenomenon.

Dr. Agllias outlines a number of steps in accepting sibling loss. Achieving peace requires viewing the estrangement objectively and assessing the family patterns, and current and historical events that contributed to the dysfunctional relationship. A sibling needs to gain insight into why the cutoff occurred to alter his or her view of the relationship and commit to living again.

To drill down and truly comprehend the collapse of the relationship, it's necessary to avoid generalizing and stereotyping a sibling's characteristics and behaviors, as well as to recognize, if possible, some positive qualities the estranged sister or brother possesses. Another important and sometimes challenging step is identifying one's own role in the breakdown. To reduce or avoid feelings of guilt and shame, a sibling often denies or minimizes his or her role in the problems. But to learn and grow from the estrangement experience, it's important to take a hard look at oneself and attempt to change the behaviors that may have damaged the relationship.

If all this seems too daunting to achieve alone, the British organization Stand Alone has compiled a list of ways to cope. The organization recommends regularly visiting a therapist or counselor who will provide a safe space to speak about emotions, practicing meditation to feel more in control of emotions and gain a sense of perspective, exercising regularly to combat the negative feelings associated with estrangement, leaning on a partner for perspective and support, and accepting feelings as they present themselves.

Another aid in processing the loss is to write as a form of therapy. Putting feelings into words—privately, publicly in a chat room, or even by filling out my survey—may bring some relief.

Arlene Smith, seventy-two, hasn't spoken to her seventy-five-year-old sister, Lorraine, in twenty-five years. When they were children, the two were both sexually abused by their father. Each woman responded to the legacy of their abuse differently. Lorraine questioned why Arlene didn't limit contact with their father, why Arlene hadn't changed her last name as Lorraine did, and why Arlene chose to maintain a relationship with relatives who did nothing about the abuse. Eventually, Lorraine wrote Arlene a brief letter in 1993 that said, "I can't be your sister anymore."

The thought that she will never see her sister again preoccupies Arlene. To cope, she filled out my survey and posted this comment on the Facebook chat room page: "I took the survey and it felt therapeutic to tell my story again." She says she also is working on a memoir about her family story as a means to deal with her losses.

The work of Dr. James Pennebaker, a pioneer in writing therapy who teaches in the psychology department at the University of Texas at Austin, confirms the value of emotional writing or narrative therapy. In a landmark research project, he identified potential health benefits from the practice of writing from the heart for twenty minutes a day. Pennebaker's research has been replicated and validated hundreds of times.

To find peace in estrangement, it's important to recognize painful triggers and avoid them wherever possible. For example, put away photos or memorabilia that create distress, or block contact on social media. One member of an estranged siblings' chat room decided to protect herself from triggers by simply dropping out of the group. In her final message, she wrote that when she wakes up and reads the painful posts, she absorbs the pain of those who are hurting—so much so, that it takes a mental toll on her. To cultivate her own happiness, she said she had to drop out of the group, explaining that she no longer wishes to try to understand the perplexing topic of sibling estrangement.

It's not easy to avoid all triggers, especially during this past year when the world is coping with a pandemic. Many of the estranged have felt increased pressure to reach out to a remote brother or sister because of the life-threatening coronavirus. First, social distancing has promoted keeping in touch with family and friends through phone calls and video chats, and the estranged may feel alienated by that message. Second, having lost their routine, many of the estranged in chat rooms report that they are lonely and dwelling on their losses, wondering whether this is the moment when their estranged family member might be more receptive to reconciliation. Finally, some have become acutely aware of their own mortality, and fear they that if they don't contact an estranged sibling now, they might not have the chance.

Birthdays, holidays, a family's traditional events, and even Mother's Day also can upset the equilibrium of the estranged. One holiday that seems to particularly irritate those estranged from a brother or sister is America's National Siblings Day, April 10. On that day, social media is flooded with happy childhood photographs of siblings together and loving tributes to brothers and sisters. The day is a painful reminder to the estranged of the void in the lives, and many who don't live in the U.S. are relieved that their country doesn't commemorate a sibling holiday.

Estranged brothers and sisters who have adjusted to their circumstances anticipate these special days and other troublesome events. I was never very good at that. Each year as my brother's birthday approached, I wrestled with the same questions over and over again: *How is Scott doing? Is he celebrating? Should I send him a card, an email, a text?*

Those at peace with estrangement don't revisit this angst every year; they create new rituals or make some gesture to recognize the loss and see it in a more positive light. Those who cope best find meaning in the estrangement experience itself. Service to others who suffer from similar losses helps heal any trauma. Estranged siblings might participate in campaigns for awareness or in groups that provide support, thus reducing feelings of isolation and gaining insights from other members.

Creating a Family of Choice

Cultivating close, healthy relationships with others outside the family helps create a sense of belonging. "Voluntary kin can serve as excellent sources of support and fulfill the roles we associate with family," says Dr. Scharp. "Many people have a difficult time separating the idea of family from biology and law. Yet there is nothing inherent about biology or the law that guarantees a happy or satisfying sibling relationship."[2]

Many survey respondents have opened their hearts to surrogates or voluntary kin:

I'm starting to realize that most of the "sister" relationships that I crave can be met through loving, healthy friendships.

I've got a family made up of friends and coworkers. I had to create a whole new family. I'm hurt, but I'm enjoying life, as lonely as it is.

"Family" means little to me. What matters is how I'm loved by the people who choose to be in my life.

Gwen Preston, a fifty-five-year-old Australian woman who describes herself as a "white, Anglo-Saxon, university-educated atheist," hasn't spoken to her older sister in fifteen years. However, when Preston was diagnosed with breast cancer, she decided to contact her sister to warn her that she, too, might be at risk. To her shock, her sister told her that she had been diagnosed with breast cancer years ago. Despite the pain of this deep rift, Preston has made peace with her estrangement:

I believe the main factor behind this estrangement is that our mother was a child evacuee during the war (from England to Australia). We were raised without aunts, uncles, or cousins, without any model for an extended family. Our family life was extremely confusing, with peaceful times and emotional neglect, arguments, and shouting matches. Mum was emotionally neglected, and she has subconsciously passed this trauma on to us.

My sister has made it clear that I am not welcome in her life. She's very jealous and dismissive toward me and other family members. She stole our father's address book, went through it from A to Z, rang all the relatives and friends, and explained that they are no longer welcome in her life.

I think about my sister, but I refuse to miss her. The "emotional bank account" is empty, bankrupt. From an early age, I got my emotional needs met and found support in the children of a neighbor family. Even though they moved away, I am in constant contact with them. We refer to each other as sisters from other mothers.

Preston has discovered that what the late Maya Angelou once said is true: "Family isn't always blood. It's the people in your life who want you in theirs. The ones who accept you for who you are. The ones who would do anything to see you smile, and who love you no matter what."

Understandably, it may be easier to maintain a relationship with voluntary kin than with an actual sibling. First, friends aren't part of the original family's history and dysfunction, and they don't have an awareness of hot-button issues. Second, as discussed in earlier chapters, siblings have to differentiate themselves from brothers or sisters and sustain some connection. To accomplish this goal, siblings typically distance themselves from one another in young adulthood and reunite when boundaries are well established. None of this is necessary with voluntary kin.

New Challenges when an Estranged Sibling Is Terminally Ill or Dies

A terminal illness or the death of an estranged sibling presents a uniquely difficult moment for a surviving sibling. Some survey respondents who experienced or tried to anticipate the illness or death of an estranged sibling fell into a world of confusion:

When I found out my sister died, I didn't feel anything. We had not talked in months. I don't feel anything. No feelings of emptiness or loss.

I haven't talked to my 81-year-old brother in four years. What do I do when he dies? If he passes before me, should I go to the funeral?

My brother is a stranger to me. He has never been loving, comforting or supportive to me. I don't think I would bother to go to his funeral.

When the final curtain is about to fall on a sibling relationship, some feel compelled to take some kind of action. Rabbi Elliot Kukla, the first openly transgender person to be ordained by a Reform Jewish seminary, works in hospice in San Francisco and he warns that contact with an estranged family member before he or she dies may not be productive. "In my experience of serving people in hospice," he blogs, "you are equally as likely to regret what you *do* in haste as what you *don't do* out of caution. Enormous harm can be done, both to the dying person and their family, if they reconnect out of a panicked fear of regret. A visit that reopens old wounds can bring more regret than no visit at all."

Rabbi Kukla suggests that it might be more helpful to write a letter or a poem or send photos of yourself to an estranged relative who is dying. The letter doesn't need to say everything, and if the letter does say "everything," it may be best to never mail it.

One woman, however, found that she was able to heal old wounds at her estranged brother's deathbed. When confronted with his terminal illness, she felt she couldn't ignore him any longer. Their estrangement began when she reported to the police that another brother had sexually abused her. The terminally ill brother took the side of her abuser and lied to the police. Consequently, she cut him out of her life. After reconnecting with her brother on his deathbed, the two were able to talk about why he lied. He apologized, and she forgave him. Eventually, he passed away in her arms, and their final reconciliation gave her comfort and peace.

Blogger Traci Foust similarly chose to see her terminally ill estranged

sister before she died. In a moving essay called "What I Said to My Estranged Sister on Her Deathbed," Foust, who hadn't spoken to her only
sister for twelve years, describes what it felt like to see her one last time
when she was jaundiced, skinny, and her breathing was ragged:

> What ignorant cowards an unfixable past can make us. My sister was barely
> hanging on. . . . "Hold me," was the last thing she said. . . . I curled the whole
> front of my body into hers, squeezing through her sickness, trying to get in-
> side all those years we had wasted.[3]

Siblings who are confronted with an estranged sibling's death often are
as stunned and shocked by grief as those relatives who maintained a close
connection. Complicating matters, an added layer of loss and regret
plagues some estranged mourners. Death closes the door on any possible
reconciliation; thoughts of *"if only"* and *"I wish"* may torment an estranged
sister or brother. "Even loving and connected relationships usually hold
some regrets," explains Rabbi Kukla. "Our lives are not tied up in neat
bows at the end; we are messy, complex beings. This is even more true in
cases of estrangement. Having a regret is not the same thing as having
made the wrong choice."

A family funeral raises even more vexing questions. *What are my obligations to the deceased and the family when we haven't spoken in decades?
Should I make an appearance at the funeral? Should I send flowers or offer
condolences? If so, to whom?*

It's virtually impossible to generalize about the emotional response or
the best course of action when an estranged sibling dies. Sister Renee Pittelli, an adult-child recovery mentor and victims' advocate, and the founder
of an online support group called Luke 17.3 Ministries, conducted one
of the only surveys on whether to attend an estranged relative's funeral.
She found that only four of seventy-two respondents who filled out her
questionnaire said they would attend the funeral of an estranged family

member. Most felt no obligation to go to the funeral or to support others in the family—no matter how long they had been cut off or who had ended the relationship. Those who did not go said they had no regrets. Some expected to be criticized or judged for not attending, but they said that would not affect their decision. Sister Pittelli explains that families often expect relatives to mourn a relative, even if the deceased was an abuser.[4] Rabbi Kukla recommends that estranged loved ones who don't attend the funeral might conduct some sort of memorial service of their own to remember the deceased.

Kathy Gibbons, fifty-three, of Spokane, Washington, has thought about how she'll feel when her estranged sister—her only living relative—dies. The two haven't spoken in five years. Gibbons says she has no idea what normal grieving over death would feel like. Gibbons has thought about her own death, too, and she believes that when she passes, her body will likely go unidentified and she will be buried in an unclaimed mass grave.

Some of the estranged who have been devastated by painful losses even go as far as banning an estranged sibling from their funeral. This extreme position calls into question the very purpose of funerals. Are they for the dying, who will have the comfort of knowing that only friends and family will attend, or are they for the living, who will have the chance to grieve and say one final good-bye?

When asked in one of her "Dear Therapist" advice columns in *The Atlantic* about banning the estranged from a funeral, Lori Gottlieb, a psychotherapist and author of the bestseller *Maybe You Should Talk to Someone*, advocates settling scores before death. "If banning them from the funeral represents a final, public acknowledgment of her pain," she writes, "the one person who needs that acknowledgment most won't be alive to see it. So maybe it's worth considering what might bring your wife even more peace than their absence at her funeral: the opportunity to be heard by them now."[5]

Finding Peace after Estrangement

When an estranged sibling finally lets go of an irreparable relationship with a sister or brother, he or she often experiences posttraumatic growth—positive change that arises from adversity. This growth occurs when the estranged sibling develops a stronger sense of self, feels greater compassion for others, and acquires a greater appreciation for life.

The opposite of estrangement is not reconciliation, explains author Laura Davis. The opposite of estrangement is peace. "Even a failed reconciliation can open a new door," she writes, "bringing deeper self-knowledge, unexpected opportunities, new chances to love, and ultimately a sense of peace."[6]

The Facebook chat room posts of forty-one-year old Canadian Stephanie Bleacher, who has commented on her journey in previous chapters, serve as a kind of diary of her suffering and recovery. She remains estranged from one of her five sisters.

In January 2018, Stephanie reported that her estrangement with her sister was poisoning the whole family. "Last night, I confronted my entire family about how I was feeling isolated," she posted. "They got very defensive and said they've tried to work with her, but she won't budge. I don't know why she hates me. I wish I could ask. I may never know." At her lowest point during her two years of posts, she admitted, "I feel constantly attacked and judged, like people think I'm a bad person. Sometimes I don't want to exist at all. The pain is unbearable."

Stephanie was determined to find joy in her life with or without her estranged sister. With the support of the Facebook group, psychotherapy, and other loving relationships, Stephanie posted her progress: "Enjoyment of life post-estrangement is possible . . . having a great time!" she wrote in August 2018. "Focusing on people who love and accept me and letting go of those who don't." Occasionally she lifted up others in the chat room when they struggled: "Hang in there, Terri. Let go of expectation. . . . Know your value and seek people who are good to you. . . . In the meantime, be good to yourself. I've been there . . . or maybe somewhere similar . . ."

Two years after her first post, she made a surprising announcement: "Hey gang," she wrote, "I'm happy to say at this time, I no longer need this group! Not because my sister and I are no longer estranged, but because I've made peace with it. *Namaste!* Love to you all on your journey."

Chapter 15

The Dreaded Holidays
for the Estranged

THE CRADLE NURSERY
Winter 2014

I lean hard on the security buzzer at the back entrance of the Cradle, but there's no answer. Tightening my scarf and pulling my jacket hood over my head, I figure the nursery must have lots of babies tonight; otherwise, one of the three nurses on duty would have buzzed me in right away. A slashing wind burns my face as the wet, slushy snow starts to seep through my boots. I hate to push the button again if they're busy, but I'm freezing, and now I wonder if anyone heard me the first time. I wait a few seconds—it seems like five minutes, at least—and then I press the buzzer again.

At last, Rosie comes through on the intercom: "Who is it?"

"You know who, Rosie," I say. "It's Sunday night. Who else would it be? It's Fern."

"Fern who?" She's cozy and warm indoors, just playing with me.

"Rosie! Quit messing around. It's freezing out here!"

She presses the buzzer to unlock the door, and I quickly grab the handle so I won't get locked out.

Walking out of the elevator on the fourth floor, I see that the nursery windows have been redecorated with seasonal paper cutouts of holiday wreaths, Christmas ornaments, menorahs, and Kwanzaa candelabras. Draped across the top of the window is a sign heralding all of the holidays: "Season's Greetings!"

In the nursery, Rosie is filling out forms at the counter.

"How many ounces did Jessie take?" she calls out to Linda, one of the other nurses on duty.

"Three," Linda says. Rosie notes the number, then looks up from her paper and sees me standing next to her. Grinning, she reaches over to dramatically brush the snowflakes off my jacket. "Sorry! Just kidding!"

"Yeah, right." I roll my eyes while unzipping my wet coat.

Looking past Rosie, I scan through the slats of the cribs. To my surprise, I count only five babies. "Quiet night," I say.

"Yeah, a few went home last week."

"Oh, great!" Then I ask about a couple of babies I cuddled two weeks ago. One mother changed her mind, Rosie says, and decided to take her son home to raise herself. The other baby found a home with a gay male couple. This is a common Cradle placement practice, given that some biological mothers prefer gay men as parents. That way, the biological mothers remain the only moms in their children's lives.

Adoptive parents working with the Cradle select their babies' names, but they're required to keep as a middle name what the biological mother chose. Once in a while, a heartbroken mother who forfeits her baby chooses a name that contains a message. One mother, for example, coined the name "Lya," telling the staff that its letters stood for "Loving You Always."

When Rosie told me the story of Lya, it struck me that adoption is another form of estrangement. I'm reminded again that the reason I volunteered to cuddle years ago was not only to mitigate the hurt of separation for these babies but also to subconsciously address the loss of connection in my own family.

"How are things?" Rosie asks as she sits down. I take the rocking chair next to her.

"Not great." I know she's really asking how Scott is doing. "Seems like I just keep trading worries."

"So what's the latest?"

I tell her about Scott's job frustrations, explaining that I wish he could do something with his two strong skills, technology and finance.

"He's pretty discouraged," I say. "But it seems like he can fix anything electronic—computers, video equipment, networks. He just doesn't know where to start. He doesn't know how to get some sort of business going. He's so demoralized—"

"Wait!" Rosie raises her hand like a stop sign. "iPhones? Can he fix them?"

"I'm sure."

"I can't get my phone to download pictures," she says. "It's such a problem. It would be great if he could straighten that out for me. Give me his number!"

I pick up my phone and share Scott's contact information with her.

"Come to think of it," Rosie adds while checking her phone, "I have a few other things he can do for me too. Do you think he'd mind giving me a ride to Lombard next week to visit a friend? I hate driving that far, and I always get lost."

I know Rosie's husband no longer works because of a disabling illness, and she supports both of them on her meager nurse's salary from the Cradle. She must *really* hate to drive that far, I think, if she's willing to find money in her tight budget to pay Scott for a ride.

"Rosie," I say, "honestly, I think he'd do anything right now. He just wants to feel productive and make some money."

One of the babies starts to howl in the corner of the nursery, and Rosie gets up to comfort him. Throughout the rest of the evening, we're preoccupied with five needy newborns, all wanting to be fed and hugged at the same time. The babies keep us hopping, and at one point, Rosie turns to me and says, "Funny how some nights, five can be more demanding than ten!"

After that busy evening at the Cradle, I completely forget about Rosie's promise to get in touch with Scott. I even forgot to mention it to him. A week later, I get an unexpected text from Rosie telling me she has just returned home after spending several hours in the car with my brother, who drove her to and from Lombard.

Rosie: LOVED Scott.

Me: Oh, great!

Rosie: Talked the entire way to Lombard.

Me: Wow! Sometimes, he's pretty quiet, so you must have really clicked. That's great!

Rosie: He's my new BFF.

How great! I'm thrilled the two of them hit it off.

A week later, on a Saturday afternoon, my phone rings. I'm startled to see that it's Rosie calling. Usually we talk only at the Cradle, so she must have something on her mind.

"Lots has happened since I last saw you," she says right after she says hello. "I need to discuss something with you."

"Oh?"

She takes a breath so deep I can hear it clearly. "My ninety-year-old stepmother-in-law died two weeks ago," she says, her voice heavy with sadness. "Then, a few days later, my hundred-year-old father-in-law went. He seemed to die of a broken heart."

"Oh, Rosie!" I say. "I'm so sorry."

I know Rosie had taken on some of the work of caring for her in-laws in recent years, especially since her husband became ill and hasn't been able to do much. She often mentions visiting their eldercare residence to check on them. As a nurse, she organized their medications and monitored their doctor appointments; of course, she also ran plenty of errands.

Now, with this call, I realize I can feel the nature of our friendship changing—but I don't know how, or why, or what to say.

"That's a lot to deal with at one time, Rosie."

"Yes," she sighs. "It's really sad."

It's not uncommon, I'm thinking, to hear about loving couples who die within days of each other, but I hadn't given much thought to how hard it is for the surviving family to mourn both at the same time.

"And there's so much to do," she continues. "I just finished planning both of their funerals, and now I have to get rid of all their stuff—which they've accumulated for *decades*—and clear out their place. I don't even know where to start."

Is she asking me for help with these tasks? I'm about to offer when she says, "And there's more."

"What's that?"

"I think we stand to receive a small inheritance. About a hundred thousand dollars."

"Oh, well . . . that's nice."

"But you know, my husband is too sick to help me with any of this."

"What can I—"

"And I really don't know anything about money," she goes on, sounding more and more overwhelmed.

Then she stops for a moment, takes another deep breath, and says, "So I was wondering . . ." Now she sounds tentative, a little nervous.

Another deep breath. "Do you think Scott would help me settle the estate?"

Really? Is *that* all? I'm happy she's thinking of Scott for work, but I'm not sure she really needs him.

"You sure you can't manage this on your own?" I ask. "That's not all that much money. I don't think it's complicated to settle a small estate like that."

"I'm not sure," she says, and then she laughs a little. "You know, if you need an injection, I'm your girl. But when it comes to money, I have no clue."

A few weeks later, Rosie and Scott both fill me in on what happened the day Scott went to Rosie's house to have a look at the task of settling the estate.

On a frigid afternoon in late December, he found his way to her modest ranch, located in Skokie. Holocaust survivors transformed this bedroom community near Chicago's northern border after World War II. Here the newcomers built synagogues, Hebrew schools, Jewish bakeries, community centers, tailor shops, and other old-world businesses. For a time, Skokie had the feel of an American shtetl.

As Scott walked up the path to Rosie's door, he passed her small garden in the front yard, which Rosie lovingly tends in the warm months. All spring and summer, passersby pause to see what's blooming in her lush, colorful array of heirloom perennials—some of which she divided and shared with cuddlers every fall. Scott noticed that Rosie had planted something else, right in the center of the garden: a sign draped with snow on this January day, benevolently announcing SKOKIE WELCOMES EVERYONE. It was Rosie's response to the anti-immigrant sentiment so troublingly evident in recent years.

Indoors, Rosie was all business, immediately directing Scott to four big, bulging cardboard boxes that had taken over her dining room table.

"What's this?" Scott asked, staring at the boxes.

"It's my in-laws' financial life," she announced without a trace of humor.

Scott was stunned. Even if Rosie knew plenty about money, he now understood why she said she had no idea how to settle the estate. Bank statements, paycheck stubs, annual reports, dividend receipts, contracts, random notes: The elderly couple's entire portfolio was stuffed into the boxes. They had never used computers; they had never organized current investment records, or even ancient ones, into files or folders.

"This is it?" Scott asked in utter disbelief. "This is all you have?"

He fished out one of the hundreds of unopened envelopes in one over-stuffed box and held it up. It was a statement from a mutual fund. In fact, most of the envelopes were still sealed, as if someone had lost interest years ago in managing or even monitoring the money.

"Isn't there any record of accounts?" he asked. "Or some sort of clear-inghouse that would show what they have?"

"Nope," Rosie said, biting her lip. "This is it."

She watched Scott fretfully as he eyeballed each of the overfilled boxes, assessing the job. She was worried he wouldn't work with her—that she would be stuck having to sort through this unbearable mess herself.

"Will you help me? I'll pay you," she pleaded, not knowing where to turn if he refused.

"I . . . I don't know," Scott said. "I don't know if I can."

"Why not?" Rosie pressed him in her usual direct manner.

"This . . . this is no small task," he answered. "It's like a forensic ac-counting job. These are the only records you have, and that means that I'm going to have to chase down every account in your in-laws' names. And I'll have to do it all on the phone. That's time-consuming, and I don't want my meter, the lawyer's fees, and the taxes to run through your hundred-thousand-dollar inheritance."

Scott looked Rosie straight in the eye and saw her deep anxiety. He grasped her fear and sadness, and he probably saw himself.

"Okay," he said, realizing he couldn't refuse her in her desperation.

Rosie let out a long sigh of relief.

Scott smiled. "I'll see what I can do."

It's the holidays, and that fact is evident everywhere—from the decorations in the Cradle Nursery window to the miniature Christmas trees in every office. It's the time of year Norman Rockwell idealized in his romanticized rendering of the family—eleven people spanning three generations—seated around the Thanksgiving table with its bounteous, turkeycentric spread of food. The 1943 painting sets the standard for what American holidays *should* look like: joyous kin of all ages, gathered to enjoy the warmth, comfort, and love only a family can provide.

This is not a familiar scene for the estranged, who are constantly reminded of their losses during the last months of each year. Seasonal advertising, holiday movies, customized greeting cards, social media—all present glowing pictures of happy families together, laughing and loving as they celebrate. Festive decorations and well-meaning greetings are ubiquitous; even National Public Radio inadvertently twists the knife. One host innocently blindsided estranged listeners with these familiar words: "Happy Thanksgiving! Hope you are spending the holiday with your family."

The estranged may be fortunate enough to have *some* of their loved ones at their holiday tables, but it's also a time when they take measure of who is missing. Their losses are captured in the haunting, poignant Civil War song called "The Vacant Chair," which describes the empty place where a beloved soldier and family member, now gone, once sat at the table.

When Scott and I were estranged, that vacant chair haunted me all year long, but my chronic sense of emptiness was especially acute from October until January. This is the first year in decades that I don't feel trepidation and dismay as the fourth Thursday in November approaches. We're not planning to bring the two families together because my children remain suspicious of our reconciliation. Still, at least, this year the holidays won't underscore my losses. I tell myself that, even if our reconciliation is temporary, I'm relieved to be released, however briefly, from that unrelenting seasonal turmoil.

The Holiday Season: Dread, Resentment, and Increased Loneliness

I remain curious to see how others who are estranged bear up to these annual hurts. In the fall, I begin to keep close tabs on the online estrangement chat rooms to monitor increasing tensions and anxieties that spill out during the drumroll leading up to Thanksgiving and the December holidays. Now that retailers are displaying festive decorations in the early fall, lengthening the holiday season to take full advantage of profits, the suffering goes on longer than ever for the estranged.

In mid-November, members of the estrangement chat rooms share a few wry jokes about estrangement and the holidays. One chat room member suggests that a way to get relatives speaking to one another again is to send out a heartfelt Christmas card with a photograph of the family with an extra child nobody knows. Another poster quips that the picture should include a new husband.

However, the mood in the chat rooms turns somber as Thanksgiving approaches. Members post dark and depressed thoughts, expressing their raw emotions to strangers online. Their grieving is palpable. Many members admit that every year they suffer from October to December, when the hurts of estrangement reach an emotional crescendo. Many say depression and low self-worth blindside them. They recognize that the holidays perpetuate the fantasy of a loving family, and most people don't have that experience. Still, some admit that they wake up during the night crying in their sleep over the devastating loss of a brother or sister.

Not every estranged sibling, however, finds the holidays a time of mourning. Some are liberated and relieved that they *don't* have to spend long days with "loved ones" and attend strained gatherings at their families' homes—though it's not easy to answer the ubiquitous question every acquaintance seems to ask: "What are you doing for the holidays?"

Even for those who severed family relations, the holidays spent alone may force a reevaluation of whether a complete cutoff is absolutely the right and healthy choice.

One distressed member makes a creative suggestion to help others in the group by asking them to reframe their holiday experiences. Instead of focusing on their emptiness and losses, she asks them to contemplate what they don't miss about the holiday dinners. Their long list includes a sister's stuffing, drunk relatives who thoughtlessly make cutting remarks, and some uncle's incessant political diatribe.

Often chat room members ask others for guidance on how to resolve problematic situations. One woman, who hasn't heard much from her siblings since her parents died nine years ago, wonders if she is obliged to maintain a holiday connection. Throughout the year, she says, there are no phone calls, no emails, no visits. But when Christmas comes around, her family holds an obligatory gathering at a restaurant for lunch. They spend one hour with each other, talk about superficial things, and exchange presents. Then everyone goes home, and they have no contact again for another year. She is tired of this pattern, and she wonders whether she should stop the charade that they have a holiday get-together or a family.

Coping with the Holidays without Family

Members debate with one another about how to handle specific problems, but as the holiday season grinds on, tensions in the chat rooms rise, and the frustrations that simmer below the surface spill out onto the pages.

One member who is getting into spats and arguments with these strangers on the page barks that she joined the group for a supportive, nonjudgmental place to vent. She begs members who can't find something constructive or supportive to say to keep their comments to themselves. The tenor of conversations in the chat rooms is less compassionate and more irritable and edgy during the last months of the year, as members struggle to maintain their balance and sanity during these difficult days.

Weeks pass, and as Christmas approaches, many who have no intention or hope of spending the day with relatives worry about being all alone. One woman rejoices that she received a coveted invitation for Christmas dinner from friends: She says she feels like she won the lottery because this alleviates the alienation, stress, and sadness she typically feels on that day. But for those who have no place to go, the talk turns to how to spend the dreary, lonely, family-focused days.

Interviewees and chat room members offer a number of suggestions about how to cope with the holidays:

- Help out at a crisis center for homeless people or refugees to surround yourself with people who, unlike family, may appreciate your time and efforts.
- Attend Christmas services and organize a peaceful day to appreciate the good things in your life, and avoid dwelling on what's missing. Go for a walk to see Christmas lights.
- Take time for yourself. Don't feel obligated to spend the holidays as one "should." Spend time with friends or watch Netflix, if you like. Take a trip, organize closets, or do projects you've put off.
- Delete social media apps during the holidays so technology doesn't add salt to your wounds.
- Start new traditions to make the holidays less stressful and more fun. Create new memories.

- Decorate your home, make really nice meals, plan some entertainments like a concert or visit the botanical gardens.
- Be grateful that you don't have to deal with family drama.

Still, many wish the calendar would fast-forward to January to skip the holiday madness. One forlorn chat room member who desperately wants company on December 25 extends a generous open invitation that reveals the deep connection she feels to this cyber community: "Hello to all members," she writes. "If there is anyone spending Christmas alone in my area or somewhere in New Mexico, you are welcome to come to dinner at my home. Hugs to all of you."

Chapter 16

The Benefits of Reconciling
with an Estranged Sibling

A few days after meeting with Rosie, Scott plunges into her boxes like a zealous Dumpster diver. He arrives early and works through the day, sorting and listing what he finds in an exemplary spreadsheet.

Around three in the afternoon, he leaves, with a promise to Rosie that he'll return early tomorrow. Once in his car, he immediately calls me.

"Oh my God!" he says the moment I answer the phone.

"What's wrong?" Instantly, I panic. I've never heard him sound like this before.

"You're never going to believe this!"

"What happened?" My heart is pounding. Even though we've been back in touch for nine months now, I'm still learning to read him—especially on the phone.

"I found an account in one of the boxes!"

"Oh." That's no surprise; it's what Rosie hired him to do. "What kind of account?"

"A *big* account."

"How much?"

"A CD worth a ton of money!"

"Wait . . . what? I thought the estate was worth a hundred thousand dollars."

"Yeah, that's what Rosie thought. But this is just *one* account, so it must be worth a lot more than that. Those boxes are stuffed with statements from different accounts."

"But some may be duplicates." I've recovered enough to provide the voice of reason. "You know, multiple quarterly statements from the same accounts."

"Who knows?" Scott sounds delighted. "I have no idea what all is in there."

The next day at three, I get another call.

"Oh my God!" It's the same happy voice.

"What? What did you find?" I ask, now that I know where this is going.

"I can't believe this!"

"What?"

"A life insurance policy worth double what I found yesterday!"

"Wait—so now the estate is at least *triple* what she thought?"

"Yep. I can't imagine what else is in those boxes."

The next day at three—yes, there's the phone.

"Oh my God!" It's his standard salutation now. "Today I really hit the jackpot!"

"What did you find?"

"A mutual fund account worth a boatload of money."

"This is unbelievable," I say, shaking my head. "Have you told her?"

"Not yet. I don't want to say anything until I have a full accounting."

"She'll be shocked! She'll feel like she won the lottery!"

"Yeah," he says happily, "this will blow her mind!"

"I can't imagine how she'll—"

"Hey," Scott interrupts, "who *are* these people? Her in-laws. What do you know about them?"

"Nothing," I tell him. It's the simple truth. When Rosie and I talked at the Cradle about her in-laws, we discussed their health and care. She never mentioned their names or what they did in life. I really don't know a thing about Rosie's family.

The "Oh my God!" calls continue every afternoon for several weeks as Scott uncovers more and more assets: bank accounts, mutual funds, bonds, limited partnerships, fur coats, art, jewelry, real estate. There's even a Picasso painting in storage. When Scott finally reaches the bottom of the boxes and tallies up the total, we learn that Rosie and her husband are suddenly worth far more than they ever could have dreamed.

This is a couple who, out of necessity, have never been anything but frugal. Rosie conscientiously has clipped coupons for grocery shopping and restaurants. Goodwill has always been her first stop for clothes shopping. They have rarely traveled, and after struggling every year to pay their property tax bill of three thousand dollars or so, they have never had enough money to even think about investing.

After discovering the full extent of the estate, Scott goes online to learn more about the in-laws. His report about her family is almost as surprising as the estate itself. Rosie's father-in-law ran a large candy company that specialized in Dutch-processed chocolate, which provided a richer, creamier taste than others. Eventually, the Fannie May candy company purchased his company, which operated some fifty shops in the Chicago area during the 1940s, '50s, and '60s. When Scott mentions the candy company, I remember that the one time I stopped by Rosie's home to drop something off, I noticed unusual decorations hanging on the wall: two antique tin molds, one for Easter bunny chocolates, another for toy soldiers.

Rosie's stepmother-in-law was, of all things, an old-fashioned gossip columnist whose work appeared in several major Chicago newspapers. She wrote about society and show business every week for sixty-five years, and she became wealthy in her own right. A shrewd investor with a knack for savvy financial decisions, Rosie's stepmother-in-law had the foresight to put her money into a limited partnership whose first project blossomed into a major Chicago restaurant chain—and an enormous, long-term windfall for the estate.

Once Scott has identified all of Rosie's assets, he needs some time to meticulously prepare his presentation for her. Finally, on a morning in early March, they sit down at her newly available dining room table to go over the inheritance. As he speaks, Rosie listens carefully. He goes through all of the accounts and numbers on his spreadsheet before giving her the final tally on the last page of his document.

As his pencil moves down the ledger lines, Scott watches Rosie's reactions carefully. Her eyebrows shoot up and her eyes grow wide as he points out the zeros before the decimal on each holding. As they add up, she tries to take in these mind-boggling figures—and an equally mind-boggling life change.

Then, at the final page, Rosie's mouth falls open. She begins to gasp for air. The news is so shocking, her reaction so physical, that Scott fears she might have a heart attack right then and there.

"*How* much?" she finally asks in a shaky voice. "How much?" she says over and over again. "How can that *be*?"

"I'm just telling you what I discovered," Scott says calmly.

"But what am I going to do?" she asks Scott, her hands shaking. Her reaction is strangely off, as if the good news she's receiving is actually bad news.

"This is wonderful," he reassures her, but Rosie is too overwhelmed to comprehend her good fortune. Instead, as she tries to grasp this new reality, she becomes fixated on the terms Scott used during his presentation that she didn't understand. Having jotted down a few words as he spoke, she fires off questions from her list: "What is a limited partnership? What's preferred stock? A real estate investment trust? What is compound interest? What is dividend reinvesting?"

Finally she throws up her hands and announces, "I simply don't know where to start." She tells Scott that her husband has always handled their money matters, and she doesn't even know how to transfer the accounts to her name.

"How will I ever manage?" She looks at Scott pleadingly again.

"Well," he says, "I can help."

On the spot, Rosie offers Scott a job as her personal financial adviser, and they begin the long process of settling the estate and managing the money. Initially the job is quite demanding, requiring daily phone calls and twice-weekly meetings. The two seem to work well together. Rosie deeply values Scott's financial knowledge and his dogged determination to discover every last dollar she and her husband should receive. Her trust in Scott—his honesty as well as his skills and wisdom—is equally valuable to him.

One afternoon in April, after several weeks of working for Rosie, Scott calls me again from the car.

"You know," he says, "now that I have a job, I've made a decision."

Scott has always struggled with decision making, so I'm curious to hear what he's resolved to do.

"I have money to pay for tuition now," he announces, "so I'm going to go back and finish my college degree."

"Oh, Scott!" I'm absolutely stunned. "That's wonderful."

"I think I can do it in under two years," he says.

"Wow!" It's all I can say as I absorb the goal he has set for himself at the age of sixty-two. I admire his resilience; I don't know if I would have what it takes to go back to school in my sixties.

I try to swallow the lump in my throat, but tears stream down my cheeks anyway.

"That's really something!" I say lamely. I want to go on, but I bite my tongue, knowing that he needs to own this decision without feeling the weight of the past.

Still I wish I could tell him what I know to be true:

Dad would be so proud of you.

After I hang up the phone, I realize the lump in my throat is a joyous mix of accomplishment, pride, and satisfaction. I replay our conversation: Scott has decided to return to school—not for Dad but for *himself*, and he called to share his exciting news with me.

It has taken us nearly a year to get to this sweet place. We have found a path through a variety of struggles, negotiating a range of emotions— anger, frustration, guilt, shame, regret, and remorse. Tensions have erupted, but when an issue divides us, we share our feelings. If one of us loses perspective, the other quickly invokes our mantra: "Move forward. Leave the past behind." We've even come up with a visual metaphor. We remind each other to pack up bitter feelings, lock them in a suitcase, and abandon the baggage on the side of the road.

Both of us carry within us the dark days, months, and years we've lost. Neither one of us wants to be robbed again of our roles as a brother or a sister.

Committing to Reconciliation

Some who reconcile eagerly hope to return to the relationship that once existed. Those siblings are nostalgic for their childhood connection, however, a reconciled relationship will never revert to what it once was. It may be better or worse, but it won't be the same.

"It's important to approach the reconciliation as a 'new' relationship, rather than with someone you've known for your entire life," says psychotherapist Alexandra Butler. "The connection that you and your sibling are building is fragile—and will ultimately take time, patience, and a commitment to each other to develop in a healthy manner."[1]

For those who choose to pursue a sibling relationship, many survey respondents report that they have found ways to establish a fresh relationship with a sister or brother:

> I wouldn't exactly call this a "reconciliation," but perhaps a surrender that I'll graciously accept. I invited my only full biological brother, with whom I was estranged, to stay in my home while he got on his feet.

> I invited my estranged sister to my son's graduation party. She did show up. (She didn't RSVP, so I wasn't sure if she would.) I put my arm around her, said hello, and exchanged small talk. That's it. Then she invited me to her son's party for the next weekend. I know it will be perfectly fine. I have control. I can leave anytime.

> I'm determined to resolve things with my sister, though it's hard to get over all the hurts and betrayals. But I'm so sad that we've missed out on so many

important events in each other's lives. We are going to do several sessions with my therapist on Skype. I hope this works.

Estrangement was very hard on me, so my reconciliation with my only brother has been very positive. With the deaths of both parents, I am the only remaining family member. We are very close now. We have been making up for lost time.

Sadly, a sibling's negative traits that fueled the original cutoff may still be part of his or her personality, and those characteristics may continue to define some reconciled relationships. Consequently, those siblings may need to evaluate carefully and regularly if their difficult sister or brother will ever change, and whether distance or a cutoff is the best insulation from toxicity or abuse.

The Long Shadow of Estrangement

As exhilarating and satisfying as it is to reconnect, it's impossible to erase the damage of estrangement to many family members. In earlier chapters, Sam and Rachel Goldman discussed how estrangement affected each of them. (Sam had withdrawn from the family because he felt judged for marrying a woman who wasn't Jewish.) Now they feel their recently established bond has brought them support, a safety net of comfort, and a sense of belonging. Yet both recognize that the consequences of their cutoff linger.

Rachel describes the toll estrangement took on her:

When my brother left his marriage of over thirty years, we were able to resume our relationship. A weight was lifted; my anxiety subsided. I'm just so grateful I have a brother now. Time heals, but scars remain. I hardly know

his children or grandchildren, and that probably won't change. It makes
me sad.

Sam deeply regrets his choices that led to the breakdown in his relationship with his sister. He continues to suffer with grief and remorse. Their reconciliation has brought some relief, however, giving him a sense of wholeness:

For decades, I felt I failed as an older brother. I felt terribly guilty, which can be a powerful motivator to change, or it can freeze a person in inaction. To my great disappointment, I chose inaction. I was angry at myself for freezing my sister out of my life, and I felt I didn't know how to change things.

Often there's a catalyst for reconciliation—some event that shakes an ingrained pattern. After I left my wife of over thirty years, I called my sister, and in that conversation, years of superficial, forced communication dissolved.

After we talked, I knew it would take a lot of work to avoid falling back into old habits. I was determined to change. Developing a relationship with a formerly estranged sibling requires recognition of one's own failings, humility, patience, persistence, and a sense of optimism. Despite all the division and sadness, it's important to believe there can be a better tomorrow.

I promised myself I would never let too much time pass before speaking with my sister. I validated her by acknowledging how important she was in my life. I apologized to her for my wrongs. I decided to always take time to visit her and be interested in her family. I knew I had to prove that I am worthy of her trust and intimacy.

I'm still haunted by the fact that so many years passed without any communication with my only living sibling—the one person on earth who most understood me. She and I shared life's biggest successes and deepest traumas. We experienced the death of our father as teenagers, the death of our mother and younger sister as adults.

When we fail in our most intimate relationships, we don't develop the confidence to succeed in other less daunting tasks. It's almost as if a momentum builds, and I recognized I had to stop that force that had tainted other parts of my life. Now that we are no longer estranged, I feel a sense of wonder at how comfortable I am in our relationship. My family is complete.

Those who reconcile often feel a sense of partnership with their siblings as they rediscover the link of their common bond of history. Reconciliation may bring relief, a lightness of being, and contentment.

The Broader Benefits of Reconciliation

Tackling and solving any intractable problem alters how we see ourselves. It's especially satisfying, even hopeful, to conquer the challenge of rebuilding a shattered sibling relationship. Renewing that bond with any degree of success produces relief, closure, and a rewarding resolution, even if the relationship is less than picture-perfect.

Many reconciled brothers and sisters, as Sam described, discover that they have a sense of accomplishment, greater self-esteem, enhanced self-confidence, and a general feeling of optimism toward the larger world. Having learned to cooperate and negotiate with each other, reconciled siblings may apply these new communication and life skills to other difficult issues. When I think of my reconciliation with Scott, I wonder if our renewed relationship may have helped him develop the confidence to take on the challenge of completing his college education.

In the best situations, reconciled siblings no longer avoid difficult conversations in their other relationships with family, friends, and coworkers. They are able to live more authentically, and they learn that there's no need to fear confrontation. Those who live authentically know a fundamental, counterintuitive, and transformative truth: Conflict may be an opportunity for growth. In any relationship, disagreements are inevitable, and they may be deeply unsettling. However, those who have lived through estrangement know the dangers of avoiding a dispute.

A clash with another person may offer insight into ourselves, raising a fundamental question: Why do I feel so strongly about this issue? A dispute may spotlight what we need to change in ourselves, as well as in the affected relationship. Often, sparring siblings frame arguments in a win-lose context when it's actually important to simply acknowledge and understand one another's thoughts and feelings. Conflict resolution, as Hicks identified in the Dignity Model, requires careful listening, which is actually a powerful statement of love and respect. A dispute and the discussion that follows it can be a pathway to greater intimacy.

Chapter 17

Other Remarkable Reunions
of Estranged Siblings

THE CRADLE NURSERY

Spring 2015

On my way into the nursery, I stop for a look at the construction paper decorations celebrating spring—the same ones that brightened the window a year ago. An explosion of bright-green buds and bursting hot-pink flowers, all popping right off their brown branches, frame the glass. I remember thinking last year that the colorful, riotously optimistic display ran counter to my anxious outlook. This year, the dazzling spring flowers are right on target, echoing the beauty of this gratifying moment in my life. So much has changed in one year, and this place has had a large role in the transformation.

"Hey, Fern," Rosie calls out when she sees me lingering at the window. I cup my hands around my eyes to peer through the glass. Rosie and the two other nurses—some with two infants in their arms—are juggling too many crying babies.

"Get in here! We need you!"

Inside the nursery, four of the seven resident babies are howling at the same time. Then, in a domino effect, they wake up the other three who were sound asleep in their cribs. Each infant seems to be competing to be the loudest. Whenever all the babies start crying at once, I think of sirens blaring in a fire station: We're all first responders.

I grab a gown to dive in and help. Some of the babies are wet, hungry, or tired; some just want the maternal warmth and love of our touch. All four caregivers are swept up in a tidal wave of baby needs.

When the noise and chaos crescendo, I call out to Rosie, "I wish I were an octopus! We need more arms!" I try to comfort the newborn I'm holding with a pacifier, but he keeps spitting it out and screaming louder. I picked him up so quickly that I didn't even see his name. "Who is this little guy, anyway?" I ask.

Rosie is too busy with her own armful to answer. While comforting a baby, she is using her other hand to press buttons on the old boom box to start some music. Finally the archaic machine starts to play, and I catch a snippet here and there of a pianist performing some Bach piece. The babies drown out the music that was supposed to soothe them, and the occasional piano notes I hear only seem to contribute to the noise.

In these moments in the nursery, I lose track of time. Seconds feel like minutes, and minutes feel like hours. The babies' desperate wails torment me.

Knowing this, Rosie calls out, as she does almost every time I'm in the nursery: "You've been doing this for years. You should be used to baby chaos by now. Don't be so sensitive."

"I can't help it," I say, and then I give her my usual response. "That's why I'm a good cuddler."

Finally, after a solid half hour of ear-piercing wails, the babies wear themselves out. One by one, their cries turn to moans, then whimpers; they sniff and shudder and, at last, the nursery becomes mercifully quiet. The nurses and I exchange quick, tentative, relieved glances. Some babies are sleeping in their bouncy seats; others are dozing in our arms. Barely breathing, we quietly creep over to the cribs and place the infants we're carrying in them, then tiptoe away, elaborately careful not to set off the alarm again. When a baby whines in his or her sleep, one of us jumps to wind up the colorful mobile that tinkles, "It's a Small World" or reset the vibrating bouncy seats. All of us need a break.

As soon as we settle into the rocking chairs, Rosie says, "Things are going really well with Scott."

"I'm so glad." I can't help grinning. "He loves working with you." Then I shake my head and add, "I still can't get over how all this turned out."

"You?" she asks incredulously. "Look at me. I'm still trying to adjust to having money."

"That shouldn't be all that tough," I smile at her. Then I add, "You know, I've been wondering. Why did you think the estate was only worth a hundred thousand dollars?"

She explains that the misleading figure was a result of her in-laws' reluctance to discuss money. Rosie tells me that she knew they were wealthy, but she assumed that whatever money they had was being eaten up by the cost of their two full-time caregivers. As a nurse, Rosie was well aware of how intensive care can run up big bills. She figured her in-laws had paid more than $350,000 a year for nursing care for the past three years. That would add up to more than $1 million, and she was sure those staggering costs had depleted their estate.

"I just can't get over all that's happened," I repeat. "So I have to ask you, how did you decide . . . I mean, why did you do this for my brother?"

Rosie looks at me directly and says, "Well, remember the first time you walked into the nursery?"

"A long time ago!" I say. "Yeah?"

"We started talking that day. We just clicked. You shared my values and my outlook. You were one of those people I felt like I had always known."

"Yes, I felt that way too," I say, gazing around the nursery, which looks exactly the same as it did on that day.

"I remember telling you, 'I'll make your schedule for you.' That way, I could make sure we worked together on Sundays."

"Yes, I've always worked your shift," I say.

"During our time together," she continues, "I got to trust and love you. We've talked about all kinds of things—recipes, plants, adoptions, children, marriages.

"So when you told me about your problems with your brother and what you were trying to do for him as he was recovering, I wanted to do anything I could to support you."

"And you did," I say. "Just by listening—"

"I know that helped," she says. A baby stirs, and both of us immediately turn our heads toward him. I start to get up from my rocking chair, but Rosie stops me: "Leave him. He's only half awake." Without missing a beat, she proceeds to her point. "And that's what we do for each other here in the nursery. We nurture babies, and then we nurture each other.

"But then I thought about things, and I figured I might be able to do more," she continues. "When I learned that I was getting a small inheritance—and I *knew* I didn't know how to settle the estate—I immediately thought of Scott. You had told me that he was a trader, and he knew a lot about money. I figured if he was anything like you said, I could work with him."

Rosie then explains that when she learned the amount of money she had inherited, she felt it came with certain moral responsibilities. She says she felt obligated to sustain her stepmother-in-law's giving spirit.

"No one was as generous as Sandy," she says. "She gave money to everyone. If someone made her a meal, she would write a check that would cover much more than the cost of the food. If she saw someone at the grocery store who didn't have enough money, she would step in and pay for everything. That's just how she was."

When Rosie first met Scott, she thought that this might be an opportunity to carry on Sandy's mission. But she says, as she thought about things, there was another reason she wanted to hire Scott that went beyond his needs. She has developed a deep empathy for survivors, having lived among them in Skokie for over fifty years. The fact that our mother was a Holocaust refugee swayed Rosie's decision too.

"I was hoping to make all of your lives a little sweeter," she says, "And actually I ended up making all of *our* lives sweeter."

This was one of those rare experiences when everyone involved benefited. "I knew a little about Scott's history," Rosie says. "I knew he needed to make money. I had the money to pay him, and I wanted him to take care of me, since my husband was ill and couldn't help me in this situation."

Then she grows quiet for a moment and shakes her head incredulously. "I can't believe what he's done for me over the last few months," she says. "He chased down every lead. He found money in accounts that I wouldn't have known even existed. Nobody would have worked harder for me than Scott. Not only did he insulate me from chores I didn't want to do, he did those tasks much better than I could have done them myself."

In the process of working together, Rosie says she has built a relationship with Scott that transcends the financial tasks he does for her every day. She says she's beginning to cherish him for the man he is now.

"Look at me," she says. "All four parents are dead. My sister lives in San Francisco. My brother lives in Arizona. They don't share my life. I don't have anybody, except my husband and children. It's lonely. I think that loneliness brought me to the nursery in the first place. I found a sisterhood here. And then the relationship with you—which I developed in the nursery—led me to this unusual connection with Scott, which gives me balance, a sense of security, and a wonderful new friendship." Rosie is describing her family of voluntary kin.

"But there's more," Rosie continues. "This is who I am: a caregiver. People who are born to care for others always see the glass as half full. We want to fix things, help people, and make a situation better." She points to an infant in a crib and adds, "If that little guy makes a big mess that I have to clean up, does that mean I won't take care of him again? Of course not.

"The way I see things, everybody makes mistakes, and nobody's perfect. Everyone needs a second chance."

I couldn't agree more. I've spent the last year trying to understand what drove my estrangement with Scott and then giving him—and us—a second chance.

The more I thought about Rosie's generous offer to Scott, the more I came to the realization that our entire situation is absolutely improbable and unpredictable. No one could have anticipated Rosie's newfound wealth or her extraordinary bigheartedness.

Rosie's unexpected actions became the unlikely cement—securing not only Scott's future but *our* connection as brother and sister. When I reflect upon all that has happened, it seems like a quirk of fate, an outlier in the realm of human interaction—an absolutely serendipitous turn of events.

But I am not alone in experiencing a remarkable twist in a sibling story. In my researching this book, for example, several brothers and sisters shared their deep sense of discontent and estrangement that seemed to go well beyond their rifts; some said they felt as if they didn't belong in their own families. That feeling gnawed at their very being, producing profound alienation and angst. Some discovered startling answers to their uneasiness through genetic testing.

Other Remarkable Reunions:
When DNA Changes Everything

Marco Bertelli's story of family, estrangement, and technology is worthy of its own book. Bertelli, the seventy-one-year-old lawyer from California who described his family in chapter 4, is the oldest of three boys and was raised in a Catholic family. Unlike his brothers, he valued education, community service, and the life of the mind. He never identified with his father, whom Bertelli describes as "a kind of Archie Bunker"—a narrow-minded bigot in the 1970s television sitcom *All in the Family*—or his brothers, who he says are like his father—"difficult, argumentative, and materialistic." He writes:

> *"How did you turn out so unlike the rest of your family?" I'm often asked. All of us have been estranged from each other at different times in our lives. At one point, my brother even said to me, "We're so different; I can't believe we're related."*
>
> *Last year, I did a DNA test on Ancestry.com. I thought I was 100 percent Italian, but the results showed I am half Italian and the rest Irish, British, and Scandinavian. I wondered,* How could this be? *I figured Rome invaded different places, and other places invaded Italy; people must have fooled around.*
>
> *Ancestry listed one person as a likely "very close family member." It was a name I knew.*
>
> Holy shit! *I thought.* Why is he on my family tree?
>
> *My mom worked as a legal secretary for this attorney before I was born. Turns out, this guy is my father!*
>
> *I have no idea what happened. My mom was a religious person and not one to fool around. Maybe she got drunk at a holiday party, and he took advantage of her.*

I doubt my biological father knew about this; my mom may not have known either. She has Alzheimer's now, so I can't ask her questions. I don't want to tell my dad; he's ninety-four and I don't want to hurt him. I haven't told my brothers.

At a recent appointment, my doctor asked: "Are there any changes in your family medical history?" "Funny you should ask," I said. When I told him of my discovery, he said he hears this story often with today's genetic testing.

In recent years, Bertelli has come to know his two half-sisters, who are intellectually inclined and much more like him than his (half-) brothers. In fact, Bertelli says he finally feels at home in his new family. His half-sisters enjoy spending time with him too, in part because Bertelli has some of the same mannerisms as their deceased father. Bertelli brings their beloved dad back into their lives.

After Marco shared his story with me, I read Dani Shapiro's book *Inheritance: A Memoir of Genealogy, Paternity, and Love*, which captures a similar experience. In the twenty-first-century world of Ancestry.com and 23andMe, Shapiro discovers, almost by accident at the age of fifty-four, that her beloved father is not her biological father. A deeply devout Orthodox Jew, Shapiro's father made sure his daughter had a strong Jewish education and spoke flawless Hebrew. Yet for Shapiro, something was always amiss. Looking back, she recalls having a sense of longing—for exactly what, she couldn't say.

"I always felt like I was different, an outsider," she writes, echoing Marco's words. She never had reason to explore or question her lineage. However, her half-sister, to whom she was never close, seemed to intuit that Shapiro was not her sister. She had suggested years earlier that Shapiro take a DNA test. Eventually, she discovered she is indeed unrelated to her half-sister and her presumptive father. Shapiro is biologically the daughter of a Christian doctor who donated sperm at a fertility clinic in Philadelphia.

For Shapiro and Bertelli, learning the truth of their ancestry has helped them understand their vexing, distant relationships with their siblings. As Bertelli explains, "Sometimes people feel 'other' and estranged from their families because they *are* 'other' and estranged genetically." Ancestry.com sent Shapiro and Bertelli on a dizzying path of self-discovery, altering their sense of family and identity and shifting the trajectories of their lives.

Chapter 18

A Family Reunion

After nearly two years—five semesters, ten courses, and countless hours of study—my brother, now sixty-five years old, is about to receive his bachelor of arts degree in business management—forty-seven years after he first enrolled in college.

Scott has decided that he doesn't want to participate in his college's processional ceremony. He says he doesn't need that kind of public acknowledgment; completing his degree was a personal goal. Still, my mother and I intend to mark this momentous milestone with a family dinner at a nice restaurant. Mom insists that all family members—even those who haven't exchanged a word in decades—be invited.

So once again, I'll have to approach my elder son, who has continued to resist any involvement with my brother or his family. Dreading the conversation, I postpone it as long as possible, instead devoting weeks of thought to what I'm going to say and what I'm *not* going to say. I promise myself I won't debate or argue with him again. That's a losing proposition. When he says no, I won't ask why or inquire when he'll put aside his grievances. Instead, I'll just say okay and let it go. I want this conversation over with as quickly as possible to contain the damage this subject invariably inflicts on my son's and my relationship.

After my mother has asked repeatedly whether my son and his wife will join us for the dinner, I realize I can't put off my request any longer. I punch his name on my phone and dip my feet into choppy waters. Right after asking how he's doing, I dive in.

"W— will you two join us for dinner to celebrate Scott's graduation?" I blurt. Fully expecting an earful, I brace myself while thinking frantically: *How am I going to tell my mother that I couldn't round up my troops?* Already I can hear her: *So once again I can't have all my children and grandchildren in one room to celebrate an important event together.*

"When is it?" There's not a hint of hostility or bitterness in his tone.

Wait! What? He acts as if this were something I routinely ask of him. He didn't even pause to think about it!

I'm so shocked I don't know what to say. I don't have an answer to "when" because I was thinking we wouldn't get past "if."

Not wanting him to know I'm stunned, I try to sound as composed as he is when I casually answer, "Uhhh, I'll let you know. It'll be next month."

As I tap the End Call button, my head is spinning. My son didn't completely shut me down, and I know my two other children will likely follow his lead. Maybe there's a chance Scott and I *can* experience some semblance of family life after all.

The five cousins have been together just once in the past few years. At a large wedding, they awkwardly greeted one another and made just enough small talk to be polite. This will be the first time in years—actually, as I look back, it may be the first time ever—that the entire group has gathered for an intimate family dinner. Five cousins, two aunts, two uncles, a few pregnant spouses, one grandmother: just us.

I'm filled with hope and possibility and, to be completely honest, great trepidation.

On this warm summer evening, the families mill around a long, narrow restaurant table, seating ourselves for our big celebration of Scott's graduation. When everyone has settled in, my brother and his family are seated together along one side, and my family lines the other. At the center of the table, Scott and I sit directly across from each other, flanked by our spouses and offspring. Mom is at my side. A photo of this scene should be captioned, "The Hatfields and McCoys *Finally* Break Bread Together!"

I look at Scott and notice that his whole face looks different; his eyelids aren't swollen, and his cheeks don't droop, as they once did when he was severely depressed. Instead, his face is lit like a jack-o'-lantern. The others at the table don't share his glow. Awkwardness sets in quickly as the cousins warily eye one another. Nobody knows where to start or what to say. It's so quiet I can hear chairs scraping against the floor as everyone adjusts themselves.

I toss out something about how I'm glad we're all here, but that doesn't break the ice. Then Scott's daughter-in-law and my daughter-in-law, both of whom joined the family in recent years and don't carry the bitter history of the long estrangement, strike up a conversation.

"When are you due?"

"Have you picked out a name?"

"Are you planning to go back to work?"

Once the others hear the two women chatting, they begin to talk as well. The din at the table grows louder, and I'm able to catch snippets of one conversation between my nephew and my elder son.

"So where did you go to school?"

"What are you doing now?"

"You have your own business?"

"Where do you live?"

It occurs to me that the two of them would have the same conversation if they had just met at a bar.

The waiter comes to the table to take orders for drinks. Some guests ask for martinis, beer, or wine to toast Scott's success, but my brother goes for his now-usual club soda with lime. The two pregnant women also refrain from drinking, but their abstinence is temporary: Scott's daughter-in-law tells mine that she misses an occasional glass of wine with dinner, and she's eager for the day when she'll have that chance again. I think about how Scott feels when he hears these casual, frequent comments about alcohol. I admire his resolve.

At the other end of the table, my younger son and Scott's younger son sit opposite each other, but they haven't said much. Both are studying the menu, probably as a convenient excuse not to talk. For all the time they spend considering their dinner options, I notice both are unprepared to place their orders when the waiter asks what they'd like.

Once the food arrives and everyone begins to eat, the tension eases. The young men, having identified their perennial favorite topic—sports—establish that they like the same local teams and fall into a deep discussion about players and coaches. The women continue to talk about pregnancy, doctors, childbirth, and babies. Half a dozen conversations buzz around us, punctuated by laughter. My experience is limited, but it seems like a normal family dinner. At last I breathe a little easier.

Before this dinner, Scott and I talked about our hopes for the evening. Each of us reminded the other not to expect much, agreeing that we simply wanted everyone to enjoy themselves. Still, Scott told me that he's hoping this dinner might change relationships in the family. He asked whether I thought the cousins, now that they're adults, might make some effort to stay in touch. "That may be pushing things," I replied, knowing that my children still harbor resentments.

As the waiter clears our plates, we present the graduate with a few gifts. Scott's children have ordered a custom frame for his diploma, with the name of his college engraved in gold.

"Oh, great!" he says with evident appreciation. "I'm definitely going to hang my degree in my office." Then he adds, "I don't generally brag, but I did get all A's."

"Wow." His elder son whistles, appropriately impressed. Then he brings his dad back down to earth: "What does your GPA average out to?"

We all know that his father's transcripts from the 1970s include classes that he failed, and the whole table joins in laughing about the GPA gap.

"Hey, I've got a solid 3.0," Scott declares, having already made the calculation.

"Now you can finally go to medical school!" I pipe up. Everyone is still laughing as Scott and I give each other a knowing smile.

As the waiter brings dessert, I try to get the group's attention. "I'd like to say a few words," I announce, clinking my water glass with my spoon. Conversations cease around the table, and all eyes turn toward me.

"I wouldn't want the dinner to pass without recognizing what we're celebrating," I say. "It's an amazing accomplishment to complete your college degree at any age. But this is extra special, given that Scott has finally met a goal he set for himself decades ago.

"In addition, having everyone together tonight is its *own* accomplishment. Scott, I'm so happy you graduated, but I'm even happier that we could celebrate together."

"Me too!" I hear Scott say. Others at the table nod in agreement.

To my surprise, my brother is savoring his moment in the spotlight. He opens a few more gifts, and reads out loud the sentiment from each card he receives. The words differ, but every message is the same: "You did it! Congrats, Grad! Super impressive!"

Finally he opens my card and reads my handwritten note:

Dear Scott,

For the last few days, I've been thinking about what this college degree really means.

For you, I think it means a lot. You no longer have a glaring shortcoming on your résumé. You have proven to yourself that you can succeed (wildly) in school. You no longer live in the long shadow of that unmet goal.

But for me, even with a college degree, I see you as I always have—as my handsome, funny, smart, irresistible big brother.

I always knew you could do it. Now you know too.

Congratulations!

> *With all my love,*
> *Fern*

There was so much more I wanted to say, but this was not the time or the place. Another day, I'll point out to Scott that what he has done is rare, and that his college graduation is just one aspect of a much larger triumph.

Not many people face their inadequacies and despair; even fewer accept responsibility for their problems. In his classic bestseller *The Road Less Traveled*, psychiatrist M. Scott Peck explains that most who suffer psychological distress ignore or work around the cues, though resolving those issues actually offer a path to growth. To avoid their problems, many may quit their jobs, move to a new town, avoid activities that sharpen the pain; some use drugs or alcohol. Even those who recognize their symptoms often impugn others or make excuses for themselves. Peck says they often blame "the world outside them—uncaring relatives, false friends, greedy corporations, a sick society—for their condition. . . . Only a few accept their own inadequacy and the pain of the work necessary to heal themselves."[1]

Scott is among those few. In taking responsibility for himself, he has changed the lives of everyone who has come to this table to celebrate his achievement. Had he not done the work to heal, our family wouldn't be here tonight.

The din at our table grows louder again. Looking around at our three generations, I feel—cautiously—that the group is cohering. Peeking at my elder son, I see that even he appears to be enjoying himself.

Now Mom clinks her water glass with a spoon and gets to her feet. "I'm so glad everyone was able to make it tonight. I look forward to meeting my new great-grandchildren," she says with a smile, nodding toward her two pregnant granddaughters-in-law. Then she adds, "And I hope we can do this again."

She casts her eyes from Scott to me and then from one grandchild to another, as if she is hitching each guest to the next with her gaze. Swallowing hard, blinking back tears, fighting a catch in her voice, our mother says it all: "Let's keep the family together!"

Epilogue

There isn't time, so brief is life, for bickerings, apologies, heart-burnings, callings to account," Mark Twain wrote more than a century ago, as he looked back on his own life. "There is only time for loving, and but an instant, so to speak, for that."[1]

Five years into our reconciliation, Scott and I text nearly every day and talk on the phone every week, sharing news of our children, our elderly mom, and other matters. Sometimes we continue to explore the rocky terrain of our shared history.

By now I would have expected that I would have adjusted to my place in my brother's life and his in mine. I haven't. I never take our relationship for granted. I can never forget the darkness of estrangement.

When I told a friend the story of our years of silence, our remarkable reconciliation, and our heartening friendship with Rosie, she said it all sounds like a fairy tale. But it isn't. Like all brothers and sisters, Scott and I are at times pulled toward each other, and other times we both need distance. A sibling relationship is a kind of living organism that is always changing.

Over the last years, we have had to negotiate many potholes, detours, and blind curves during our reconciliation, and we have even teetered on the brink of estrangement again. Two years ago, for example, we had a bitter, brutal argument that arose over a holiday party guest list—something that often divides families. Voices raised, we staked out our entrenched positions with harsh words. As the fight became dangerously heated, my heart pounded and my breathing turned ragged, and we both spewed venom. Rage coursed through me. Finally, recognizing that we were both saying things we would later regret and that we were too upset to *really* hear each other, I said, "I can't talk to you right now." Then I pressed the End Call button on my phone.

During the next few days, I felt sick every time I thought about him and the fight. But I wasn't about to call him; I was still too angry to have a civil conversation. I needed time, and I figured he did too. I replayed the rancorous exchange, ruminating over every hurtful detail. I worried about the frightening possibility that we were about to retreat into our own lives again.

But on a Monday morning five days after the fight, Scott surprised me. The phone rang, and when I saw his name on the caller ID, I picked up the call.

"How you doing?" he asked, without even saying hello.

"Not great. How about you?"

"Yeah, not great either."

During the days when we hadn't talked, we both recognized that our relationship was far more important than the need to win an argument. With measured words, we admitted having said things we wished we hadn't. Then we set about the task of compromising and compiling a mutually agreeable guest list.

The famous twentieth-century child psychologist Bruno Bettelheim explains that in the fairy tale "Hansel and Gretel," siblings transcend their "immature dependence on their parents and reach the next higher stage of development: cherishing the support of their age mates."[2] Maybe, through this fight, Scott and I reached that higher stage.

The ups and downs of these reconciliation years have allowed me to develop a better understanding of why estrangement was so intolerable to me—why I, unlike so many others who are estranged, could never detach and cut my brother out of my life.

First, he is my only brother, and that reality intensified my need for him. Others who are estranged may garner comfort from their relationship with another brother or sister or a group of friends. But for me, without my only sibling, I lost several roles and a crucial sense of belonging. My place in the family diminished.

But there was another psychological reason I could never let Scott go. As the youngest in the family, I couldn't easily differentiate between my parents and my brother; all members of my family were older and wiser than me. I viewed all three as potential guides in a terrifying world I couldn't navigate alone. Because my parents couldn't always provide consistent love, security, and stability, I shifted my needs to my older brother, hoping he could give me some of what our parents couldn't. That was unfair to both of us.

Still, throughout my adult life and our estrangement, I continued to cling to the hope that he would give me, among other things, the love I craved in childhood. Therefore, no matter how distant we became, I never wanted to give up on him. Eventually, our reconciliation helped me to see my brother in his proper role. I came to understand that he, too, was a child who had experienced the same emotional void. He could never be a parent to me; at best, he could only be my brother.

Ironically, during our reconciliation, I was able to provide for Scott some of what I had wanted from him when we were children. When his world was collapsing, I offered him safety, steadiness, and security. That created an opening—an opportunity to develop an adult sibling relationship, a place where we could find each other once again.

My volunteer work at the Cradle was a moment in time that altered three lives: Rosie's, Scott's, and mine. For six years, from 2009 to 2015, I cuddled babies at the venerable Evanston institution that has been placing babies in adoptive homes for more than a century. In recent years, however, as the stigma of "the unwed mother" has dwindled, fewer women are placing their babies for adoption. When they do, they tend to ask a relative in their extended family to raise their child. Consequently, the nursery, which once teemed with babies, is often dark, and the Cradle doesn't have the same need for cuddlers anymore.

Even though several years have passed since I volunteered in the nursery, the experience transformed me. Nurturing and loving babies in their time between birth and family placement enhanced my capacity for empathy, enabling me to offer others what I experienced within its pink walls. I feel a profound gratitude for my own transformative experience in the nursery's distinctive culture, which cultivated comfort, support, and strength. I regret that others aren't likely to benefit from this mostly female environment. Even now, my mind often returns to those two-hour shifts on Sunday evenings; I feel myself sitting on the white rocking chairs, enveloped by the cacophony of life: young and old, needy and nurtured, abandoned and accepted.

Rosie and I maintain our friendship by getting together whenever we can. Last year, on a scorching Memorial Day afternoon, she helped me in my mother's garden, preparing the soil for spring plantings. After raking and weeding for an hour in the harsh sun, Rosie, Mom, and I retreated into the comfortably air-conditioned house. Sitting in the den, we drank ice water, cooled off, and talked.

"I've told you this before," I said to Rosie, "but I want you to know that Mom and I are grateful for what you've done for Scott."

"You know," she said, "he tells me he's a changed man. But I never knew him as he was; I only know him as he is now. That's all that matters to me. I don't know what I would do without Scott." Rosie has employed him for two years and hopes to continue indefinitely. "Really," she continues, "he's like a brother I never had."

"Like the brother *I* never had too!" I add, bringing a laugh that underlines the gratitude all three of us feel for this happy ending.

My three children were initially resistant to the reconciliation, but only my elder son opposed any relationship with Scott. Even he, however, finally decided that my brother has proven himself. When my son and his wife had their first child in October of 2018, he announced that every family member who hadn't been involved in his childhood would be absolved of all earlier transgressions. With the birth of his daughter, my son fully welcomed his uncle back into the family.

Another family relationship has improved drastically as a result of my brother's and my reconciliation. My own smoldering anger toward my mother has dissipated; I no longer feel betrayed by her actions during the estrangement. My research for this book has given me a deeper understanding of and empathy for her wrenching circumstances. She was doing her best to maintain some connection with both her children.

I hope I never face my mother's choiceless choice, but I know that if I were caught between feuding children, I would do everything possible to facilitate a reconciliation. If that failed, I—like my mother—could never choose one over the other. I would do what she did in trying to maintain some sort of relationship with both—an extremely difficult negotiation in the hostile and bitter battleground of estrangement.

What's even more surprising than recovering our relationship is that I finally persuaded my mother to replace the old wooden door on her house. Now a fresh white fiberglass model with a colorful Tiffany window and side lights cheerfully welcomes anyone who comes to visit her home. Mercifully, it opens and closes smoothly, silently, without any nuance or subtext.

When I considered writing a book about our evolving relationship, I met Scott for breakfast to discuss the possibility. With trepidation, I asked, "How would you feel if I were to write a personal account about our estrangement and reconciliation?"

He surprised me. "I'm okay with it," he said casually.

I explained that I would tell our story and explore estrangement in general, so that readers would gain an understanding of the sad phenomenon.

"Well, if you need subjects, just let me know," he offered. "Every family in my neighborhood has a story."

When I signed a contract to write the book, I asked Scott if he would fill out my survey and give his perspective on our long cutoff. He agreed and answered the questions in his usual taciturn way, with only one or two words. But one of his responses revealed how profoundly the estrangement had haunted him too.

The survey question: "How often do you think about your estranged sibling?"

His unexpected answer: "Every day."

After he generously participated in the survey, I pressed him for an even greater contribution. On the phone, I asked if he would give his perspective by writing the book's afterword.

He was quiet as he thought about my request, clearly uncomfortable with the idea.

Maybe, I thought, *he has given me all that he can, and I've reached the limit of our relationship.*

"I don't think so," Scott finally blurted out. "I can't do that!"

"Why not?" My tone dripped with hurt.

"Because I'm not *you*." He dug in with irritation.

"What? Why would you say that?" I felt the hairs on my neck stand up. "I would never ask that of you. I don't want you to be me."

Then, because I know him so well now, I couldn't stop myself from adding a jab: "And *I'm* not *Dad* either!"

"I know." He laughed a little and added, "I mean, I'm not much of a writer."

"Well, you don't have to be. I'll back you up. I can edit what you write."

Still skeptical, he said, "But I won't know what to say."

"You don't have to do it alone. I'll help you sort out what's most important."

"*We'll* figure it out?" he asked incredulously. "Together?"

"Sure," I reassured him, adding, "And I'll make you look good too. . . . I promise."

"Okay!" he said, as if he were linking his arm in mine.

Moments passed. I waited.

Then, at last, he followed up his consent with five remarkable words.

Words he'd never said during our childhood.

Words that, through forty years of estrangement, were utterly inconceivable.

Words that, during our reconciliation as he clawed his way out of despair, I didn't dare dream.

"You know, Fern . . ." He swallowed hard and took a deep breath. "I'd do anything for you."

Afterword

When my sister asked me to write the afterword for this book, I had some worries. I was never very good at talking about my feelings, and I never felt confident about my writing. But I said I'd do it, so here goes.

For most of my adult life, I basically had no relationship with my only sibling, my sister. I was the cause of our estrangement. Part of the reason for the cutoff was our father. He was a very difficult, stubborn person, and he had a certain way of doing things. It was always his way or the highway. I felt he didn't value me because I didn't do what he wanted and follow in his footsteps by going into medicine. He was always disappointed in me. He couldn't see me or appreciate me for who I am.

Throughout the years, my father and I had many terrible arguments, and he hurt me many, many times. I remember when I went to college when I was eighteen, I felt like I had finally escaped. I was so relieved I didn't have to deal with all the drama anymore. But it didn't stop. He and I continued fighting. Finally, when I was in my twenties, I took control of the situation and protected myself by choosing to cut off all contact with him.

But that choice spilled over into my relationship with my sister. It wasn't easy for anyone to maintain a connection with our father, who always had to be right. He was quick to cut people out of his life when they didn't do things his way. But my sister somehow figured out how to have a relationship with him. She even gave our father a chance to know her children, three of his five grandchildren. My two sons would never get to know their grandfather. I felt jealous.

When I look back at my life, I see that I pushed my sister away. I didn't want to deal with my father, and she was still connected to him, so I cut her out too. In fact, I pushed everyone away and went into my own world. When any situation came up that I didn't know how to handle, I dealt with it by removing myself. I used alcohol as my escape.

There were so many problems with that choice, but the worst of it was that I became used to drinking by myself. I never drank during the day, but I looked forward to it when it got dark and I could relax and have my Crown Royal on the rocks. In time, I felt like I didn't need anybody. I became more and more isolated and depressed.

I stopped drinking five years ago. It was hard to quit because it had been a habit for so many years. Every night, it helped me get to sleep. Also, I was never all that comfortable around people, and drinking helped me be social. With a few drinks, I could go into a bar by myself and talk to anyone who sat next to me. Now I don't have the urge to drink, but I still think about it. It was a big part of my life and everything revolved around it. I am not close to some of my old friends anymore because they still have the same lifestyle.

During all the years I was drinking, I didn't talk to my sister. I never felt comfortable about the estrangement with her. She and I weren't really close when we were younger. But when we didn't talk at all for so many years, I felt I was missing a part of my life, a piece of me.

Now everything has changed.

Last summer, for example, we moved our ninety-three-year-old mother out of her home of fifty years. Then we had to get the house where we grew up ready to sell. This huge, stressful task ate up a lot of days. We had to sort, clean, and run all kinds of trash to the dump. I know many siblings who fight over who does what and who gets Mom's stuff, but my sister and I managed to get through the entire experience without any major problems.

We talked and texted every day, figuring out who would do what on the long "to do" list. We had to change Mom's mailing address, shut off the landline, cancel her cable TV, figure out what furniture to take to her new home, and set up the moving company.

We laughed about the long-expired cans of Campbell's tomato soup that Mom stashed on the bookshelves in the den and the cans of Valvoline motor oil that were there when we moved into the house in 1967. We rolled our eyes at each other as Mom insisted on keeping her 1983 World Jewish Congress calendar *and* the souvenir pouch she bought on a trip to see her cousins in Uruguay thirty years ago. We put off cleaning the dreaded basement as long as possible because we worried we might find a dead body there.

I'm grateful my sister never gave up on me. When I hit rock bottom, I knew I needed help, but I didn't know where to turn. After all the years of cutoff, I never thought my sister would have anything to do with me again. But when I was most desperate, she came back into my life. I wouldn't be where I am today without her love and her belief in me.

We grew up together and we went through a lot during those years. She probably knows me better than anyone. I feel balanced that we have a relationship again. Now I can discuss anything and everything with her. I'm only sorry it took us so long to find each other. After years of living without being brother and sister, we are finally true siblings.

Unfortunately, the estrangement took a toll on the whole family. Our five children, who are cousins, probably won't ever be close, and that makes me sad. We lost the chance to build that family bond when they were young. I don't have the relationships I'd like with my niece and nephews either. I can't go back and fix all that. I can't change the past, but at least I know I'll always have my sister.

When we were younger, our father always told us we should have some sort of legacy; we should leave the world a better place than we found it. I didn't become a doctor as my father wished, but I did other things *I* value. I became a loving husband, father, and grandfather. I'm proud of these contributions, but I also want to leave something beyond my family. I hope this book is part of my larger legacy and helps others understand the complicated, often hidden reasons siblings have for cutting off their relationships.

Above all, I hope our story holds out the possibility—even for brothers and sisters who have been complete strangers to each other for decades—that they, too, might return by the road they came.

Scott Schumer
August 1, 2019

Acknowledgments

Reconnecting with Scott and writing this book required both of us to trust each other—a great challenge after so many years of disconnection, resentment, and injury. It also forced him to revisit discomforting experiences and past pain. He did so steadfastly, while providing me with support, encouragement, and a droll sense of humor. By consenting to my telling his story, my brother has taken responsibility for his own life and has committed himself to an act of genuine atonement. He is trying to make whole what was broken. In so doing, he is offering himself as a template for resilience and recovery. I'm deeply grateful to him for his willingness and dedication to this project.

I'm also grateful to my mother, Edith Schumer, who has been the subject of many of my books. Several have been deeply personal and have forced her to relive painful parts of her past. Throughout my writing career, she has been unflaggingly supportive and encouraging, even though some of the content of my books may have been uncomfortable for her. Her generous support is testimony to her belief that my words might make a larger contribution. Someone once said, "When there's a writer in the family, there will be trouble." I hope it hasn't been too much trouble for my mother.

This work would not have been possible without the many estranged siblings who participated in my survey and those who generously shared their feelings in online chat rooms. I hope this book gives back to them some of what they've given to me. Maybe the knowledge I've shared here takes a few of the blind curves out of the road.

My circle of family and friends always shepherds me through all of my book projects. They include Susan Remen King, Ann Sherman, Marcy Kaplan, James B. Lieber, Dr. Linda Stern, Adrienne Behrens, Karen Berkowsky, Ross Chapman, Kate Chapman, Keith Chapman, Alex Butler, Isabelle Chapman, and Dave Uberti. Many other friends, too numerous to name, have supported me as well.

Back in 2017, during a lunch with my agent, Marian Young, I shared the remarkable story of my sibling estrangement and reconciliation. I wasn't thinking about writing a book on the topic, but Marian jumped on it. She has enthusiastically believed in the book and its importance from the start . . . so much so that I've often wondered if this is the same skeptical agent I have known and loved. I treasure our twenty-two-year partnership and friendship, and I can't imagine where I would be without her.

Thanks to editor Carole DeSanti, who seized upon the idea, sensing this topic would attract a wide audience. Georgia Bodnar has been an editor extraordinaire. She has invested much time and emotional energy to cultivate its potential. I'm honored I had the opportunity to work with someone who cares as deeply about this project as I do. The manuscript was greatly improved by her critical eye and meticulous editing. I also am grateful to Gretchen Schmid and all the others in the editorial, sales, publicity, and marketing departments at Viking who worked hard on this book.

For all my projects, my great friend Susan Figliulo is always my first reader. I depend upon her for lively commentary about content, her critical eye, and her great sense of humor. Whenever I get stuck, she helps me find a writing path and, in the case of this book, a title!

Finally, thanks to my husband, Bruce Wasser, who, for years, has had to live and breathe sibling estrangement in my personal and professional life. I am deeply grateful to him for listening, supporting, and influencing my work—gifts he gives me every day.

Notes

Introduction

1. Kylie Agllias, *Family Estrangement: A Matter of Perspective* (New York: Routledge, 2017), p. 46.

Chapter 1: The Challenges of Sibling Relationships

1. Theodore Lidz, *The Person: His and Her Development Throughout the Life Cycle*, rev. ed. (New York: Basic Books, 1983).
2. David Brooks, "The Nuclear Family Was a Mistake," *The Atlantic*, March 2020.
3. Brooks, "Nuclear Family."

Chapter 2: Different Types of Estrangement

1. Dr. Kristina Scharp, interviewed by the author via email, June 2, 2020.

Chapter 3: The Grief of Estrangement

1. Kip Williams, "Kip Williams Media Contact Overview," last edited January 29, 2020, Social Psychology Network, williams.socialpsychology.org.
2. "Welcome to the Harvard Study of Adult Development," 2015, Harvard Second Generation Study, www.adultdevelopmentstudy.org.
3. Robert Waldinger, "What Makes a Good Life? Lessons from the Longest Study of Happiness" (presentation, TEDxBeaconStreet, Brookline, MA, 2015); Robert J. Waldinger, George. E. Vaillant, and E. John Orav, "Childhood Sibling Relationships as a Predictor of Major Depression in Adulthood: A 30-Year Prospective Study," *American Journal of Psychiatry* 164, no. 6 (June 2007): 949–54, https://ajp.psychiatryonline.org/doi/full/10.1176/ajp.2007.164.6.949.
4. René M. Dailey, "Confirmation from Family Members: Parent and Sibling Contributions to Adolescent Psychosocial Adjustment," *Western Journal of Communication* 73, no. 3 (2009): 273–99, http://dx.doi.org/10.1080/10570310903082032.
5. J. N. Melby et al., "Adolescent Family Experiences and Educational Attainment during Early Adulthood," *Developmental Psychology* 44, no. 6 (2008): 1519–36, https://doi.org/10.1037/a0013352.
6. E. E. Werner, "Resilience in Development," *Current Directions in Psychological Science* 4, no. 3 (June 1995): 81–84, www.jstor.org/stable/20182335.

7. Milevsky, A. (2005). "Compensatory Patterns of Sibling Support in Emerging Adulthood: Variations in Loneliness, Self-esteem, Depression and Life Satisfaction." *Journal of Social and Personal Relationships* 22, 743–55.

Chapter 4: Risk Factors for Sibling Estrangement

1. Kylie Agllias, *Family Estrangement: A Matter of Perspective* (New York: Routledge, 2017), p. 19.
2. J. Jill Suitor et al., "The Role of Perceived Maternal Favoritism in Sibling Relations in Midlife," *Journal of Marriage and Family* 71, no. 4 (November 2009): 1026–38, https://doi.org/10.1111/j.1741-3737.2009.00650.x.
3. Ali-John Chaudhary, interviewed by author via telephone, April 28, 2020.
4. Judy Dunn, "Sibling Relationships in Early Childhood," *Child Development* 54, no. 4 (August 1983): 787–811, https://doi.org/10.2307/1129886.
5. Helgola G. Ross and Joel L. Milgram, "Important Variables in Adult Sibling Relationships: A Qualitative Study," in *Sibling Relationships: Their Nature and Significance across the Lifespan*, ed. Michael E. Lamb and Brian Sutton-Smith (New York: Psychology Press, 1982), pp. 225–84.
6. Joshua Coleman, interviewed by the author via email, June 2, 2020.
7. Dr. Karen Gail Lewis, interviewed by the author via email, June 2, 2020.
8. Anonymous, "A Letter to . . . My Estranged Brother," *The Guardian* (London), May 12, 2018.
9. Mark Sichel and Alicia L. Cervini, "The Family Myth," no date, Psybersquare, www.psybersquare.com/family/myth.html.
10. Harriet Lerner, *Why Won't You Apologize?* (New York: Gallery Books, 2017).

Chapter 7: Estrangement and Self-Esteem

1. Kylie Agllias, *Family Estrangement: A Matter of Perspective* (New York: Routledge, 2017), pp. 47–48.
2. Laura Davis, *I Thought We'd Never Speak Again* (New York: HarperCollins, 2002), p. 47.

Chapter 8: Social Media and the Estranged

1. Dr. Brian A. Primack, interviewed by the author via email, June 3, 2020.

Chapter 9: Reconnection and Reestablishment of a Sibling Relationship

1. Donna Hicks, *Dignity* (New York: Yale University Press, 2011).

Chapter 10: Estrangement and Mental Illness or Addiction

1. Bruce K. Alexander et al., "Effect of Early and Later Colony Housing on Oral Ingestion of Morphine in Rats," *Pharmacology Biochemistry Behavior* 15, no. 4 (October 1981): 571–76, https://doi.org/10.1016/0091-3057(81)90211-2.
2. Robins, L.N., Helzer, J.E., Davis, D.H. "Narcotic Use in Southeast Asia and Afterward. An Interview Study of 898 Vietnam Returnees." *Archive of General Psychiatry* 32 (8), Aug. 1975: 955-61.
3. Susan M. McHale, Kimberly A. Updegraff, and Shawn D. Whiteman, "Sibling

Relationships and Influences in Childhood and Adolescence," *Journal of Marriage and Family* 74, no. 5 (October 1, 2012): 913–30, https://doi.org/10.1111/j.1741-3737.2012.01011.x.

4. Dr. Gabor Maté, "The Power of Addiction and the Addiction to Power" (presentation, TEDxRio+20, Rio de Janeiro, June 11, 2012).

5. Nicholas Kristof, "How to Win the War on Drugs," *The New York Times*, September 22, 2017.

Chapter 11: Estrangement's Ripple Effect in the Family

1. Dr. Zina McGee, interviewed by the author via email, June 13, 2020.

2. Robyn Fivush, Marshall Duke, and Jennifer G. Bohanek, "'Do You Know . . .'": The Power of Family History in Adolescent Identity and Well-Being," *Journal of Family Life*, February 23, 2010.

Chapter 12: A Balance Between the Individual and the Family

1. Kaitlyn Greenidge, "Could Our Sibling Bond Survive This U-Haul?" *The New York Times*, September 21, 2018.

2. Murphy, D.C. (2003), "Emotional Cutoff and Domestic Violence." In P. Titelman (Ed.), *Emotional Cutoff: Bowen Family Systems Theory Perspectives* (New York: The Haworth Clinical Practice Press), 337–50.

3. Ora Peleg, "The Relation Between Differentiation of Self and Marital Satisfaction: What Can Be Learned from Married People over the Course of Life?" *American Journal of Family Therapy* 36, no. 5 (2008): 388–401, https://doi.org/10.1080/01926180701804634.

4. D. C. Murphy, "Emotional Cutoff and Domestic Violence," in *Emotional Cutoff: Bowen Family Systems Theory Perspectives*, ed. P. Titelman (New York: Haworth Clinical Practice, 2003), pp. 337–50.

Chapter 13: A Limited Relationship with a Difficult Sibling

1. Ali-John Chaudhary, interviewed by the author via telephone, April 28, 2020.

2. Alexander Butler, interviewed by the author via telephone and email, April 28, 2020.

Chapter 14: An Irreparable Sibling Relationship

1. Lynne Marek, "Closing Time: Stories from Chicago's Famed Trading Floor," *Crain's Chicago Business*, June 13, 2015.

2. Dr. Kristina Scharp, interviewed by the author via email, June 2, 2020.

3. Traci Foust, "What I Said to My Estranged Sister on Her Deathbed," *MamaMia*, October 22, 2013, www.mamamia.com.au/said-estranged-sister-deathbed/.

4. Sister Renee Pittelli, Luke 17:3 Ministries, accessed August 19, 2020, www.luke173ministries.org.

5. Lori Gottlieb, "Dear Therapist: My Dying Wife Has a Challenging Request for Her Funeral," *The Atlantic*, October 7, 2019.

6. Laura Davis, *I Thought We'd Never Speak Again* (New York: HarperCollins, 2002), p. 310.

Chapter 16: The Benefits of Reconciling with an Estranged Sibling

1. Alexandra Butler, interviewed by the author via telephone and email, April 28, 2020.

NOTES

Chapter 18: A Family Reunion

1. M. Scott Peck, *The Road Less Traveled*, 25th anniversary ed. (New York: Simon & Schuster, 2003).

Epilogue

1. Mark Twain to Clara Spaulding, August 20, 1886, Mark Twain Boyhood Home & Museum, Hannibal, MO.
2. Bruno Bettelheim, *The Uses of Enchantment: The Meaning and Importance of Fairy Tales* (New York: Vintage Books, 2010), p. 166.